Growing Up Again

Growing Up Again

Parenting Ourselves, Parenting Our Children

JEAN ILLSLEY CLARKE
and
CONNIE DAWSON

Second Edition

Hazelden
Publishing

Hazelden Publishing
Center City, Minnesota 55012-0176
hazelden.org/bookstore

Library of Congress Cataloging-in-Publication Data
Clarke, Jean Illsley.
    Growing up again : parenting ourselves, parenting our children /
Jean Illsley Clarke and Connie Dawson. — 2nd ed.
      p.   cm.
    ISBN 1-56838-190-5
    1. Parenting.   I. Dawson, Connie.   II. Title.
HQ755.8.C55   1998
649'.1—dc21   97-48978
                                                                        CIP

Editor's note
Hazelden offers a variety of information on chemical dependency
and related areas. Our publications do not necessarily represent
Hazelden's programs, nor do they officially speak for any Twelve Step
organization.
    All the stories in this book are based on actual experiences. The
names and details have been changed to protect the privacy of the
people involved. In some cases, composites have been created.

01 00 99 98   6 5 4 3 2 1

Book design by Will H. Powers
Illustrations by David Spohn
Cover design by David Spohn
Typesetting by Stanton Publication Services, Inc.

We dedicate this book to our children and their children, for being who they are, and for inadvertently pushing us to figure out our lives.

Contents

Contents

Preface

When trade publisher Dan Odegard called to say that Hazelden wanted a new edition of *Growing Up Again,* he asked if we authors had anything new we wanted to say. The answer was an immediate yes.

Connie had pursued her study of adoption and the many ways that it demands special parenting. Jean and Dr. David Bredehoft had completed their research on overindulgence, that confounding phenomenon that seems to be more and more widespread.

Recent births and the deaths of friends and relatives have pushed us to expand the Ages and Stages section of the book: astounding research about the significance of the prenatal experience needs to be considered, and the end of life, whether it arrives in later years or follows an illness during an earlier decade, are unique stages of life and need to be recognized as such.

Our colleague Jim Jump suggested the metaphor of the highway as a way of thinking about the nurturing and structuring behaviors. We have expanded that idea into a graphic representation that helps parents recognize not only daily habits of caring for themselves and others, but also intergenerational patterns of parenting that they may wish to keep or change.

The second edition of *Growing Up Again* includes new examples of nurture, structure, and discounting and a concise way to identify those behaviors in solving a vexing problem.

We also give direct attention to the human hungers for stimulation, recognition, and certainty and how the need to satisfy those hungers can sometimes show up in confusing ways. Recognizing the potency of the hungers can help unravel the cause of puzzling behaviors.

Growing Up Again readers have added richness to the book with their contributions. Barbara Beystrom offered the helps for handling parenting conflicts in merging families. Sandy Keiser urged us to include charts on denial and double binds and submitted prototypes. Mary Kaye Ashley responded to the request for guidelines on supporting children's spiritual growth.

So we have expanded what Gaye Hurtig calls "the helpful landscape of growing up again." Here it is—new help for the all-important challenge of parenting our children and helping ourselves grow up again. Make it yours.

Connie and Jean

Acknowledgments

We thank the many people who have offered their thinking and support for the new version of this book, especially Joan Comeau, Susannah Temple, Eveline Goodall, Drew Betz, Ruth Harms, Carole Gesme, Sandy Keiser, Deane Gradous, Cally Fuchs, and Lu Soley.

We are grateful to the people who willingly made contributions to the various new sections of the book.

Deep thanks to Laurie Kanyer, Kathie Arcide, Sandy Keiser, Millie Dash, Elaine Childs-Gowell, Marcy Wineman Axness, Russell Osnes, Jeanne Wiger, Susan Clarke, Ruth and Ken Lough, and Patricia Allen for drawing on their experience to provide information for the pre-natal Becoming chart.

For sharing their experiences and sound thinking on the foster and adoptive parenting chapter, Connie thanks Alyce Mitchem Jenkins, Marcy Wineman Axness, Mary and Terry Paananen, Myrth Ogilvie, Jeff, Laurie and Jake Dagenhart, Mark Henningsen, Dennis Thoennes, Ph.D., Tom Matlock, Sherrie Eldridge, Christine Ternand, M.D., Diana York, Barbara Beystrom, Shirley Bullock, Sandy Keiser, Eleanor McFarlane, Darlene Fairbanks, Marilyn Sackariason, Mahima Price, the hundreds of workshop and class participants and the attachment therapists and therapeutic foster families in Evergreen, Colorado. Special thanks to Jean Paton and Betty Jean Lifton for their contributions and mentorship.

The writing of the section on Death, the Stage of Integration, coincided with the deaths of friends Joe Lawrence and Joe McFarlane, who taught us about the meaning of life through their dying, and their wives, Maggie and Eleanor, who helped us understand the journey. Thanks to the Crone Circle of Evergreen, Colorado. The thoughtfulness of an indomitable group of crones from many places, most particularly Ruth Robinson, Nancy Parsons-Craft, Barbara Sternberg, Anne Anselment, Delphine Bowers, Shauna Adix, Susan Ann Stauffer, Ruth Lough, and Elders Dick Lundy, Russell Osnes, and Ken Lough is much appreciated.

For their insights on overindulgence we want to acknowledge the hundreds of people who have shared their experiences and their wisdom during workshops or as part of the research group. Jean is grateful to Phil Margolis and Bernie Saunders and especially to Heidi Caglayan who contributed to and expanded upon the early thinking about overindulgence. Big thanks to David Bredehoft, Ph.D., of Concordia College in St. Paul, MN, for doing the overindulgence research with Jean. We also appreciate Alison Anderson, Adam Erickson, Kevin Schlieman, and Robert Cullen for the hundreds of hours spent in coding and inputting data for the research project, and Sheryll Mennicke, Ph.D., and Alisa Potter, Ph.D., for help with the analysis and interpretation of the data.

Thanks to Gressa Rowland, Jennifer Clarke, Gary Rowland, and Gaye Hurtig for their editing help. Athalie Terry and Barbara Beystrom deserve huge gratitude for their unflagging tenacity in facilitating the reworking of the manuscript.

Last, but most importantly, we thank our children, Tom, Mary Claire, Charles, Marc, Jennifer, and Wade and (our children-in-law) Kathy, Rocky, Indira, Gary, and Amy. And we thank our most delightful teachers, our grandchildren David, Elly, Tom, Emma, Anya, Sean, Gressa, Freya, Disa, and Addie.

Growing Up Again

SECTION I

Getting Started

Like every parent, I want nothing so much as my children's well-being. I want it so badly I may actually succeed in turning myself into a contented and well-adjusted person, if only for my children's sake.

JOYCE MAYNARD

Introduction

This is a book of hope—hope for adults who grew up with parenting that they want to avoid passing on to their children. It is also for adults who want to grow up again, whether they have already begun that journey or whether they have only a whispered wish to get what they needed earlier in life.

We wrote this book because we believe that children are important and adults are important. And we believe that families are the primary places where children learn how to be adults.

We respect families—their strength, their tenacity, their attempts to create systems where human beings can learn, grow, love, and care for themselves and each other.

We believe that adults of any age can grow and that every day is a good time to rejoice in our being, to celebrate what we do well, and to go about changing any parts of our lives that we want to do better.

Using the Book

We wrote the book using ideas drawn from many sources and from the experiences of many people. There are lots of examples of "what to do" as well as "what not to do," because we believe that any person or book that tells us what is wrong needs to offer ways to do things better. Some examples are arranged in charts that let you scan the material and pick out the topics most interesting to you. The chart format also helps you locate examples you may want to explore further at a later time.

Since it's often easier to learn by doing instead of reading, activities in the appendices help you practice new behaviors or move to a deeper level of understanding.

Many examples are organized by age. You can use these examples two ways. If you have a child that age, use the ideas to help you think about the way you parent. Or use them to think about your own journey. If you received the positive parenting described, celebrate getting what you needed. If you didn't get all the positive parenting you needed, give yourself those healthy messages as you read.

You may say, "Yes, but that's not the way it was for me." That is why you are reading this book. We are talking about *now,* not *then,* what is, not what was. And *now* you deserve loving, caring messages, and this is the time you can give them to yourself.

You can approach this book in a number of ways. Use it to

- improve the way you interact with your children no matter what their ages,
- improve your skills for taking care of yourself,
- evaluate the way you were parented, and
- discover ways to heal from the uneven parenting in your family of origin.

Even and Uneven Parenting

We refer to parenting that has been less than adequate as uneven, not as dysfunctional.

Please notice that we refer to parenting that has been less than adequate as uneven, not as dysfunctional. If our families had not functioned, we would not possess many of the skills that we do have. Somehow our families were functional. Some parts of them worked. A negative label is a burden that doesn't help anyone.

Here are some beliefs common to people who received uneven parenting:

- *I am not lovable.*
- *There is no way out.*
- *Nobody can tell me what to do or tell me what not to do.*
- *I don't know what to do.*
- *I don't know what is normal.*
- *I don't know who I am.*
- *I don't trust anyone but myself to be in control.*

If you received uneven parenting, you can use this book to help yourself and your children.

Children deserve helpful, "even" parenting, and adults deserve to be able to break the chain of uneven parenting, a chain that may be newly forged or that may have been passed down for generations. You can identify your own learnings about even and uneven parenting by doing the exercise on page 275 in the appendix.

About Shame and Guilt

You may say, "But I already should know how to raise children" or "I have already made so many mistakes, I don't even want to think about it. I feel too ashamed."

This is the place for a few words about guilt and shame. Guilt is about our behavior. It is useful. It helps us feel uncomfortable when we have made a mistake and motivates us to start anew or make amends.

Shame Isn't All Bad

Shame is a judgment about who we are, more than about what we do. It can be helpful or unhelpful. Feeling ashamed can be a part of how we live appropriately in society. Fear of doing something that would bring shame upon ourselves or our families—such as running naked through the street, cheating on a test, stealing, or exploiting others—makes us think twice about doing it. In this way, shame can guide us away from behaviors that harm other people or make us outcasts in our cultures.

Shaming can also be used to stop a behavior that needs to be stopped. The two-year-old boy dashing toward a busy street needs to be stopped. A huge, forceful, angry yell will cause him to freeze in his tracks. In this way shame can be used very sparingly to help keep another safe.

Shame That Destroys

Employing shame to control people, however, is a misuse of power. When Gandhi was asked how so few British could control the enormous numbers of Indian citizens, he replied, "They humiliate us to control us." So it is with anyone who intentionally, or out of deep and unexamined old learning controls another by means of humiliation. Sharp anger, a searing jibe at someone's very essence, name-calling, setting someone apart as unacceptable, rejection, all of these behaviors and many more render others helpless. This is the aberration of shame from which so many of us must work to release ourselves.

When we take humiliating messages into ourselves and let them define our being, shame's nagging voice pushes us to hide or lash out. This kind of shame can immobilize us completely and cause us to avoid growth. When we feel ashamed, we feel alienated from others. Our other feelings—guilt, joy, anger, fear, and sadness—can be shared in ways that help us feel connected with other people. But we hide our shame; it isolates us.

When our sense of self becomes too closely linked with our doing, our accomplishments, we shame ourselves inappropriately. Then, when we don't do well or fear that we won't do well, our very being, our very worth feels threatened. No wonder we are tempted to avoid responsibility and hide or quickly throw shame onto others.

Think of inappropriate shame as a response to the lack of unconditional love. Children need to be loved so well that they can learn to love themselves. Those of us who often feel ashamed didn't get that love or didn't get enough of it or didn't believe it. So we try to buy love by doing things and we learn to distrust love that is freely offered. In addition, those of us who have experienced much criticism come to hear any directive as critical and therefore as a threat to our being, as shame producing.

Moving On

If you experienced unhelpful shaming or uneven parenting, use this book to help you parent your children without shaming them and to help yourself recognize shame and replace it with love and joy.

We start our book with the Nurture section, which is about unconditional love, but you can use the book in the order that works best for you. We have grown throughout our writing of this book. Now it is yours.

chapter 1

Learning to Parent Our Children and Ourselves

The Dream

As parents, we plan to provide our children whatever we lacked growing up. We want them to experience love and joy, to be successful and happy, to have a sense of self-worth. We want them to have self-esteem, to believe in themselves, and to feel both lovable and capable.

To achieve this work of wonder, we intend to copy the parts of the parenting we received that helped us and then improve on the rest. We dream. We think and talk about how lovingly we will parent.

The Shock

When our first child arrives, we come face to face with the reality that parenting is much more than a loving dream. It is the daily demand of knowing what to do, when to do it, and how to do it, and then doing it. These demands continue in some form as long as we or our children live. Some parenting tasks we do over and over in monotonous repetition. Others we do only once. Some jar us with their unexpectedness and with how unprepared we are.

Some days we find ourselves doing the very things we vowed we would never do.

We don't always know what to do. Some days we find ourselves doing the very things we vowed we would never do, and we feel guilty, remorseful, and unable to change. Or we give in and deliver the same abuse inflicted on us, defending it as "character building."

We need to learn skills, often many skills, that we did not learn in our families when we were growing up.

Nurture

Humans are born with few skills and have a great variety of needs. One thing children always need is unconditional love. They need it to thrive and grow, to learn to love themselves and others. They need the words and touch and care that say, *I love you; you are lovable.* We call this essential contribution to children's growth and well-being *nurture.*

Structure

But unconditional love is not enough. Children also need to learn limits, skills, and standards. They need to be safe, to learn healthy habits, to develop a sense of who they are and who others are, to learn values and ethics, to develop character, and to become responsible for themselves and to others. Children need parents to convey the message, *You can do this; I will teach you how; you are capable.* The parenting skills that support the development of these skills in a child we call *structure.*

How Nurture and Structure Work Together

Nurture and structure work together to shape the personality. If you think of the personality as a body, nurture provides the soft tissue and muscle and structure acts as the skin and bones. Nurture lets the body move with freedom and grace. When children receive and accept nurture in abundance, they develop a base of self-value and self-love that makes it easy for them to love and care for themselves and to love and care for others. Every experience of accepting love strengthens the muscles of the personality.

Structure, then, gives shape to the personality, providing the skeleton that holds us upright and the skin that contains us. Structure forms the framework and the boundaries of the personality. Like nurture, structure is built from many, many small experiences. We started building it in the family we grew up in, and we continue to build it bit by bit all our lives. People with well-developed structure define their sense of self from within and have strong character. They are clear about who they are and who other people are in relation to themselves. We say such a person has "plenty of backbone."

If a child does not have enough nurture experiences to keep the muscles of the personality strong, the skeleton of the structure will still allow the child to function. The child, however, will feel a hollowness or lack of joy in life, and lack loving response to others.

Adults with less structure than they need do develop a framework, but it is not strong enough to keep appropriate boundaries. They may inappropriately wander into other people's physical or psychological territory. "He pokes his nose in where he doesn't belong." The skin of the personality may be delicate and easily torn as they allow other people to invade their boundaries. We say such persons are "thin-skinned."

Building Nurture and Structure

Think of each structure and nurture experience as a unit of growth. The human infant arrives with a unique set of characteristics and proceeds to build an identity and self-esteem by accumulating, one bit at a time, life's many experiences and by making decisions about those experiences. While we parents cannot predict with certainty that our children will have high self-esteem, be joyful, or succeed, we can continually strengthen our ability to offer a balance of sound structure and loving nurture, and not just do whatever is easiest for us.

How do we learn the skills to give our children the structure and the nurture they need for their well-being? Some skills we learned from our parents. Some we learn by observing our own children and figuring out what works. Some we learn by getting information from others and then thinking about it. If our families weren't good at providing us with appropriate nurture and structure skills, we can learn new ones now.

One caution—some people who received neglectful, abusive, or smothering parenting are so determined not to do the same to their children that they "parent by doing the opposite." The hazard is that they often go too far. Parents who grew up in an atmosphere of rigidity and criticism may set too few limits and standards. They end up throwing out helpful structure along with the rigidity. Parents who were not nurtured well and did not receive unconditional love themselves, may smother their children with attention in an attempt not to be neglectful. Or, if they were hampered by indulgent, overprotective love, they may withhold love to ensure that they are not smothering. Children need a balance of nurture and structure, and so do adults.

In the process of learning to provide for our children, we need to learn better nurture and structure skills for ourselves as well.

The Hope

Becoming contented and well-adjusted is a process filled with hope and is as important for us as it is for our children. The decision to rebuild ourselves, to grow up again, can be a sudden one, but the process is not. There is no quick fix. There is no magical, sudden way to borrow the needed skills and to reclaim our self-confidence and self-esteem. We must do it ourselves step-by-step; we must build from within. Responding to someone else's urging us to "build our self-esteem" by thumping our chests and shouting "I am the greatest" is questionable at best and harmful at worst. On a day when we are feeling directionless, depressed, or suicidal, simulated self-esteem could add to our despair or further alienate us from our feelings.

> *The decision to rebuild ourselves, to grow up again, can be a sudden one, but the process is not. There is no quick fix.*

True self-esteem comes from within and is not competitive. If it depends on being greater than others, it is "competitive-esteem" or "other-esteem," not "self-esteem." Self-worth is claimed, bit by bit, by practicing being capable, by affirming ourselves in ways that are meaningful to us, and by learning to believe that we are lovable.

Competence and a feeling of well-being or self-esteem are important for both children and parents. We build our self-esteem by recognizing the positive and the negative messages and experiences life has offered us, and by making healthy decisions about those offerings. Nurture and structure help us do this. A balance of loving nurture and consistent structure helps us satisfy our basic hungers for stimulation, recognition, and certainty. We will explore those next.

chapter 2

The Hunger for
Stimulation, Recognition, and Certainty

This Isn't How I Thought It Would Be

Love my children? Yes, of course, I love them. But parenting isn't what I thought it would be!

Listen to the laments:

My Marcie whines and demands, especially when I don't have time to give to her.

I give lots of attention to my Josh, but he always wants more.

Andrew just seems flat. I offer him the same thing over and over and he doesn't respond, so I leave him alone.

Flat? I wish my Noah had some of that. He keeps our house in a state of uproar.

Well, my Elena flouts the rules and laughs at my anger.

Not my Brian. He takes punishment seriously, but it seems like I'm always after him about something.

Any of that sound familiar? And to add to the problem, not only could Marcie and the other children be any age, but also with some slight alterations, the laments could refer to a spouse, a friend, a partner, or a work mate, or even to yourself.

If you have a similar lament, it may be time to try out some different ways of parenting or of understanding yourself. It may be time, in the rhythm of your life, to grow up again.

Hearing these laments as part of the "SRC triangle" can help us deal with them. *SRC* stands for the psychological hunger for stimulation, recognition, and certainty. These three human hungers, present in all of our lives, are so powerful that sometimes they even push aside needs for sleep or food.

If these hungers aren't readily satisfied, at any age, we pursue them; we need to feel alive (stimulated) and acknowledged (recognized) and safe (certain). If we can't get the one we need, we try to make do by substituting one of the others. This works to a certain extent, but is never really satisfying because the three hungers are distinct and equal in importance.

Think about these three hungers as the three points on a triangle.

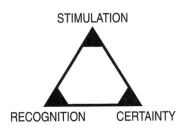

STIMULATION

RECOGNITION   CERTAINTY

Let's do something! At one point is stimulation, the hunger to be energized and vital.

Look at me! At another point is recognition, the hunger to be acknowledged and considered valuable.

Who's in charge here? The third point holds certainty, the hunger for a framework in which to feel safe and confident and to get stimulation and recognition safely and appropriately.

You can use this book to help you think about the following questions:

- Am I providing a balance of stimulation, recognition, and certainty for my children?
- Is one of them easier for me to offer so that I offer it at the expense of the others?
- Is one of my children clamoring for me to meet one of the hungers because she isn't getting enough of another?
- When children are not responding well to our offers, we can remember that children, like adults, have widely different temperaments. The book by Helen Neville and Diane Clark Johnson *Temperament Tools, Working with Your Child's Inborn Traits*[1] helps us do just that.
- Am I putting one of my unmet hungers onto the children instead of noticing what they need?
- Do I have stimulation, recognition, and certainty balanced in my own life?
- Am I accepting the satisfaction of one hunger in place of another when I could do something to get that hunger met directly?

The three hungers are equally important. Children and adults may crave more of one than another, at any one time, but we can't always recognize that. Therefore, it is safest to offer a balance of all three.

Let us look at each example. Every one could be about a child or an adult.

Recognition—the hunger to be acknowledged—*Look at me!*

My Marcie whines and demands, especially when I don't have time to give to her.

Marcie's whining and demanding may be saying, "I need more recognition from you. I feel scared and angry when I'm not sure if you value me." The response: more time with Marcie, more loving (I recognize your need to be acknowledged for who you are), and more noticing and commenting on what Marcie does (I recognize your accomplishments).

I give lots of attention to my Josh, but he always wants more.

Josh has lots of recognition already, so his bid for more may be a signal that he has been given a kind of recognition that does not support his growth. He may even receive too much recognition and believe that he is the center of everything.

Instead of recognition, does Josh really need more or less stimulation? If his life does not offer enough things to do and to think about, offer more stimulation. On the other hand, if his life is too filled with transitions with no time to hang out, to integrate, to think or play through his experiences, he may be overstimulated, feel overwhelmed, and need less stimulation.

Or does Josh feel uncertainty? He may need to be taught the skills to comfort himself or to initiate his own activities. Or the family rules may be too rigid so he seeks the reassurance of recognition because the rigidity feels as if it is squeezing him to be someone other than he is.

Stimulation—the hunger for the contact that is vital to life—*Let's do something!*

Andrew just seems flat. I offer him the same thing over and over and he doesn't respond, so I leave him alone.

Babies who are not touched and talked to languish or die. Andrew went flat. Children and adults go flat or they agitate or manipulate when life is too monotonous, too repetitive, beyond boring. We all need variety, action, challenge, excitement, touch. Andrew may need all of those.

Flat? I wish my Noah had some of that. He keeps our house in a state of uproar.

Noah, who creates too much excitement, may be saying, "There is too much or too little stimulation here so notice what I need!"

Or he may be saying, "Since you don't recognize me in other ways, I've found a way to get your attention."

Or he may be asking for stronger boundaries and clearer rules—better structure—so he can learn to contain himself.

Certainty—the hunger for physical, social, and psychological systems that keep us safe and make life predictable—*Who's in charge here?*

Well, my Elena flouts the rules and laughs at my anger.

If Elena flouts the rules and then laughs, and if she is older than two, she may need better structure. Her parents can develop consistency if the structure has been lax. Or they can loosen up the rigidity, if the structure has been rigid. Too many limitations often result in rebellion, passivity, or manipulation rather than safety.

Not my Brian. He takes punishment seriously, but it seems like I'm always after him about something.

Brian, who gets punished often, may be saying, "I'm uncertain about the structure in this family."

Maybe the parents are inconsistent or don't agree on family rules. Brian may need clear, safe rules regularly enforced.

Or Brian may be saying, "Recognize me. This is the only way I get you to notice me."

Or he may be creating contact in a life that has too much or too little stimulation.

SRC for Adolescents

"But," you say, "my teenagers want to be with their friends, not with me. They think I'm irrelevant. So I've been backing off."

Don't back off. Stay connected. The recently released National Longitudinal Study on Adolescent Health[2] is based on interviews of 12,118 adolescents, grades seven through twelve. These teenagers report that connectedness with their parents in either dual-parent or single-parent families tops the list of protective factors for the teenagers' health. Those teens who are in regular touch with their parents and feel valued by them are less likely to smoke, drink, or experiment with drugs and early sex.

Adults Have Needs Too

Adults have these hungers too. Have you attended a meeting where the structure was so unclear that it took a whole morning for the group to decide what to do? William, who attended just such a meeting recently reported on how people responded to the uncertainty. Some people addressed the lack of certainty directly:

- *Can't we set some goals and get going?*
- *Let's divide up into smaller groups and decide what to do.*
- *We could do this just like we did the last time.*

When that didn't work, some people tried for recognition:

- *I feel uncomfortable because we haven't introduced ourselves.*
- *I need to change rooms.*
- *Can we wear name tags?*

Some people raised the stimulation level by doing a lot of side talking, pointing out of the window, interrupting, and disagreeing with everything. After a structure was finally created, when goals were identified and a way to meet them was constructed, individuals settled down and the group went about its work and play. The next time you are in a situation where it feels like people's needs are not being met, think about the SRC triangle, think about your own needs, and then decide what to do.

So, here it is. A triangle that offers options. A helpful way to look at our own behavior and that of others. A hopeful guide to help us get our needs met and improve the ways we interact with others.

The Nurture section of this book helps us look at how we offer recognition and stimulation with some structure. The Structure section offers ways to provide certainty by strengthening boundaries and sorting out rules as well as offering stimulation and recognition.

The Denial section offers a framework for exploring how we might sabotage our good intentions to improve our parenting or change the way we care for ourselves.

The sections on Prenatal and Birth Experience, Growing Up Again, and Adoption remind us that each period of our lives presents us with special needs and special opportunities to find stimulation, recognition, and certainty.

We will explore Nurture first.

Human Hungers

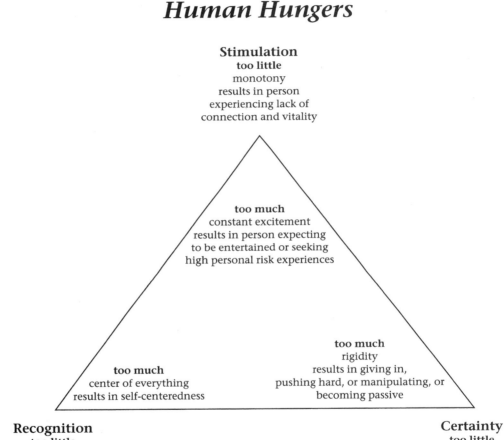

Stimulation
too little
monotony
results in person
experiencing lack of
connection and vitality

too much
constant excitement
results in person expecting
to be entertained or seeking
high personal risk experiences

too much
rigidity
results in giving in,
pushing hard, or manipulating, or
becoming passive

too much
center of everything
results in self-centeredness

Recognition
too little
isolation
results in person feeling
ignored, devalued, unimportant

Certainty
too little
abandonment
results in uncertainty,
lack of order and
direction,
chaos

Adapted from Eric Berne's book *Transactional Analysis in Psychotherapy,* New York, Random House, 1961.

SECTION **II**

Nurture
The Gentle Side of Care

Great love can both take hold and let go.
O. R. ORAGE

chapter 3

Nurture
What It Is and Why We Need It

Nurture: Acts of Unconditional Love

Nurture is all the ways we offer positive recognition and stimulation. It includes giving love to ourselves and others. Nurture is important because it helps people of all ages thrive and develop. It offers us the hope, joy, and self-confidence to be ourselves, to be successful. Nurture helps us develop our uniqueness and helps us believe we deserve to become skillful. Nurture is about *being*. It does not need to be earned. If structure can be seen as the skin and bones of life, nurture is the soft tissue that fleshes out the body and helps the bones move freely. We store it, bit by bit, as the basis of our self-esteem.

> *Nurture is all the ways we offer positive recognition and stimulation. It includes giving love to ourselves and others.*

In this section we will consider

- Nurture—what it is and why it is important
- Care and support—expressions of unconditional love
- The Nurture Chart—ways people get recognition and stimulation
- Distinctions between care and support
- The Nurture Highway
- How to help children accept love
- Nurturing other adults and ourselves

Young children need to be nurtured, to be touched, noticed, and cared for. Nurture provides them with the attention and contact they need in order to stay alive and to live fully. Nurture is so essential that children who are not noticed and are touched very little fail to thrive. These children may even die.

Attention (or recognition) and contact (or stimulation) help children live. Of course, some forms of attention and contact are much healthier than others. Children who are hit, treated harshly, or violated sexu-

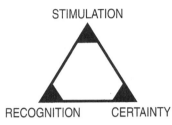

STIMULATION

RECOGNITION   CERTAINTY

ally *are* touched and noticed. They often, but not always, manage to grow up. In the absence of positive touch and care, those children "make do" with the harsh contact available to them. They live, but often without hope, joy, confidence, and competence.

People whose childhood was filled with unconditional love, with gentle care and loving touch, pass it along naturally to their children. Others of us, although we may be determined to give our children the good parenting we did not have, often don't know how. Learning new ways takes determination, time, thought, and sometimes discomfort. There is, however, joy in this process. It comes as we watch our children thrive and as we learn to nurture ourselves and become truly more confident and hopeful.

Care and Support: Expressions of Unconditional Love

We begin our discussion of love by looking at what children need. You can use these chapters to help you nurture your own children, to think about the ways you were nurtured, and to improve the ways you nurture yourself. After we have considered the ways children get or don't get loving care, we will consider adults whose lives lacked or lack healthy care and what they can do to heal themselves. Perhaps the child in you needs extra care and support.

True nurturing comes in two forms, assertive care and supportive care. *Assertive care* means that the caregiver notices, understands, and responds to the cues and needs of the child. The caregiver determines what the child needs and responds to those needs in loving, trustworthy, and reliable ways. *Supportive care* is the act of offering care that the child is free to accept, reject, or negotiate.

The foundation of both assertive care and supportive care is unconditional love. Its expressions are many:

- "I love you and care for you because you are here."
- "I love you because you are you."
- "You deserve love. No strings attached."
- "I love who you are."

- "I love and care for you willingly."
- "I love you."
- "I'm so glad to know you."
- "I'm glad you're my child."

Unconditional love has no price tag. It uses no yardstick to measure worth. It is given freely, as often and as much as needed. Children who receive this kind of care thrive, master their developmental tasks in natural ways, and are free to be fully loved. This opportunity to thrive may be the greatest gift parents can give.

Loving nurture includes giving love and care by

- providing nutritious food and opportunities to strengthen body, mind, and spirit,
- encouraging the accomplishment of developmental tasks, and
- providing environments and activities that feed souls rather than bleed them.

The Decision to Love

Love is all around us and its supply is inexhaustible. But just because love is always possible does not mean we believe it is an option for us. Giving and receiving unconditional love is something we decide to learn and practice. Love is not made real just because we say the words of love. Unconditional love must be communicated in words *and* transmitted through our actions.

> *Giving and receiving unconditional love is something we decide to learn and practice.*

Loving words need to be matched by loving behaviors. A hand on the shoulder, an offer of help, time for listening, warm eye contact, and the many, many other ways we show love back up what we say. Children who hear and feel unconditional love have the opportunity to learn how to give unconditional love to themselves and others. They can learn to believe in their being and respect the being of others.

Unconditional love is not always easy to convey. When someone we love is behaving badly and trying our tolerance, it may be more difficult to act out of our unconditional love. Loving is a skill that is learned and practiced. We *decide* to stay in a position of unconditional love while dealing with distressing behaviors.

Giving someone the gift of unconditional love doesn't mean always agreeing, or accepting any behavior no matter how hurtful, or accepting substandard performance of tasks, or hiding our anger. It does mean being honest, working through differences, negotiating and renegotiating agreements, holding one another accountable, and staying respectful in the process.

Children who hear loving words yet are disregarded, abandoned, or exploited learn to be suspicious of love. They learn that love is confusing and not to be trusted. They may want to believe the words and may pretend to believe, but they don't really learn about unconditional love. As adults, they will need to learn to love themselves and others and, through practice, build the muscles of giving and receiving love and concern without expectation of a reward or having to pay back.

Misguided Love

Nurture is a loving gift—unless it becomes twisted and out of balance. Here are some things to watch for:

- Besides offering assertive and supportive care to our children, we find fun in indulging them at times. But it is important to examine how often and why we do this. If we give to our children because it feels good to us, but does not meet the child's needs, it is a message to our children that they count only as a reflection of us. When we learn to meet our own needs directly, we no longer want to overindulge our children.

- Some parents put their children first in order to play the martyr.

> *Some parents put their children first in order to play the martyr.*

Such parents do not truly value themselves and seek validation from their children. Hence, they do not want to deny the children's wishes or risk their wrath. Children with parents who undervalue themselves will not learn to value the parents, themselves, or others. Lacking a model for true self-worth, a child tries to construct a sense of self by copying the parent's martyrdom. Or, seeing the futility of that, the child may try the opposite: running over the needs of others to get what he or she wants. Parents who overindulge, for any reason, often raise children who are selfish and unappreciative of others. (See section IV on overindulgence.)

- Some parents are not consistent in offering unconditional love and instead alternate between ignoring a child's needs for care and overindulging the child. Others alternate supportive care with care that has strings attached. "I'll love you if you do things my way."

The Nurture Chart

Parents can offer recognition and stimulation in either helpful or unhelpful ways. The Nurture Chart shows six methods of contact: *Abuse, Conditional Care, Assertive Care, Supportive Care, Overindulgence,* and *Neglect.* The following pages define the six methods of contact and explain the organization of the Nurture Chart. Use these pages to help you understand ways you can use the Nurture Chart.

Six Nurture Positions

The six ways of offering, or failing to offer, nurture are arranged from harshest contact to the absence of contact. The two in the center of the range, *assertive care* and *supportive care,* offer stimulation and recognition appropriate to the child's age and development.

ABUSE CONDITIONAL CARE ASSERTIVE CARE SUPPORTIVE CARE OVERINDULGENCE NEGLECT

Abuse is harsh contact. Abuse involves physical invasion, tissue damage such as shaking, burning, or hitting, and sexual touch. It also includes other painful, invasive behaviors such as humiliation, sexual innuendo, laughing at pain, threats of harm, scolding for being in pain, and ridicule. Even though abusive attention is harsh, children will make use of this kind of attention to stay alive in the absence of any other recognition.

Conditional care is nurture provided only when a child earns it. The implicit demand is "I'll take care of you if you'll take care of me" or "I'll care for you if you are good, bright, quiet, etc." Conditional care ties love to behavior.

Assertive care meets the other person's needs directly. The caregiver provides nurturing without asking the recipient for permission, because the caregiver judges the care to be necessary and appropriate to the child's development and recognizes that the recipient is unable to provide that self-care.

ABUSE

CONDITIONAL CARE

ASSERTIVE CARE

SUPPORTIVE CARE

OVERINDULGENCE

NEGLECT

Supportive care is the loving presence of the person who offers help. It responds to requests for aid and offers help that may be accepted, declined, or negotiated.

Overindulgence is the patronizing, sticky love expressed by giving too much too soon or too long. It is given to meet the needs of the giver and undermines the competency of the recipient.

Neglect describes caregiving that doesn't notice or meet the child's needs because the parents are too busy or are preoccupied meeting their own needs or are physically or emotionally absent.

Notice that the extremes of abuse and neglect are very similar. Both fail to meet the needs of the child.

How to Use the Nurture Chart

ABUSE   CONDITIONAL CARE   ASSERTIVE CARE   SUPPORTIVE CARE   OVERINDULGENCE   NEGLECT

To use the Nurture Chart on pages 28–29 most effectively, it's important that you wait until you are familiar with the chart before you make judgments about your parenting or identify the parenting in your family of origin. Children experience combinations of the six methods of contact at home, at school, and elsewhere. Furthermore, most adults use more than one position on the continuum. The center two, Assertive and Supportive Care, offer the most healthy structure. Since every child responds to, interprets, and makes decisions in ways that reflect his or her uniqueness, your child's decisions may not match those on the chart.

> *Assertive and Supportive Care offer the most healthy structure.*

Vertical Columns

- The top cell in each column describes the general characteristics of that position.
- The second cell down gives an example of the words and behaviors typical of a parent offering that way of nurturing.
- The third cell suggests the underlying message a child might hear. Bear in mind that how the message is heard varies from child to child.
- The fourth cell lists common ways children respond to being nurtured in this way.
- The bottom cell describes decisions children typically make in response to the particular way of nurturing. There is a tendency for these early decisions to be carried forward into adulthood. You can think about your own old decisions and examine them now in the light of the Nurture Chart.

Horizontal Rows

- You can look across any row to compare the six ways of nurturing.

THE NURTURE CHART, page 1

Joy, hope, self-confidence, and self-esteem grow from care and support. Despair, joylessness, and loneliness flow from abuse, conditional care, overindulgence, and neglect.

ABUSE	CONDITIONAL CARE 	ASSERTIVE CARE 
Characteristics:		
Abuse involves relating to a child by assault, physical or psychological invasion, direct or indirect "don't be" messages. Abuse negates the child's needs.	Conditional care requires the child to earn care or pay for care in some way. The care the parent gives the child is based on the parent's needs and expectations, not on the child's needs.	Assertive care recognizes the child and the child's needs. The parent decides to nurture in this way because it is helpful to the child, responsive to the child's needs, and appropriate to the circumstance. It is comforting and loving. It is freely given. 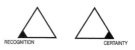
Example: School-age child has a badly scraped arm.		
Parent does not care for wounds. Says, "Stop sniffling or I'll give you something to cry about." Yells at or shakes the child.	Parent says, "Stop crying or I won't bandage your arm."	Parent cares for the wound in a loving way. Says, "Your arm is scraped! I'm sorry."
Children May Hear the Following Underlying Messages:		
You don't count. Your needs don't count. You are not lovable. You don't deserve to exist. To get what you need, you must expect pain.	I matter and you don't. Your needs and feelings don't count. You can have care as long as you earn it. Don't believe you are lovable; you have to earn love.	I love you and you are lovable. You are important. Your needs are important. I care for you willingly.
Common Responses of Children:		
Pain in the heart, as well as pain in the scraped arm. Fear, terror, rage, withdrawal, loneliness, despair, shame, confusion about reality.	Pain in the heart, as well as pain in the scraped arm. Fear, terror, anger, mistrust of own perceptions, shame, feelings of inadequacy, suspicious of love.	Pain in the arm and warmth in the heart. Feels comforted, accepted, important, satisfied, relieved, secure, safe, loved.
Decisions Often Made by Children:		
I am not powerful. I deserve to die, or the reverse, I will live in spite of them. It's my fault, or I'll blame everything on others. I'll be good, or I'll be bad. Big people get to abuse, or I can abuse those smaller than I am, or I will never abuse. I won't feel or have needs. Love does not exist. I am alone; I keep emotional distance from, and don't trust, others. I blame or strike or leave first.	I am what I do. I must strive to please. Big people get what they want. I can never do enough. I must be perfect. I don't deserve love. There is a scarcity of love. I must be strong. Love obligates me and is costly. I don't trust. I do keep emotional distance, run away, or blame others.	I am important. I deserve care. It's okay to ask for what I need. I belong here. I am loved. Others can be trusted and relied upon. I can know what I need. It's okay to be dependent at times.

SUPPORTIVE CARE 	OVERINDULGENCE ☾	NEGLECT ✳
Characteristics:		
Supportive care recognizes the child and the child's needs. It is care the child is free to accept or reject. It offers help, comfort, and love. It stimulates children to think and to do what they are capable of doing for themselves.	Overindulgence is a sticky, patronizing kind of care. It promotes continuing dependence on the parent and teaches the child not to think independently and not to be responsible for self or to others.	Neglect is passive abuse. It is lack of emotional or physical stimulation and recognition by parents who are unavailable or who ignore the needs of the child. These parents may be "there, but not there."

Example: School-age child has a badly scraped arm.

[Parent has already taught child how to clean a scrape.] Says in a concerned and loving tone, "I see you've scraped your arm. Does it hurt? Do you want to take care of it yourself or would you like some help from me?" Offers a hug.	Parent rushes to child. Says, "Oh, look at your arm, you poor thing. That really stings! I'll bandage it. Go and lie down in front of the television and I'll do your chores for you."	Parent ignores the scrape. Says, "Don't bother me."

Children May Hear the Following Underlying Messages:

I love you, you are lovable. You are capable. I am willing to care for you. Ask for what you need. Your welfare is important to me. I am separate from you. I trust you to think and make judgments in your own best interests.	Don't grow up. Don't be who you are (capable). My needs are more important than yours (or) your needs are more important than mine. You don't need to care for yourself; someone will care for you.	Don't expect to be recognized. Your needs are not important. You are not important. You do not deserve to exist. Expect to suffer to get what you need. Be confused about reality.

Common Responses of Children:

Pain in the arm and a heart filled with confidence. Child feels cared for, comforted, challenged, secure, and trustworthy.	Pain in the arm and uncertainty in the heart. Self-centered satisfaction, temporary comfort, self-righteousness. Later on: confusion, woefulness, helplessness, obligation, resentment, defensiveness, and shame. Not knowing what is enough.	Pain in the heart, as well as pain in the scraped arm. Feelings of abandonment, fear, shame, rage, hopelessness, helplessness, abject disappointment.

Decisions Often Made by Children:

I am loved. I can know what I need. I am capable. I can be powerful. I am not alone. It's okay to ask for help. I am both separate and connected. I can decide when to be dependent and when to be independent.	I am not capable. I don't have to be competent. I don't have to know what I need, think, or feel. Other people are obligated to take care of me. I don't have to grow up. I must be loyal to my indulging parent. To get my needs met, I manipulate or play a victim role. It's okay to be self-centered. Later on: be wary and don't trust.	I don't really know who I am or what's right. I am not important. I am not lovable. I die alone or survive on my own. It isn't possible or safe to get close, to trust, or to ask for help. I do not deserve help. What I do doesn't count if someone has to help me. Life is hard.

chapter 4

Assertive Care and Supportive Care

Alike but Different

Both assertive care and supportive care are provided willingly with no strings attached. However, they differ in subtle and important ways. Assertive care is a *loving response* or *loving intrusion*. Supportive care is an *offering, lovingly given.*

Infants require care. They signal their needs by crying or fussing. When the furnace breaks down and Dad puts warmer clothes on Sally before she starts to cry from the cold, Dad has made a loving intrusion. He has given assertive care. Baby Sally cries and Dad offers her a bottle. She refuses it and Dad tries gentle rocking. She fusses for a bit, then settles into his arms, satisfied. He has made loving responses and given supportive care.

Support helps young children start making decisions and it encourages them to think about how they feel and what they need. Little Jenny, a toddler, has been busy exploring the objects on the end table after dinner. She starts to fuss and looks tired. Dad says, "Jenny, I have a rocking chair and a big hug for you. Do you want to rock?" Jenny gets to choose whether to be rocked, fuss some more, or wander off to another activity. If her fussing increases, Dad will switch from support to assertive care.

As children grow older they need more support and less intrusion, but even big, competent kids appreciate assertive care now and then. Judy's teenage son Eric had been making his own lunches. One morning, knowing he had dedicated the evening before to studying for a daunting math test, Judy made his lunch and left it in the refrigerator. When Eric rushed to the kitchen to make his lunch, Mom pointed to the refrigerator. Eric on seeing his lunch ready and waiting, said, "Way cool!" Judy's loving decision to make his lunch signaled her empathy for his distress. She didn't ask if he needed help. She decided he needed a bit of care. And he felt cared for and affirmed.

When parents take good care of their children, the children grow up knowing how to take good care of themselves. As children are able to be more responsible for meeting their own needs, parents decrease the amount of assertive care they provide and increase the amount of support they offer. The growing relationship between parents and adult children becomes primarily one of support in both directions.

chapter 5

Life Examples of the Nurture Chart

Using the Nurture Chart

Since most parents use all six ways of interacting with children sometimes, it is helpful to think of the Nurture Chart as a highway.[1] The center two positions are the driving lanes, conditional care and overindulgence are the shoulders, and abuse and neglect are the ditches. When we have been driving on a shoulder or are in a ditch, we need to move back to the middle, but try to avoid overcorrecting onto the shoulder or into the ditch. The goal is to stay in the driving lanes as much as possible.

You can assess and improve your skill at offering care and support to children by thinking about the following examples of common parenting situations. Decide if the assertive and supportive care suggestions would be helpful if your current family were in that situation. If not, rewrite those messages and behaviors in a way that would be more appropriate for your family. Remember to base your decisions on unconditional love.

EXAMPLE 1

Situation: One-year-old girl puts everything in her mouth.
The parent:

   Abuse: Screams at child and hits objects out of her mouth.

   Conditional Care: Frowns, says, "I don't love you when you do that. Be a good girl and stop."

   Assertive Care: Takes all hazardous or breakable objects out of rooms where child plays. Admires child's ability to explore.

Supportive Care: Offers a wide variety of objects that are safe for child to mouth.

Overindulgence: Lets child ruin things because "she wants to chew on everything."

Neglect: Doesn't notice child tasting colored tissue paper, cigarette butts, aspirin, dishwasher soap.

EXAMPLE 2

Situation: Four-year-old boy plays dress up in women's clothes.

The parent:

Abuse: Says, "You're a little queer!" Snatches jewelry off child and beats him.

Conditional Care: Says, "Act tough like a real boy should or you're no son of mine."

Assertive Care: Says lovingly, "I see you like playing dress up." Offers hug.

Supportive Care: Provides a variety of dress-up costumes.

Overindulgence: Buys six fancy costumes that reflect "real boy" activities such as a cowboy suit, pirate outfit, Superman costume.

Neglect: Provides no props for fantasy play.

EXAMPLE 3

Situation: Seven-year-old child feels sad about being excluded by friends.

The parent:

Abuse: Says, "I don't blame them. Who would want to play with a crybaby like you?" Hits child on upper arm or twists his ear.

Conditional Care: Sighs, says, "I'd always hoped that you would be popular."

Assertive Care: Says, "I love you and I think you are wonderful. I'm sorry they left you out. What are some other things you can do today?"

Supportive Care: Says, "I remember a time when I was your age and was sad about being left out. It felt icky. Remember that I'm on your team. Anything you want from me?"

Overindulgence: Says, "I'll get you some new toys and then your friends will want to play with you."

Neglect: Doesn't notice or says it doesn't matter.

EXAMPLE 4

Situation: Family is moving to different town and eight-year-old child does not want to move.

The parent:

Abuse: Says, "Don't be a crybaby. If you're going to whine, I'll give you something to cry about."

Conditional Care: Says, "I have a lot to do so be a good kid and help me pack."

Assertive Care: Sees child's tears. Holds and comforts child and reads her a book about a child's experience with moving and talks about it.[2]

Supportive Care: Says, "Leaving the place you live and your friends is tough. Want to plan some special ways to say good-bye to your friends?" Parents do some good-bye ritual about leaving the home and invite the child to join them.

Overindulgence: Says, "I feel sorry for you. I moved twice when I was your age. You can have your choice of the bedrooms and all new furniture."

Neglect: Fails to notice child's distress.

EXAMPLE 5

Situation: Ten-year-old wants to play a French horn.

The parent:

Abuse: Says, "You want to play a horn?" in a ridiculing way. Laughs at child.

Conditional Care: Offers no praise, focuses on mistakes, or urges other activities instead. Says, "I don't have the money for a horn because you need better skis."

Assertive Care: Says, "On Friday we'll go to the music store and find out about renting a horn."

Supportive Care: Says, "How will you learn to play? Can you get lessons at school or shall we look for a teacher?"

Overindulgence: "Here, I got you a trumpet. It's a very good one. It'll be easier for you to carry than a French horn."

Neglect: Ignores child's request, or promises to get an instrument and forgets.

EXAMPLE 6

Situation: Child is experiencing onset of puberty.

The parent:

Abuse: Teases about acne, budding breasts, or voice change. Touches child in sexual manner.

Conditional Care: Says, "I see you're are starting to mature. I hate to see you grow up."

Assertive Care: With a loving voice, says, "I notice your body is changing. You are entering adolescence and becoming more grown up. That's a wonderful, important change. I love who you are." Continues to touch child in a nurturing, nonsexual way acceptable to the child.

Supportive Care: Says, "I'd like to celebrate this important milestone. How would you like to celebrate, or do you want to leave it to me?"

Overindulgence: Says, "I see you're starting to mature. I'm glad! Now you can have boy-girl parties. Let's plan one for this Friday."

Neglect: Doesn't notice or withholds touch. (Some parents confuse nurturing touch and affectionate touch with sex and stop touching their teenage children of the opposite sex. During puberty, however, most kids feel insecure and need the reassurance of continued, safe, parental touch.)

EXAMPLE 7

Situation: Teenage son is surrounded by pressure to use alcohol.

The parent:

Abuse: Regularly searches teen's personal belongings, listens in on phone conversations. Slaps him around after hearing there was beer at a party he attended.

Conditional Care: Says, "I love you as long as you don't drink." Or, "You'll be the death of me if you drink."

Assertive Care: Does not offer liquor to teenagers. Offers car when appropriate so teen doesn't have to ride with peers who are drinking. Affirms love for and importance of the teen on ongoing basis.

Supportive Care: Does not drink or uses in moderation, never to intoxication. Acknowledges peer pressure to use. Asks how to be of help. Encourages teen to develop a variety of skills and awareness for coping with pressure. Celebrates successes.

Overindulgence: Offers to buy liquor for teen.

Neglect: Drinks to excess, is emotionally and/or physically absent, doesn't notice kid is drunk.

Test Your Knowledge

For examples 8–11, write in the space provided the nurture position that best describes the response. If the responses of assertive care and supportive care don't fit your circumstances, rewrite them. Compare your answers with those provided. Remember that tone of voice and body language can change how a message sounds.

EXAMPLE 8
Situation: Fourteen-year-old boy shows signs of alcohol and other drug use at home and school.
The parent:

1. Takes child to qualified person for assessment of problem and recommendation of solution and insists upon treatment if that is indicated. If not, insists that child stop alcohol and drug use. _____
2. Yells and lectures child about not using. Shakes him by the shoulders. _____
3. Says, "I can't believe any son of mine would do what you're doing." _____
4. Searches out alternative community supports for child and self. _____
5. Looks the other way. _____
6. Takes the blame on self. Listens endlessly to excuses, tolerates irresponsible behavior, and protects son from negative consequences. _____

Answers: (1) Assertive care (2) Abuse (3) Conditional care (4) Supportive care (5) Neglect (6) Overindulgence

EXAMPLE 9
Situation: Child is disabled.
The parent:

1. Does not provide care, support, or protection for child. _____
2. Calls child gimp, cripple, peg leg, half-wit. Cares for child roughly. _____
3. Withholds comfort when child is suffering. Praises child when he denies grief and sadness. _____
4. Offers a variety of opportunities for child to grow and thrive. _____

5. Does not expect child to be responsible for his own feelings or behavior. Does things for the child that child is able to do for self. _____

6. Teaches child to cope. Validates child's feelings. _____

Answers: (1) Neglect (2) Abuse (3) Conditional care (4) Supportive care (5) Overindulgence (6) Assertive care

EXAMPLE 10
Situation: Teenager acts severely depressed.
The parent:

1. Doesn't notice or says, "I see you're growing up. I hope you make it." _____
2. Says, "Come back when you're cheerful." _____
3. Says, "Don't mope around here. You have nothing to be depressed about." _____
4. Commiserates. Lets child stay alone in room. Buys expensive presents. Says how bad life is. _____
5. Takes child to a professional for assessment and gets therapy if needed. Makes necessary changes in the family system. _____
6. Only assertive care is appropriate. Getting help is not optional. _____

Answers: (1) Neglect (2) Conditional care (3) Abuse (4) Overindulgence (5) Assertive care (6) Supportive care

EXAMPLE 11
Situation: Teenage daughter has been raped.
The parent:

1. Says, "You can't expect people to respect you now. Let's not tell anybody about this." _____
2. Provides opportunities to listen to or to talk with her. Offers to be available. Does whatever is necessary to heal self. Family participates in a community education effort to prevent rape. Daughter can join the family in the program if she chooses. _____
3. Beats her or blames her for attracting the rapist. _____
4. Sends child on a trip to Europe to get her mind off the rape. _____

5. Gets professional help for whole family. Uses all resources, personal and external, to help daughter, self, and family heal. _____

6. Doesn't notice. Since daughter is used to neglect, she doesn't tell. _____

Answers: (1) Conditional care (2) Supportive care (3) Abuse (4) Overindulgence (5) Assertive care (6) Neglect

EXAMPLE 12

Situation: Your child wants clothes that your family cannot afford.

For each position, answer the question: What would I do if I were to be abusive, provide conditional care, provide assertive care, etc.?

Abuse: _____

Conditional care: _____

Assertive care: _____

Supportive care: _____

Overindulgence: _____

Neglect: _____

List a problem situation from your own parenting. Describe how you might show each of the six responses in your situation.

_____

_____

Think about what you need to stay in the driving lanes.

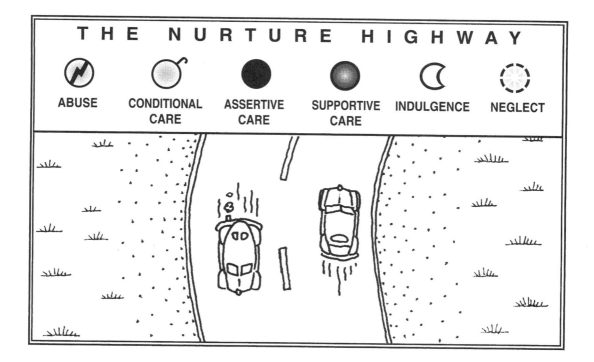

The Nurture Highway

On the Nurture Highway, assertive care and supportive care are the two safe driving lanes. They are the two most helpful ways of offering recognition and stimulation. Conditional care, *I will only love you if . . .* , and overindulgent care, *I love you so much I'll give you more than you need,* are the questionable shoulders of the road. Abuse and neglect are the ditches and sometimes necessitate a tow truck of support or outside help to get back on the road.

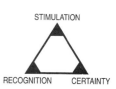

    Equate parenting to driving. Think of caring for your children as driving your parenting car, staying on the road as much as you can, and getting whatever help you need to stay there. Most drivers hit a shoulder now and then; the challenge is to get back on the road without overcorrecting and hitting the opposite shoulder or ditch. Anyone who has driven a lot knows it is possible to end up in the ditch without any intention of getting there. Letting your children know that you are aiming to stay on the road can help them understand your parenting goals.

You can make a Nurture Chart for yourself as often as you need to. Teach your children to evaluate what kind of nurture they are getting outside of your family. Teach them to expect care and support and to recognize and reject abuse, conditional love, overindulgence, and neglect.

chapter 6

When Love Doesn't Stick

Sometimes the love we send by word or deed isn't heard and internalized by the receiver as we intended. Children who grow up with *conditional care* and other shoulder-and-ditch experiences learn to let in only part of the love that's available, only as much as they feel is safe.

Helping Children Accept Love

If you think your child is rejecting love or converting nurturing messages to criticism, or if the child is not accepting the love you offer or is feeling ashamed, ask yourself: *Is the child being abused by someone else? By someone who is cruel and mean? Or by someone who does not understand developmental needs and is interfering with them?* If this is true, protect your child and get help.

Has your own parenting been uneven? If so, tell your child that you have been inconsistent and are going to change. Then follow through. Also try the following:

- Report to your child that you are not sure he or she heard your nurturing message. Ask your child to listen as you say it again. Do not wait for a response.
- Touch your child gently and repeat your nurturing message directly and softly. If that doesn't work, shout or sing it.
- Tell your child you think your nurturing message wasn't heard in the way you meant it. Say you would like to try again. Word the message differently. Don't expect a response right away.
- Say the message to yourself. Does it sound nurturing to you? If not, try to restate it in a nurturing way.

- Say that you are making changes in the ways you express nurturing. If your child is old enough, ask how you could say it better.
- Be sensitive to the expressions of caring that your child seems to prefer. Some children like to hear it, some to see it, and some to feel it.
- Ask your child to tell you what kind of loving he or she prefers you give.
- Point out ways that you are accepting love for yourself.
- Point out examples of other people, children or adults, accepting love.

When Love Seems Threatening

If the suggestions listed above don't work, you may be interacting with a child who doesn't trust love or finds it threatening. Then you may be dealing with a very early trauma experience or a later attachment problem. Children who experienced prenatal or perinatal trauma or later abuse and neglect or who experienced unalleviated physical and emotional pain frequently decide it isn't safe or wise to trust anyone to care for them. (See chapter 24, Becoming: The Prenatal and Birth Experience and section 8 on adoption.)

These children may be terrified to let anyone give them assertive and supportive care. They don't believe they deserve it. In their minds, opening to love and care means giving power to someone who can hurt them, ignore them, or leave them. They believe they have to be in control. In the most serious cases, opening to love and care means experiencing the fear of losing complete control. No wonder they shield themselves from love and care by armoring their hearts and bodies with industrial-strength Teflon. They believe it is a matter of life and death. Attracting negative attention, even if it means setting people up to abuse them, is not only familiar; it is within their ability to control.

Remember this: In order to help a child recover from such an early self-destructive decision, parents need to be understanding of the child's experience without commiserating. They must challenge the child to reconsider early decisions and allow time to make new ones. Just feeling sorry for the child won't help. It invites the child to feel and act like a victim and avoid taking responsibility to overcome the negative experiences. It *might* help to say, "I'm sorry that happened to you. It should not have happened. We won't let it happen here."

Parents can connect empathically while continuing to expect the child to contribute to the family and show law-abiding behavior. This is a hard job for parents. They'd like to make up for past hurts by giving their love freely, but that is only half of the cure. The other half is structure (see section 3). Parents must get their own love and support while the child tests the family rules and personal boundaries to make sure their love is safe. Children who feel like orphans are often receptive to helpful structure long before they can accept nurture without being fearful.

Bonding and Attachment

The definitions of "bonding" differ widely. In this book, *bonding* means the immediate, outside-the-womb, physical reconnection between baby and mother and the physical connection between baby and father. If the bonding period is missed but followed soon with confident and loving care by parents or long-term caregivers, possible deficits resulting from a lack of immediate physical connection can likely be overcome. Dr. Martha Welch's book *Holding Time*[1] can help with problems of bonding.

> *In learning to connect with others, a process called* attachment, *whereby children learn about trust, is especially important.*

In learning to connect with others, a process called *attachment,* whereby children learn about trust, is especially important. Attachment develops between child and caregiver(s) over the course of the first year of life. Babies develop a working model for future relationships based on their infant perception of how trustworthy and reliable their earliest caregivers are. That working model becomes the glasses through which they see themselves and others and affects the way they engage in relationships as adults.

The Attachment Dance

Developing an attachment relationship is like learning to dance with a new partner. With a familiar partner, we swoop and glide across the dance floor with confidence and exhilaration. With a new partner, we may stumble and make our way jerkily. So it is with attachment.

Dancing partners develop their dance by learning each other's cues and signals. Babies and caregivers develop their attachment by the use of cues and signals too. Remember that the baby's goal is to keep caregivers close enough to do what the baby is helpless to do alone. When caregivers are sensitive to the baby's cues for help, and when caregivers respond in a timely and reliable way, the baby is likely to decide she is safe and life is good. The baby feels effective and securely attached.

Hope and Help for Children with Rough and Bumpy Starts

When for any number of reasons the care is untimely, inconsistent, abusive or neglectful, dangerous or absent, babies may decide not to trust adults to care for them. They may decide to find other ways to cope, to get care while protecting themselves from hurt. They develop an insecure attachment relationship. For a much more thorough understanding of attachment, read Robert Karen's book *Becoming Attached*.[2]

This insecure child may change early decisions as a result of subsequent and persistent parenting. This includes implementing nurture and structure so well that the child, over time, learns to trust the adult not only to be present, but also to be competent.

Deep attachment wounds often require professional help in order for the child to decide to let trustworthy and reliable parents do the parenting. This may be especially true for foster and adopted children, children who sustained long or multiple separations from caregivers, or children whose early infancy was spent with a parent who was severely depressed or emotionally absent because of chemical abuse or overinvolvement with career. The list also includes infants and very young children who had surgery without benefit of anesthesia, children with unknown histories adopted from other countries, and children of parents whose parental rights were terminated because of abandonment, abuse, or neglect.

The *now* parenting of these children calls for extraordinary patience and skill, and what would be adequate for a child with good attachment experiences is not enough. Parenting children with unsatisfactory attachment backgrounds involves challenging their prior decisions and wearing them down. If you are the parent of such a child and if what you are doing isn't working, if the parenting you inherited from your parents isn't doing the trick, you'll have to find others who know how to help you. For further help, see chapter 27 on adoption.

It's Never Too Late

If you feel you may have attachment difficulties yourself, there are several things you can do.

- See a therapist who understands attachment problems and how to work with them.
- Research your earliest history, including your time in the womb if you can. Old family friends or family members often have pieces of your early puzzle they'd be willing to share. Be aware that this topic may not be welcomed by some who have the information.
- If you were adopted, ask social service workers at the agency or in the county of your relinquishment to allow you access to all information in your file to which you are legally entitled. If you were adopted from another country, find out if the agency has information not yet shared about your early experiences. Ask adoptive and foster parents to help you research. (See chapter 27 on adoption.)
- If you were in foster care, visit former foster caretakers and ask for their memories of you. Ask about the foster family. Let yourself know how you think the foster mom or dad would have cared for you.

Whether an attachment problem is yours or your child's, get the help you need. The sooner, the better. Older children and adults have to want the help and contract with a therapist and work hard on improving their lives.

If your start in life was rough and bumpy, you don't have to let it stay that way.

> *If your start in life was rough and bumpy, you don't have to let it stay that way.*

chapter 7

Nurturing Other Adults and Ourselves

Adults need nurture too. People of all ages need stimulation and recognition. The art of nurturing adults consists of an elegant balance between being sensitive about when to offer assertive care and when to offer supportive care. Not too little, not too much. If we don't know how to offer either, we can practice and learn. If we offer too much, we are resented as patronizers, enablers, codependents, or benevolent dictators. To be good at offering care to others, we watch for clues and listen for requests. We need to offer what other people really need, or ask them what they need instead of giving them what we need to give.

Assertive and Supportive Care

When do we give adults assertive care? When they are ill, stressed, lost, tired, in danger, hurt, wounded, or frail. Or when they are parents of infants or of newly adopted children. When people are grieving a loss, they need others to care for them. We may send flowers, drop a note, bring chicken soup, or extend an invitation to a movie. We also offer care to people with whom we have a close relationship. We may create an ongoing contract that doesn't need to be negotiated daily; for example, I wash your car, you wash my clothes.

While *assertive care* means the caregiver decides what someone needs and provides it, *supportive care* is help that is offered. It may be accepted, refused, or negotiated. For example, Lynn's friend Maria recently lost her mother. Think about these responses to Lynn's offers:

> *We need to offer what other people really need, or ask them what they need instead of giving them what we need to give.*

Offer is made and accepted.

Lynn says, "I'm sorry about your mom's death. I'd like to help. If you have people flying in for the memorial service, I will be happy to make airport runs." Her friend says, "Thanks," and gives her flight times.

Offer is made and refused.

Lynn notices her friend's distress. She asks, "Are you okay? Do you want to talk?"

Her friend replies, "I'm fine," and Lynn says, "Okay, if you want to talk later, let me know."

Maria has decided not to accept Lynn's offer to talk, but the door is left open if Maria changes her mind.

Offer is negotiated.

Perhaps the help Lynn offers is not what her friend needs. "I'm willing to bring dinner to your house tonight."

"Thanks for the offer. Actually, what I need more than dinner is someone to drive the kids to their lessons this evening. Would that work out for you?"

Lynn checks her schedule and says yes, she can, or sorry, she can't.

Support is characterized by respect. Each person recognizes the other as responsible and each retains a sense of personal power and integrity.

> *Support is characterized by respect.*

Practicing Assertive Care and Supportive Care for Other Adults and Ourselves

The ability to offer both assertive care and support to other adults springs from a willingness to extend unconditional love that rests firmly on our knowing who we are and what our needs are. Confronting alcoholism is assertive care. Offering encouragement when a friend with a drinking problem seeks help is support. Taking a hot meal to a family with a new infant is assertive care. Offering to babysit is support. Giving a surprise birthday party is assertive care. Offering to plan a celebration is support.

Once you have thought more about your ability to offer care and support, look at the following examples of nurturing that we can offer to other adults and to ourselves. Practice discriminating among the positions. Notice when you use positions you want to change and when you use positions you want to keep.

EXAMPLE 13
Situation: Wife asks husband for help with children.
The husband:

Abuse: Hits or ridicules wife when she asks for help.

Conditional Care: Says, "I'll help with the kids when you earn more money than I do."

Assertive Care: Says, "Children need care from dads." Participates in all aspects of child care.

Supportive Care: Negotiates with wife about child care. Praises the quality of her care in front of the children.

Overindulgence: Gives expensive presents instead of helping.

Neglect: Works long hours, travels, spends long hours at bars, sports, or civic organizations; comes home late and leaves early.

EXAMPLE 14
Situation: Married daughter suffers miscarriage at four months of pregnancy.
The mother:

Abuse: "I told you taking that exercise class would be a bad idea."

Conditional Care: "Don't cry." (Implies I can only love you when you're happy.)

Assertive Care: "I'm coming down to help you recuperate and deal with your other children."

Supportive Care: "Talk it over with your spouse and let me know what help you can use, and I will figure out what I could do to help you."

Overindulgence: "Oh, you poor baby! I'll pay for you to go to the best specialist money can buy."

Neglect: Doesn't talk about the miscarriage. Ignores it completely.

EXAMPLE 15
Situation: Parent has been denying own needs based on the belief that the children's needs come first, then my spouse's, then mine.
The parent:

Abuse: Thinks, "I'll work as long as I need to in order to provide what my spouse and children want." Works self into illness.

Conditional Care: Believes, "I'm not a worthwhile person unless I sacrifice for my family."

Assertive Care: Says, "I recognize my needs and get them met and help meet the needs of all family members. All of our needs are important. We work together to get them met."

Supportive Care: Seeks membership in an appropriate support group.

Overindulgence: Shops, works, eats, takes pills, or drinks compulsively to ease the stress.

Neglect: Continues to act on the old belief.

Test Your Knowledge

Assign nurture positions for the following examples. Compare your answers to the ones provided. Trust yourself to know what the responses mean to you.

EXAMPLE 16
Situation: Partner is addicted.
The addicted person's partner:

1. Excuses partner to children. _____
2. Says, "Here is where you can get help." _____
3. Says, "I am getting help for me and the kids. I want you to come with us." _____
4. Ignores partner's addiction or furthers own addictions. _____
5. Says, "I will love you when you shape up." _____
6. Alternates criticism and cold silence. _____

Answers: (1) Overindulgence (2) Supportive care (3) Assertive care (4) Neglect (5) Conditional care (6) Abuse

EXAMPLE 17

Situation: Parent to self, "If I stop keeping up appearances and covering for other family members' unhealthy behaviors, I will have to take care of myself directly and I don't know how to do that."
The parent:

1. Says, "I just don't see this as a big problem." _____
2. Says, "I will focus even more attention on looking good." _____
3. Says, "I will find a number of people who will support me, so I have several choices." _____
4. Says, "I am going to see a counselor or therapist and face whatever I have been avoiding in myself." _____
5. Becomes chronically ill with a stress-related condition. _____
6. Says, "I'm only okay as long as I'm taking care of others." _____

Answers: (1) Neglect (2) Overindulgence (3) Supportive care (4) Assertive care (5) Abuse (6) Conditional care

Nurturing Ourselves: Personal Rules for Love

If you have difficulty extending assertive care and support to yourself or accepting care and support from others, pause now to think about why this is difficult.

Care and support are based on unconditional love. If, as children, we didn't feel loved unconditionally, it may be hard to recognize and accept unconditional love when others offer it to us. If our being loved hinged on how useful we were to our families, we may hold our breath and wait for the other shoe to drop when someone says, "I love you." We wonder, *What will I have to do to deserve this?* or *What is this going to cost me?*

If long ago we had to accept that adult needs came ahead of ours, we learned not to expect or trust love and support. Now we will have to learn to believe in unconditional love and that may take awhile. But we can do it and the more we learn to accept unconditional love for ourselves, the better we will be able to offer it to children.

Recovery from Overindulgence

Another way that adults put their own needs ahead of the needs of children is to overindulge. When people who have been abused, criticized, or loved in conditional ways recognize the harm done to them and decide to recover, they can find support, recognition, and help. But, people who were overindulged often find it difficult to recognize the debilitating nature of their experience; they recognize it later, and it's especially hard for them to find recognition and support.

People who were overindulged say, "My parents gave me everything I wanted. They really loved me! How can I call that bad?" When overindulged people do begin to recognize that they were cheated, it is usually difficult for them to get encouragement and help from others. Tell another adult how you were abused and you will get sympathy. Tell the same adult about your overindulgence and the response is often jealousy or criticism for being spoiled. "Tough! I wish I'd had it that good." People often do not recognize the damage from being overindulged, but recognize it we must, or we stay stuck in the pain of being only partly grown up, bound by the sweet, sticky ropes left from our overindulged childhood. To learn what happened to 124 adults who were overindulged in childhood, read chapter 16.

Sex and Nurturing

Each person has favorite experiences and environments that feel nurturing: a long walk, candlelight, an exhilarating day of skiing, being listened to, touching and being touched. Since touching and warm, responsive connections with others are such a big part of how nurture is given and received, many adults have assumed, because of how they grew up, that they must accept or seek sexual touch in order to be nurtured. Sexual activity can be nurturing within the context of a loving relationship, but substituting sexual contact for nurturing leads to all sorts of problems, from personal feelings of hollowness to the destructiveness of incest. It is never okay for anyone in a position of trust to misuse that trust in a sexually exploitative way, especially if it is represented as nurture. People who use sex in an

> *Many adults have assumed, because of how they grew up, that they must accept or seek sexual touch in order to be nurtured.*

addictive way need to find a skilled therapist. Adults can meet their needs for physical nurture in many ways.

Here are a few:

- getting a therapeutic massage,
- asking for hugs from friends,
- fostering nourishing relationships with people who love and accept them for who they are, and
- caring for their bodies in a loving way by eating and exercising wisely.

Choosing to Be Lovable

"I am loved, I am lovable, I am loving." These are the unconditional love decisions. Here are some personal rules that flow from these decisions:

- I accept love freely.
- There is an infinite supply of love.
- I give love freely.
- I surround myself with loving people.
- I protect myself from unloving people.

If we received uneven parenting, we decided on other rules that made sense at that time, but those rules may keep love away. They reflect our "giving up on love" or our "longing for love."

Read the following situations. Look at the decisions that these people made and the new rules they have chosen for themselves as grownups. We can borrow ideas from them to help us grow up again.

Alice: "My parents said they loved me so I don't examine what they did. I just passed their kind of love on to my children, but I still feel hollow."

New rule: I am lovable. I examine my legacy and am doing my healing. I am learning about joy and finding it for myself.

Devon: "My parents didn't love me, but I pretend they loved me. I can't stand for me or anyone else to know they didn't so I'll act as if they did or I'll act as if I don't care."

New rule: I am lovable and I care about being loved and I can attract loving people into my life now.

Bart: "My parents never told me that I did well, that they loved me, or that I was important to them, so I don't tell anyone I love them now. I'm afraid they'll think they're better than me and will leave me."

New rule: I affirm myself and accept affirmations from others. I tell others how much I appreciate them, admire them, love them.

Frank: "My parents never told me they loved me so I decided to get love from others. I will do anything for anyone who will say, I love you."

New rule: I am lovable and I deserve love. I am lovable just the way I am, and I don't deny my needs or values to please others.

Candy: "My parents tried hard to buy my love so I didn't trust their love or tell them I loved them. Now I fear that if I tell others how much I love them, they will no longer need me."

New rule: When I love you and want you to love me, I will tell you that.

Henry: "My parents abandoned me so I decided that I don't deserve love. If you love me, I am afraid you will leave me, so either I will force you to leave me, or I will leave you first."

New rule: I will accept your love and do the healing I need to do to be able to stick around.

Ed: "I felt ashamed because I didn't feel loved. Now I try to earn your love by anticipating your wants and needs. If you have to ask me to do something, I feel like a failure for not having noticed your need. If you tell me that you love me, I have to figure out something to do to deserve it."

New rule: I accept your love freely. I expect you to ask for what you need.

George: "My parents were impoverished, emotionally and economically, so I decided that I wasn't lovable and that I needed to earn whatever love I would get."

New rule: Real love is free! I can accept it but I can't buy it, and I don't need to make trades for it.

Kate: "I felt ignored so I connected any way I could. I got in fights or I settled for sex instead of love."

New rule: I find positive ways to get attention. I know the difference between sex and nurturing. Now sex enhances love; it doesn't replace it.

Marty: "My family gave me everything, did everything for me. I loved it! I also loved them. I assumed the world owed me. I hit the world outside of my family unprepared to fail in all of the incredible ways that people fail, so I blame others for my failures."

New rule: I am responsible for my own needs. I accept help from others and appreciate it. The universe does not revolve around me; I am part of it. I am important and other people are important.

These new rules make useful daily affirmations if we have chosen them freely and desire to incorporate them into our lives. You may want to make your own new rules and affirmations as Alice and the others did or you may prefer to use the ones in the Ages and Stages chapter (page 211). (See also Developmental Affirmations in appendix B.)

Making Your New Rules about Love

Now think about your own situation and the old lifesaving decisions and rules that you made about unconditional love. Look at what really happened. Grieve anything you didn't get that you needed and anything you did get that hurt you. Elaine Childs-Gowell's book, *Good Grief Rituals,*[1] has many suggestions about how to grieve well.

Your parents may not have had the nurture they needed and they may not have been able to give it to you, but the truth is, you have never been unlovable, even if you felt unloved. You deserve to do whatever you need to do to grow up again and feel lovable. If some of your old rules are outdated, outworn, or confusing, see them for what they are. When you recognize a decision or a rule that now works against you, use that as a signal to stop neglecting yourself or defending your parents and make some new rules that make sense to you now as an adult and as a parent. The new rules can be a part of your healing, growing process.

> *Your parents may not have had the nurture they needed and they may not have been able to give it to you, but the truth is, you have never been unlovable, even if you felt unloved.*

After growing up again, Alice said, "I believed they loved me. They told me that. But I had big, empty places in me because they neglected me. After I learned to recognize the neglect, I came to accept the love they did give and stopped neglecting myself. Now it is my job not to pass the neglect on to my kids." Devon said, "Now I am free to feel loved. I don't have to pretend I don't care anymore because I don't have to protect my parents anymore. For the first time I believe they did love me and in some ways they did the best they could to show their love."

Whether our parents loved us or whether they didn't is no longer the question. Now the issue is, Do we love ourselves and do we accept love from everyone who is willing to give it?

Accepting Love from Others

As we change any confusing rule we may have in our heads about deserving love and being lovable, we will be able to drop any "don't trust" rules that we have used to filter out love from others.

Those of us who grew up needing to earn love from our parents became suspicious when it was offered to us by others. We passed love through a carefully constructed filter in our heads, a filter we built because we decided that unconditional love didn't exist. At least not for us.

When we hear "I love you," do we ask ourselves, *What does this person want from me?* Do we meet loving messages with the suspicion that the terms of that love are not on the table? Do we even convert the love offered to us into criticism or feel ashamed because we are not truly good enough to merit it? When someone offers us support, those of us with highly developed filters are likely to decline the offer. Instead of welcoming aid and checking to see if it is freely given, we reject it. We automatically say, "I'm fine, thanks," or "I'll be all right," or "I don't need any help."

Very serious business! When we throw away nurturing, we filter out the very love we long for, the love that is the foundation of our self-esteem.

Some of us decided to cope with being unloved and feeling ashamed by being "perfect," being "good," being "right," or being "better." This makes our self-esteem competitive and bases it on the performance of others instead of on belief in our inherent capableness and lovableness.

Until we recognize, believe, and accept straightforward, clean, nurturing love, we rob ourselves of our birthright—to be loved and to believe that we are lovable. If you are tempted to ignore your new rules about accepting love, or if you convert a nurturing message into a shaming one, do this instead:

- Tell yourself to let the message in and notice how it feels.
- Ask the sender to repeat the message, and listen carefully.
- Say, "Thank you."
- Ask yourself if this person is trustworthy or if the love has a price tag. If it does, take in the love if you want it, but protect yourself from the price.

> *Until we recognize, believe, and accept straightforward, clean, nurturing love, we rob ourselves of our birthright— to be loved and to believe that we are lovable.*

Remember, we all deserve love; we all deserve to grow up again. When we accept our longing for love, why do we continue to keep ourselves from getting and giving that life-sustaining support? Sometimes we need to learn and apply new beliefs and skills.

Love Is Not Enough

Love is not enough. All nurture and little structure make a floppy, boundary-weak child and adult. On the other hand, all structure and little nurture often result in stiffness. Nurture encourages us to hear and believe positive structure. When we feel loved we are not apt to hear the "Do this" or "Do this differently" of structure messages as criticism or shaming. When we know we are lovable, we feel worthy and expect to ask for and get structure. A balance of nurture and structure helps give children a chance to grow up as balanced adults, capable of giving and receiving love and of choosing a quality of life that satisfies their needs.

The stimulation of love and the accompanying recognition are never enough, because we also hunger for the certainty provided by structure.

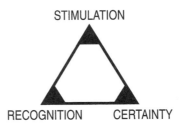

STIMULATION

RECOGNITION   CERTAINTY

SECTION III

Structure
The Firm Side of Care

*Keep in mind always the present
you are constructing. It should be
the future you want.*
ALICE WALKER

chapter 8

Structure
What It Is and Why We Need It

This section explores structure, that is, the mechanisms, the external rules, and the boundaries that provide the safety and the environment in which children and adults can get their recognition and stimulation needs met in healthy ways and can develop or improve their own internal structures.

What Structure Is and Why We Need It

Self-discipline is the name that some people give to their *internal* structure, the values and behaviors they employ to take care of themselves and other people. The *external* structure that parents provide for their children (the care and the teaching and the rules) helps children create *their* own internal structure or self-discipline.

Parents may feel confused about how to provide external structure because today there are not commonly accepted cultural standards about the job of parenting. In an effort to cast out the "old" criticism, controls, and "shoulds," some of the ways we knew to set boundaries and standards were lost. We threw the baby out with the bathwater.

> *Parents may feel confused about how to provide external structure because today there are not commonly accepted cultural standards about the job of parenting*

Today the messages about how much structure to give children are often contradictory. Some sources tell us to support and encourage a child by accepting the child's behavior, no matter how irresponsible or disrespectful. Others insist that we be tough and demand excellence in order to raise strong children. Actually, neither of these build flexible internal structures or self-esteem. Helping children become sure of themselves as lovable, capable people is a long-term process of providing love, teaching skills, *and* holding children accountable.

Meanwhile the media encourage us to expect quick relief of any distress by leaving, or by escaping through drugs, or by reacting to conflicts with violence—without attention to underlying causes of distress. Notice that on television almost all problems are solved in thirty or sixty minutes.

> *Our culture currently expects us to be able to slide rearing our children in among career advancement, community obligations, and personal interests without missing a step.*

Also, our culture currently expects us to be able to slide rearing our children in among career advancement, community obligations, and personal interests without missing a step. A little quality time whenever we can work it in and the children should be all right. Right? Wrong. Parenting children takes time and effort and plenty of both. No wonder doing good parenting feels like a counterculture activity.

In this section we will explore

- Structure—what it is and the hunger for it
- The Structure Chart—ways people get structure in their lives
- How to build negotiable and nonnegotiable rules
- Consequences of breaking rules
- The Structure Highway
- Using the Nurture/Structure Highway to assess our nurture and structure
- What to do when parents disagree about rules
- The connection between structure, shame, and victim blame
- Growing up again in the safe lanes of the Nurture/Structure Highway

The Hunger for Certainty

Certainty, which is a basic human hunger, is primarily provided through structure. Both physically and emotionally, we need the safety and protection of structure to survive. The opposite of structure is chaos. Life with chaos and uncertainty is life without predictability or stability, and in such conditions people use most of their energy searching for or trying to build stability and predictability. They have little energy left over for growth and joy or for truly connecting with others.

Structure helps us function effectively. Since young children cannot provide it for themselves, they must learn about it from adults. Giving structure to infants and very young children means meeting their emotional and physical needs in a consistent way. Later on, parents expand the ways they offer structure to children to include teaching them how to do tasks skillfully; to think clearly; to collect and assess information; to identify options; to set goals; to organize; to start, perform, and complete tasks; to manage materials, tools, time, ideas, and feelings; to be responsible; to honor commitments; and to develop morals and values.

> *Structure helps us function effectively.*

Parents teach children how to break a large task into small, manageable units and arrange them in a meaningful order. They teach children problem solving. In terms of personal boundaries, they teach how to negotiate, to say yes to healthful relationships and no to destructive ones. As adults teach rules and skills and right from wrong, children, over time, learn how to keep themselves safe, to do things well, to think clearly, to get their own needs met, and to live respectfully with others.

Structure: A Combination of Rules and Skills

Clear, consistent structure is affirming to adults and children. It lets us know we are loved, important, and capable. It keeps us safe and gives us freedom. If we didn't receive positive structure in childhood, we can learn to provide it for ourselves as we provide it for our sons and daughters.

> *Successful structure is built from a combination of rules and skills.*

Successful structure is built from a combination of rules and skills. This section focuses on rules—what kinds there are, how to make them, how to evaluate them, and how to be sure they build self-confidence and competence instead of doubt or shame. There are many places outside of this book for parents to learn how to teach children the skills they need, everything from building a kite to programming a computer. How-to-do-it skills are not the focus of this book, although the Growing Up Again and Again section includes information about which skills are appropriate to teach at what age.

Rules and skills should reinforce each other. Parents enforce rules not only to establish protection but also to set standards for doing skills well. We need to ask, "Have we been accepting or rewarding substandard or antisocial behavior?" For children, the rules establish the limits and the how-to-do-it skills are added bit by bit to strengthen their total structure. As children become more and more skillful and responsible, they learn about making and observing their own rules, setting their own standards, and living by their own values. They learn how to take care of themselves. While we help our children build their structures, we can improve our own ways of taking care of ourselves and of being responsible toward others.

The Importance of Boundaries

Think about the importance of providing clear boundaries for children. Watch youngsters at play in places with fences and places without fences. Where there is a fence, youngsters use the entire space. When a fence is lacking, they avoid the perimeters and restrict their play area.

The rules parents set for children are like the fence around a playground. With boundaries, children feel secure and cared for, free to explore what they and others are and are not permitted to do. Territory outside the boundaries lacks the protection and predictability that lie within the boundaries.

If there are no fences, no boundaries, children become wary. They limit their spontaneity, their curiosity, and their willingness to try new things. Or they become reckless and uncaring about their welfare. On the other hand, if the fences we build are too restricting, if the boundaries are too tight, children are apt to overadapt and become passive, or to demand attention with rebellious behavior.[1]

When loving and consistent boundaries are set for them, children learn gradually to set their own boundaries, to value themselves. They build their self-esteem. They get *stimulation* and *recognition* in safe ways.

Not all children are fortunate enough to live with loving limits. Some children are taught boundaries and limits by adults who are judgmental and who criticize mistakes harshly. Some children are never really told what to do and what not to do, but are expected to know anyway. These children, when they don't do things the parents' way, may be told that they are stupid or bad. Some children are taught with super-rigid rules, with punishment unrelated to the deed, or with threats of abandonment or actual abandonment.

Fight, Flee, or Flow: Learning How to Be Safe

Children learn to be safe by following and being obedient to some nonnegotiable rules. For example, in the United States, a nonnegotiable rule is, *Drive on the right-hand side of the street*. Some rules, internalized early and thoroughly, become automatic. Thus an experienced driver does not have to waste energy deciding where to drive, but follows the safe driving rules automatically.

> *Children learn to be safe by following and being obedient to some nonnegotiable rules.*

However, the skill of obedience alone is not enough to keep people safe. When danger threatens, the impulse to fight or flee floods the body with ready energy. But survival in the urban jungle requires different skills than the ones our ancestors used in dealing with wild animals. Now the best way to survive is often not to fight or flee, but to flow. This requires thinking skills and self-discipline to overcome the impulse to fight or flee. These flowing skills are taught over many years indirectly by our modeling and directly as we urge children to use their words instead of their fists; to negotiate, cooperate, and sometimes yield; and to hold their boundaries without violence. A book that can help young children establish their boundaries is *Telling Isn't Tattling*.[2]

The structure of nonnegotiable rules teaches the obedience needed for safety. Being allowed to believe that they do not have to follow the rules adults set for safety puts children at risk. Children who do not learn how to flow are also at risk. The thinking involved in negotiating rules helps children sort out how and when to fight, to flee, or to flow.[3]

How Children Develop Their Own Structures

Since children need to develop their own structures in order to survive, they build with the materials offered to them. If they don't get enough structure-building blocks from consistent, appropriate rules, they incorporate heavy blocks of rigidity or sharp blocks of criticism. Children may appear structurally sound and fit, but the rigid and critical blocks often produce inflexibility or sharpness—an inability to make appropriate decisions that take full account of the situation, others' needs, and their own needs.

Look at five adults who were parented in rigid and critical ways: Ben has a stiff body and doesn't show or feel much emotion. Sarah cries easily and criticizes herself relentlessly, while Nancy clamps her mouth in a tight line and is overly judgmental of others. Nathan has set beliefs, and ridicules other points of view. Shirley parents her children as if they were living in some earlier decade.

Children also incorporate inadequate structural blocks. These children develop structure that works, but not well. Their boundaries have weak spots and their internal support lacks strength. Look at some of those adults: Frank doesn't expect to pick up his own clothes at home or do his share of work on the job. Marcie interrupts complete strangers to give them her opinion. Jack's teammates complain that he hogs the ball. William takes offense at any slight and starts a fight. Ann asks her husband to decide for her what she thinks about things.

Those of us who were parented in ways that are not supportive to us now can rebuild our own internal structures as we parent our children. We can grow up again at any age. You can use the Structure Chart to help you do that.

The Structure Chart

There are six basic ways people offer, or fail to offer, structure as shown on the Structure Chart on pages 68–69. The positions on the chart are *Rigidity, Criticism, Nonnegotiable Rules, Negotiable Rules, Marshmallow,* and *Abandonment.* The following pages define the six positions and help you understand how to use the Structure Chart.

Six Structure Positions

The Structure Chart arranges the six positions from left to right in order of strictness, from most strict to least strict. The two in the center of the continuum, **nonnegotiable rules** and **negotiable rules**, offer structure appropriate to the child's age and development.

RIGIDITY   CRITICISM   NONNEGOTIABLE RULES   NEGOTIABLE RULES   MARSHMALLOW   ABANDONMENT

Rigidity is the most strict. In the rigid position, the rule is more important than the child and enforced without regard to the child's needs.

RIGIDITY

Criticism may be more flexible than rigidity, but it involves ridicule, name-calling, and grandiosity and suggests how the child can fail.

CRITICISM

Nonnegotiable rules tell children what to do to be safe and successful. These rules are made for the child's welfare and are routinely enforced. They teach children to be obedient, but they do not teach children how to think. The thinking has already been done by the adult.

NONNEGOTIABLE RULES

Negotiable rules teach children how to think and to be responsible. Starting in small ways when children are little and expanding as children grow, the process of negotiating rules teaches children what to consider as they set their own boundaries and build their own internal structures.

NEGOTIABLE RULES

Marshmallow parenting patronizes or gives in to the demands of the child. It teaches that the child need not follow rules or become capable.

MARSHMALLOW

Abandonment occurs when the adults fail to make and enforce the rules that protect the children. They also fail to provide opportunities for the children to learn skills appropriate to their ages.

ABANDONMENT

Notice that the structure offered at both extremes is very similar. Rigidity and abandonment both fail to meet the child's needs.

How to Use the Structure Chart

RIGIDITY   CRITICISM   NONNEGOTIABLE RULES   NEGOTIABLE RULES   MARSHMALLOW   ABANDONMENT

> *Negotiable Rules and Nonnegotiable Rules offer the most healthy structure.*

Become familiar with the Structure Chart before you make judgments about parenting or identify the parenting in your family of origin. Since every child responds to, interprets, and makes decisions in ways that reflect his or her uniqueness, your child's decisions may not match those on the chart. Children experience combinations of these styles at home, at school, and elsewhere. Furthermore, most adults use more than one style of structure. The center two, Negotiable Rules and Nonnegotiable Rules, offer the most healthy structure.

Vertical Columns

- The top cell in each column describes the general characteristics of that position.
- The second cell down gives words or behaviors typical of a parent offering that way of structure.
- The third cell suggests the underlying message a child might hear. From your own experience or knowledge, you may be able to add other possible messages.
- The fourth cell describes common responses of children who have received this type of structure.
- The bottom cell lists the decisions children often make in response to that style of structure. This is the most

important item in the column, because these decisions usually carry into adulthood and are acted upon in one way or another. If rigidity, for example, was part of your personal early experience, notice if you are living out some of those decisions now.

Horizontal Rows

- Look horizontally across any level to compare the differences and similarities among the six positions.

THE STRUCTURE CHART, page 1

Children internalize protection, safety, freedom, success, and self-esteem from nonnegotiable rules and negotiable rules. Despair and failure come from rigidity, criticism, marshmallowing, and abandonment.

RIGIDITY   **CRITICISM**  **NON-NEGOTIABLE RULES**

Characteristics:

Rigidity, supposedly for the child's welfare, springs from fear. It consists of old rules "written in concrete" sometime in the past and usually for someone else. These rules often ignore the developmental tasks of the child. Rigidity threatens abuse or withdrawal of love to enforce compliance; it doesn't believe children should have a say in working things out.	Criticism labels the person with bad names rather than setting standards for acceptable behavior. Criticism often includes global words such as "never" and "always." It negates children and tells them how to fail. Ridicule is a devastating form of criticism that humiliates and invites contemptuous laughter from others.	Nonnegotiable rules are rules that must be followed. Children count on these rules to put order in their lives, to provide safety and security, to help them know who they are, to help them make decisions, and to build their own self-esteem. Even though nonnegotiable rules are firmly set and firmly enforced, they are not "rigid" and can be rewritten for the welfare of the family and its members.

Example: Thirteen-year-old drank alcohol.

Parent says, "If you ever touch alcohol again, don't bother coming home."	Mother says, "You're always doing something stupid. Now you are drinking. You're just like your dad."	Parent says, "You may not drink alcohol until you reach the legal age. We expect you to honor this rule. If you do not honor the rule, there will be very tough consequences."

Children May Hear the Following Underlying Messages:

You are not important. Don't think. Don't be. Don't exist. You will be punished or abandoned if you make a mistake. Don't trust your own competence.	Don't be who you are. Don't be successful. Don't be capable. You are not lovable.	Your welfare and safety are important. Your parents expect you to be law abiding. Your parents are willing to be responsible and enforce the rules.

Common Responses of Children:

Feels oppressed, distanced, angry or rageful, scared, hopeless, imperfect, discounted, mistrusted, abandoned, no-good, powerless.	Feels powerless and diminished, rejected, hurt, humiliated, squashed, angry or rageful, unimportant, inadequate, scared, discounted.	Feels safe, cared for, powerful, helped, responsible, confident, accounted for. May feel frustrated, irritated, and resistant at times. Learns to follow rules and be responsible.

Decisions Often Made by Children:

Rules are more important than my needs. I am not wanted. My parents don't care about me. I will let others think for me. I will comply, rebel, or withdraw. I will blame myself.	I'm supposed to know what I don't know. I won't ask for help. I will try harder, be strong, be perfect. If I don't do things right, I am a bad person. I can't be good enough. I am hopeless. Why bother?	There are some rules I have to follow. I can learn from my mistakes. I am a good person. I'm lovable and capable. They care about me and take care of me.

NEGOTIABLE RULES   MARSHMALLOW    ABANDONMENT

Characteristics:

NEGOTIABLE RULES	MARSHMALLOW	ABANDONMENT
Negotiable rules teach children how to think clearly and to solve problems, helping them raise their self-esteem. These rules are negotiated. The process of negotiating provides children an opportunity to argue and hassle with parents, learn about the relevancy of rules, assess data on which to base decisions, and learn to be increasingly responsible for themselves.	Marshmallow parenting grants freedom without demanding responsibility in return. It sounds supportive, but it implies the child does not have to or is not capable of following rules. It discounts the child's ability and gives the child permission to be irresponsible and to fail, to be helpless and hopeless. At the same time, it lets the parent look good or play the martyr or feel in control.	Abandonment consists of lack of rules, protection, and contact. It tells children that adults are not available for them. If teasing is used when a child needs structure or approval, that teasing constitutes abandonment.

Example: Thirteen-year-old drank alcohol.

NEGOTIABLE RULES	MARSHMALLOW	ABANDONMENT
Parent says, "There are kids whose number one priority is drinking. When do you think it is okay to be with kids who drink? How can you find kids who don't drink so you don't spend all of your free time with the ones who are drinking?"	Parent says, "If all the kids drink, I suppose you can," or "You're too young to drink and drive, so you can have a kegger here," or "Kids will be kids!"	Parents says, "I don't want to talk about it." Parent is not available (either physically or emotionally), is drunk or mentally ill, or ignores or teases the child.

Children May Hear the Following Underlying Messages:

NEGOTIABLE RULES	MARSHMALLOW	ABANDONMENT
You can think, negotiate, and initiate. Your needs are important and others' needs are important. You must deal with how things really are. You are expected to be powerful in positive ways for yourself and others.	Don't be competent or responsible. Don't be who you are. Don't grow up. You can have your way and be obnoxious and get by with it. I need to continue taking care of you. My needs are more important than your needs.	I am not willing to care for you. I don't want you. Your needs are not important, mine are. No one is here for you. You don't exist.

Common Responses of Children:

NEGOTIABLE RULES	MARSHMALLOW	ABANDONMENT
Feels respected, cared for, listened to, powerful, important, loved, intelligent, safe, and sometimes frustrated. Learns to evaluate rules and participate in the making of rules as well as to follow rules and be responsible.	Feels patronized and encouraged not to grow up, remains incompetent in order to please parent. Feels unsafe, undermined, crazy, manipulated, discounted, unloved, unsatisfied, and angry.	Feels scared, terrified, hurt, angry or rageful, rejected, discounted, baffled, unimportant, upset. Perhaps suicidal.

Decisions Often Made by Children:

NEGOTIABLE RULES	MARSHMALLOW	ABANDONMENT
It's okay for me to grow up and still be dependent at times. I can think things through and ask others to think with me. I continually expand my ability to be responsible and competent.	I must take care of other people's feelings and needs, or I don't need to care about anyone but me. I am not capable of learning how to value and take care of myself. If help is offered, I mistrust it or at least expect to pay a price for it, but I don't expect helpful structure from others.	Don't ask for or expect help. No one cares. If I am to survive, I will have to do it by myself. If help is offered, mistrust it. Help and trust are jokes.

chapter 9

Negotiable and Nonnegotiable Rules

Using Rules as Structure Tools

Once we decide to replace rigidity, criticism, marshmallowing, and abandonment with negotiable and nonnegotiable rules, we need to think about

- What are rules and why are they important?
- What are nonnegotiable rules?
- Which rules are nonnegotiable?
- What are negotiable rules?
- How do we negotiate rules?
- Which rules are negotiable?
- How do we keep rules current?

What Rules Are and Why They Are Important

A rule is a boundary or limit that sets a standard and has consequences for compliance and for noncompliance. Rules are established to provide safety and to hold people, ourselves included, accountable.

> *One way parents set solid boundaries is by making and enforcing rules appropriate to a child's age and abilities.*

One way parents set solid boundaries is by making and enforcing rules appropriate to a child's age and abilities. When rules are humane and made for the safety and protection of the child, children learn that they deserve to be safe and that their parents love them. And they learn even more. They learn that they deserve to feel successful, to be successful, to be proud of accomplishments, and to live richly, mindful of themselves and others.

Clear, positive rules help children develop a personal framework for getting their needs met and for keeping themselves physically and psychologically safe from harm. Children who acquire helpful rules and boundaries from their parents avoid unsafe situations. They have a low tolerance for the invasion of their personal boundaries by people who want to take advantage of them. They are good at inviting positive people and experiences into their lives and at keeping negative experiences and people out.

> *Children who acquire helpful rules and boundaries from their parents avoid unsafe situations.*

Rules help us teach children about safety and limits. Also, in the process of teaching rules, parents give children a supply of helpful information about themselves and their environment that they can store for later use. Before children can make sense of a rule and internalize it, they need adequate information from parents to help them realize that a particular rule is for their welfare.

Nonnegotiable Rules: Keeping Children Safe

Let's review the difference between negotiable and nonnegotiable rules before we explore when to use them. Think of nonnegotiable rules as commands or demands, and negotiable rules as guidelines that apply to any situation where you bargain on what to do.

Nonnegotiable rules are boundaries or standards of behavior that we insist upon. Some of us have difficulty in making and enforcing nonnegotiable rules because we are reluctant to think of them as commands or demands. So we tell children how we feel rather than what to do: *When you yell at each other, I feel uncomfortable;* rather than *Each of you think about what you want and then talk it out; don't yell it out.* (See Encouraging Responsibility through Language in appendix A.)

When demands are not abusive or used with rigidity, they teach the value and importance of being healthy, interactive family members and law-abiding citizens.

Parents Decide Which Rules Are Nonnegotiable

Each family has to decide which rules are nonnegotiable and which are negotiable. Making those decisions—and knowing when to change nonnegotiable rules to negotiable rules as the children grow—is part of the art of parenting.

Here are eight areas suitable for *nonnegotiable* rules. One example for each area is given.

Health: "You will stay in bed when you have a fever."

Safety: "You may not drive if you have been drinking."

Legality: "You may not drive without a valid license."

Ethics: "I will not call your boss and lie for you."

Religion: "You are expected to attend services with the family until you are fourteen."

Family Traditions: "We all go to Grandma's house on her birthday as long as she is well enough to have us all."

Parental Preference: "You may not turn the volume high on your music when I am in the house."

Community Customs: "This is a quiet neighborhood. If it is a special occasion and you let the neighbors know ahead of time, you may have a party and loud music that lasts until midnight once or twice a year."

Some of these examples may not fit for your family. Remember that nonnegotiable rules differ from family to family. Children need to learn that families do things differently and that their family is unique.

List examples of the nonnegotiable rules that you have or wish you had in your family. You may think of additional categories.

Health:

Safety:

Legality:

Ethics:

Religion:

Family Traditions:

Parental Preference:

Community Customs:

Other:

Other:

In order to decide which rules are to be negotiable and which are to be nonnegotiable, parents need to be clear and straight about their own values and about what is safe and what is unsafe, what is helpful and what is not helpful. Those of us who grew up without being taught to assess danger need to consult with other people who are already good at it. Check out your reality in regard to safety with as many other people as you need to. Do not discount your needs or your child's needs for safety and protection.

To help all family members be clear about family rules, post the important ones, both the negotiable and nonnegotiable rules. (See Sample Rules Chart in appendix A.)

Negotiable Rules: Teaching Children to Think

Negotiable rules are mutually agreed upon; both parents and children offer ideas and make judgments. Sometimes, as parents, we avoid negotiating rules because we believe that to negotiate with kids means to give in or show weakness. Actually, the opposite is true. When we negotiate rules that are appropriate for kids to help decide, we teach our children how to think clearly. We show strength in our willingness to hear their needs, to understand their reality, and to rethink our own positions. Negotiation stimulates children to think responsibly and to acquire new information.

> *When we negotiate rules that are appropriate for kids to help decide, we teach our children how to think clearly.*

How Does the Negotiation Work?

Negotiating rules means making contracts. Contracts help parents and children be more clear about who is responsible for what. Sometimes it helps to clarify responsibilities by writing a contract. (See Using Contracts in appendix A.)

Topics covered during negotiations include What? How? When? Where? Who? How much? How long? Then what? Why? Parents ask questions about the child's request because they need information with which to determine the limit or boundary needed for the child's protection and safety. At the same time, parents are teaching children about the kinds of data needed to solve problems.

Notice how the parent questions the child in the following example.

Bill, a fifth grader, is expected to negotiate with parents before accepting social invitations. This is the rule. Here is how the contracting negotiation might go. Notice how many family rules are covered.

Bill: "Sam has invited me to go to the lake this weekend. Can I go?" (where)

Parent: "Well, the family isn't doing anything special, so tell me what you know about the trip." (what)

Bill: "His mom and dad and two other friends are going." (who)

Parent: "Which friends? Do I know them?" (who)

Bill: "You know Joe, but I don't think you know Kelly. He is Joe's friend." (who)

Parent: "Yes, I remember Joe. What else can you tell me?"

Bill: "We'll leave Friday after school and get back Sunday evening." (when, how long)

Parent: "Is there a phone where we could reach you in an emergency?" (how)

Bill: "I'll find out."

Parent: "Are you all riding in Mr. and Mrs. Albert's car and do they use seat belts?" (how)

Bill: "Yes. And I'll need enough money for food at McDonald's on the way up and back." (how much)

Parent: "Okay. I'll give you that. Will you ask the Alberts how early you'll get home Sunday evening? It's a school night." (how long)

Bill: "I'll find out after practice tonight." (when)

Parent: "When will you do your weekend chores?" (when)

Bill: "I'll ask Lily to do the sweeping for me, and I'll do some Thursday night. Maybe you'll help me out if I do extra next week?" (who, what, when)

Parent: "Yes, I will. Okay, I expect you can go. We'll talk again after you know about the phone and the time you get home. Find out what you'll be doing so we'll know what to pack." (when, what)

Negotiation ends when the parent and child are both satisfied and when the contract is clear about who will do what, or when the parent decides the situation is no longer suitable for negotiation. For instance, in the previous example, if Bill would not be home before eleven o'clock on Sunday night, his parent would have said that he could not go. Parents are responsible for a child's health. Bill's parent believes that a fifth grader needs to be at home and in bed well before eleven o'clock on a school night. Nonnegotiable rules always underpin negotiations.

Negotiating teaches children how to think, encourages them to be responsible, and sets the expectation that they will use their energies and power in positive ways. Also, parents can remember that as children grow up and have less physical touch from their parents, one way they get recognition and make contact is by challenging, arguing, and hassling. For kids who like to connect with their parents by hassling, the process of negotiating provides a constructive ground on which to do that.

During the negotiating process, children learn they can count on their parents. They also learn important lessons in life: *I win sometimes, you win sometimes, we both win sometimes. I can feel good about winning. I can learn to handle disappointment. I don't always have to win. I can learn skills for cooperation.*

> *During the negotiating process, children learn they can count on their parents. They also learn important lessons in life.*

If both parent and child feel as if they've lost, it's time for parents to take another look at the household rules and at their ability to negotiate clear contracts and enforce rules with love and structure, not punishment and criticism.

As children grow older it is important to increase the number of negotiable rules, making some of the formerly nonnegotiable ones negotiable. Consider the skill and maturity level of the child when deciding to do this.

Which Rules Are Negotiable?

Following are seven examples of areas suitable for negotiation. Either a parent or a child can initiate the negotiations.

Money

Family rule: *We are all to be suitably dressed, and we have this much money in the family budget for clothes.*

Parent opens negotiation: "You have this many dollars for your share of the clothing money this fall. The things you want cost more than this amount. Let's talk about what we can do."

Child opens negotiation: "All of the kids on my team have special athletic shoes. I want some too."

Grades

Family rule: *If you let your grades slip, you must spend more time studying.*

Parent opens negotiation: "It's been two weeks since your last report card. How are you doing on bringing up your grades?"

Child opens negotiation: "I've been studying for two hours in my room each school night since the last report card. I'm doing better now and I want to cut down on the study time."

Convenience

Family rule: *Seventeen-year-old Rod drives his younger brother Jason to practice.*

Rod opens negotiation: "I'm going to the speech regionals next weekend. I'd like to be excused from taking Jason to practice. Can someone else take him?"

Parent opens negotiation: "Rod, Mrs. Smith is wondering if you can take Christopher to practice too. Do you think that you could handle both boys?"

Chores

Family rule: *Everyone helps with chores.*

Parent opens negotiation: "Here are the chores that have to be done this weekend. Let's decide together who does which one when."

Child opens negotiation: "I'm bored with my chore. I'd rather do something that's fun."

Skill Level

Family rule: *Jason can bike within a half-mile radius of home, crossing the highway only at the stoplight.*

Jason opens negotiation: "I know how to ride my bike really well and I follow the safety rules. Can I bike to Lake Independence with my friends on Saturday?"

Parent opens negotiation: "Jason, I see that you are handling your bike really well. Want to take a bike trip with me Saturday to see if you are ready for a larger territory?"

Maturity Level

Family rule: *As children grow, they learn new skills and get new responsibilities and privileges.*
Child opens negotiation: "I think I'm old enough to shop for Mom's birthday present alone."
Parent opens negotiation: "If you feel ready to shop for Mom's birthday present alone, you could do it today while I'm at the hardware store."

Social Manners

Family rule: *Social manners and customs should be appropriate to the situation. Teenage son wants to wear his earring to Grandma's reception.*
Parent opens negotiation: "We are going to see Grandma. I know that you like wearing your earring, but I'm afraid Grandma and her friends will misunderstand the statement you are making."
Son opens negotiation: "I suppose you'll ask me not to wear my earring when we see Gram. I wish she'd get used to it."

List some of the negotiable rules you have or wish you had in your family. You may think of additional categories.

Money:

Grades:

Convenience:

Chores:

Skill Level:

Maturity Level:

Social Manners:

Other:

Other:

Keeping Rules Current

Sometimes after children have been observing a rule or keeping a contract for a while, they start breaking it. As long as youngsters see a rule as reasonable and workable for them, they are apt to comply. But when they begin to feel the rule is too restrictive or does not account for their increased abilities to be responsible for themselves, they may resist or defy the rule by breaking it or forgetting it. When children do this frequently, it's time to examine the rule. Perhaps the rule is no longer appropriate. Or children may be signaling about some other distress in their lives and parents will need to investigate that. Or children may be initiating a hassle about the structure to meet their stimulation or recognition hungers.

When your child breaks the same nonnegotiable rule or a contract two or three times, say, "It's time to discuss this situation. We will look for new information—information we didn't consider when we first made this rule. Let's meet tomorrow." Remember that updating or negotiating a rule is best done when people are calm rather than in the heat of disagreement or resentment.

As parents, you may decide to reassert the rule and stiffen the consequences, particularly if the safety of your child is involved. Or you may decide that a rule you negotiated giving the child more responsibility needs to be made nonnegotiable for a while or renegotiated, since the child has shown an unwillingness to keep the contract.

If the child is an older teenager, you may renegotiate the rule if it truly seems to be outdated, or you may keep it as something the teen can push against. Some adolescents need to push on rules as one way they separate themselves from their families. Will that be unpleasant? Probably, but some teens seem to need to be irritated with their parents in order to separate and become themselves. So feel free to hold fast to some nonnegotiable rules. For example: No parties when parents are not at home. No smoking in the house. Do your own laundry.

> *Feel free to hold fast to some nonnegotiable rules.*

Probably the most useful information a parent can have in deciding which rules should be nonnegotiable and which should be negotiable is what developmental tasks are appropriate for what age. Parents need to know what to expect from children of various ages and stages of development. (See chapter 25 Ages and Stages.)

chapter *10*

The Lessons of Discipline

The structure we provide for children teaches them many life lessons. The skills and standards they acquire become part of their internal structure for being competent. The rules adults provide help children learn how to be safe and responsible, how to interact with others, and how to care for themselves and others.

But what if children don't follow those rules? Then parents offer *discipline,* which is another chance to teach. This word *discipline,* derived from the word *discere,* to learn, reminds us to ask, "What are the children learning? What are we teaching?" First of all, what are we teaching about rules?

What Does Your Family Teach about Rules?

Think about what your family is teaching about rules and how you feel about rules. Listen to what the adults in your family are saying or doing (teaching) about rules.

- That rules are a burden? *Oh, groan, we just got another set of rules and regulations at work. This means more meaningless paperwork.*
- That you should know the rules without asking? *I made a mistake at work. It was something we have never done before, but I should have known.*
- That rules are stupid or thoughtless in design? *What a stupid rule! I wonder who thinks up these things!*
- That it's okay to break rules as long as you don't get caught? *Padding my expense account gets by my new supervisor. She doesn't notice.*

- That they are to be broken, finessed, or ignored? *Well, there is another rule we will have to get around.*
- That rules benefit adults at the expense of children? *You know the rule. Children don't ask questions when adults are talking.*
- That they are made to be helpful? *I'm glad there is a rule that we all drive on the same side of the road.*
- That rules should be evaluated? *That rule no longer seems to fit. Let's think about how to change it to be more helpful.*
- That you value your family rules because they protect and respect everyone in the family? *I'm glad we have a no put-down rule in our family. It helps us think about how to be helpful instead of blaming each other.*

If your family or school teaches that rules are a burden or are to be avoided or manipulated or if you or your child bristles at the mention of the word "rules," you may choose to avoid the word and ASK the *Do you remember . . .* or *Can you think why . . .* questions.

- *Do you remember when we talked about put-downs?*
- *Do you remember when we practiced petting the kitty gently?*
- *Do you remember where to put toys when you are through playing?*
- *Can you think why I need to know one day ahead when you plan to take cookies to school?*
- *Can you tell me why everyone writes on the chalkboard where they are going and when they'll be back?*
- *Will you tell me three reasons it is important for you to refill the gas tank when you have used the car?*

How do *you* feel about rules? If you do not view rules as your friends, maybe you need some friendlier rules. If the children are not following rules, is there some reason you are not expecting rules to be followed routinely?

If you have been modeling how to break or get around rules, don't expect children to follow your rules until you change your behavior.

What Does Your Family Teach about Successfully Following Rules?

All behaviors have consequences, positive or negative. If we as parents forget to provide positive consequences, expressions of trust, thanks, or approval when children perform well, we neglect a powerful method of encouraging children to be competent and to build their own positive structure. Sometimes parents don't notice good behavior because they take it for granted. Yet children need response; if they are not recognized for good behavior, they will get attention in some less desirable way. Sometimes parents inadvertently set up unhelpful behaviors by not setting clear expectations. For example, a mother who asked a child to do one chore and then assigned another chore as soon

> *All behaviors have consequences, positive or negative.*

as the first one was completed taught the child not to finish. This was not the lesson the mother intended. The child's behavior changed when the mother gave specific directions about the number of chores to be done or about the length of time she expected the child to help.

What Does the Family Teach about Breaking Rules?

When children defy or neglect to follow healthy, helpful family rules, the children lose. They lose those opportunities to be celebrated as growing, contributing family members. They lose the chance to incorporate those building blocks of internal structure.

All behaviors have consequences, and adults can choose which consequences children will experience, which lessons children will learn when they break rules. Parents need to remember that anytime a child misbehaves, the *child* has a lesson to learn or a problem to solve.

Does this take time and energy on the part of the parent? It does. And it is important. It is vitally important. Even the children know that. When the *Minneapolis Star Tribune* invited students to write about student misbehavior and disruptive classmates, nearly five thousand essays poured in from elementary and high school students. Hundreds wrote that *kids are disruptive because they pay no consequences.* Others complained that *misbehaving students have not been taught respect at home and lack structure.* "Structure" was the word they used! Most of them agreed that misbehaving peers interfere with their learning, dampen their enthusiasm, and just plain make them mad. One fourth grader said, "I have experienced disruptive or misbehaving classmates during the day. I think the teacher should put a brick wall around each of our desks."[1] Because other students lack internal structure and the classroom lacks safe structure, this ten-year-old would settle for a rigid structure—physical brick walls.

Natural Consequences

Sometimes parents allow the child to experience natural consequences which are either positive or negative and happen as a direct result of a behavior. Many times, experiencing the natural results of misbehavior is the best lesson a child or an adult can learn: when he studies and does well on a test, when she pushes someone and gets pushed back, when he forgets his lunch and goes hungry, or when she speeds and gets a ticket. The learning that results is about choice and responsibility.

When natural consequences of misbehavior are allowed, it is not to make children miserable but to allow them to experience just enough discomfort to cause them to examine how their behavior defeats them. If the adults take the discomfort upon themselves, the child gets off scot-free. Parents need to remember to be agents of support, not repositories for the child's discomfort.

Often reminding a child of a natural consequence is all that is needed. Five-year-old Joshua nagged at his father, "Tie my shoes."

> *Natural consequences are not always safe or appropriate.*

"That's your job. I'm tying my own shoes."

"I'm not going to tie mine."

"Then I guess you will learn what happens when you step on your shoelaces."

Dad's response was matter-of-fact, neither harsh nor solicitous. Josh tied his own shoes.

Yet natural consequences are not always safe or appropriate. Responsible parents do not allow a child to run into the street in order to experience the natural consequence of being hit by a car. Nor does the parent notice a destructive pattern of chemical use and allow the natural consequence of death without attempting to intervene.

Logical Consequences

Logical consequences are sometimes used when natural ones would be dangerous, too long in coming, or a great inconvenience to the rest of the family. Logical consequences should be reasonable, related to the offense, respectful of all concerned, and made known in advance.

Look at what parents said about the differences between logical and natural consequences.

- Natural consequences automatically follow a behavior. Logical consequences are related to the behavior, focus on responsibility, and help the child repair the damage done.
- Failing a class because of not studying is a natural consequence. Having to stay home on weeknights to study is a logical consequence of the failure.
- Having to walk home or call for a ride is a natural consequence of letting the gas tank run dry. Earning enough money to fill the tank and not being allowed to drive until that happens is a logical consequence.

In making contracts about behavior with our kids, we spell out the logical consequences we will impose if the contract is not kept and if the natural consequences are not safe or are inconvenient for the parent.

The Trouble with Logical Consequences

Whenever possible, parents need to involve the child in identifying logical consequences. If the parent chooses consequences, the child does not have to think about how to become responsible and respectful. The child can treat the consequence as a penalty or punishment and reject any discomfort by projecting it onto the parent.

The lack of an obvious way to connect the consequence with the behavior is another trouble with logical consequences. Taking away television privileges for fighting may seem logical to the parent, as it will reduce the influence of violence presented on TV. The child, however, may not see how television and fighting are connected.

Grounding a child for using bullying language may seem a logical result of not getting along well with peers, but it doesn't teach the child what to do instead.

While we cannot expect children to be happy about negative consequences of their behavior, we can help them to understand the reason for the consequences. If children view the consequences as punishment, they will often blame us and feel entitled to reject responsibility for their acts and to repeat them or to get even with the adults.

Sometimes the consequence that looks logical to the parent discomforts the parent more than the child. How many parents have grounded a child for a week only to find themselves miserable with the arrangement? How many parents threaten a consequence they do not want to carry out?

What Does the Family Teach about Focusing on Solutions?

Instead of focusing on consequences, many misbehaviors can be dealt with directly by focusing on solutions. Sometimes we ask children to calm themselves, to take time out, before we do our teaching, but remember that time out is not discipline. Discipline follows time out.

> *When we focus on solutions, we teach children to think and to be responsible.*

When we focus on solutions, we teach children to think and to be responsible. What do we do about spilled milk? What do you think will happen the next time you want to go to the store if you continue whining today? What do you need in order to be ready for the school bus on time? Do you remember the four steps to cleaning your room? How can you rearrange your schedule so you can get enough sleep? What arrangements do we need to make so we don't get angry with each other about use of the car, laundry, borrowing clothes, doing chores, and so on?

What about Problems That Can't Be Fixed?

When objects are broken, feelings are hurt, or reputations are damaged, there may not be a way to "fix" the problem. It's time to teach the positive lessons learned from making amends. Making amends helps the child in several ways. The child experiences discomfort as he or she faces the impact of the behavior. Self-confidence is restored as the child thinks of ways to make restitution. The outcome is positive because the loser behavior is amended by winner behavior and the child's sense of competence and self-esteem is enhanced.

Remember the four guidelines for choosing how to make amends.

1. The offending child must think of options for making amends. The adult may help.
2. The person who was hurt or offended must agree to one of the options offered or may suggest an option only after the offending child has thought of two or more.
3. The amending behaviors must be related to the offense, reasonable, legal, and appropriate.
4. If the offending child is young, the adult must agree to the amending action chosen.

We can learn more about helping children make amends by reading *Restitution: Restructuring School Discipline* by Diane Chelsom Gossen.[2]

What about Punishment?

Punishment is treatment that is harsh or unrelated to a child's behavior. We punish when we feel powerless, when we haven't carried through with consequences, or when the consequences haven't been effective with that particular child. Punishment may relieve the punisher of angry feelings; but, if helping children see the error of their ways is our goal, punishment is the least desirable way to achieve our aim. Discipline, on the other hand, takes more thought and is intended to help children see that it is in their best interest to change. The wish to punish may be a clue that we need new rules or more skills in order to continue teaching our children. Or our anger may be a clue that we have forgotten that when a child breaks a rule it is our job to keep the discomfort on the child, not to take it onto ourselves. It is hard to get angry if we are busy saying, "This is my son's problem, not mine. How do I get him to realize that what he did is a loss to him?"

Looking Behind the Misbehavior

When a child is not responding positively to consequences or changes in structure, it is time to look behind the misbehavior and ask some questions.

1. What is our discipline teaching?
2. Is the discipline we are using taking the child's temperament into account?
3. Is the child's behavior a signal that one or more of the basic human hungers are not being met?
4. Is the child's behavior reflecting some problem in the family system? Perhaps a problem such as drugs, alcoholism, illness, death, or poverty. Perhaps things kept secret such as adoption, homosexuality, alcoholism, criminal activity, incest.
5. Is there a problem in the neighborhood or school, such as violence, bullying, shunning, or scape-goating?
6. Do I need more support?

Are There Consequences for Parents?

Parents sometimes forget that they will experience positive and negative consequences for keeping or not keeping their part of the parenting bargain. (See Using Contracts, appendix A.)

When a family is first introduced to the idea of family rules as contracts, as situations with rewards and penalties for both parents and children, the children often retort, "Ha! There are no penalties for adults. When grown-ups break agreements with kids, they get by with it." But after thinking about it, the kids realize that they do penalize adults when adults don't keep their part of a bargain. The kids admit, "When parents don't do their part, I don't trust them as much, or I'll take longer to do the work they ask me to do."

We need to keep our part of every negotiated contract or own up to breaking it and make amends or accept the consequences.

Sometimes consequences for adults are as obvious as when a child confronts a parent with, "You didn't do your part." More often the child penalized the adult with the natural consequence of passive behavior such as ignoring rules, forgetting, sullenness, lack of trust, messiness, tardiness, insolence, failure at school, or flouting family values.

As parents, we need to keep our part of every negotiated contract or own up to breaking it and make amends or accept the consequences. If we neglect to hold ourselves accountable, children may learn that accountability is only for youngsters and that they will not need to be accountable as they get older.

Some Important Rules for Living Can't Be Enforced by Parents

Many rules that parents believe are important are unenforceable. These are rules for living that parents believe are wise and significant and that they hope their children will internalize. Children, in some wise part of themselves, know that they need these "voices in their heads" even though they may deride and resist them when they are offered.

Listen to the wisdom of Annie and Corky.

Eve and her friend were driving to the lake for the weekend. Eve's nineteen-year-old daughter, Annie, and her friend, Corky, were in the back seat. In the front seat, the older women chattered away and, in back, the younger two did the same. Suddenly, Eve overheard Annie's friend say, "I wish my mother had told me that." And Annie said, "So do I."

"Whoa," Eve thought, "I'm interested in this!" So, begging their pardon for intruding on the conversation, Eve asked Corky what she wished her mother had told her.

"Not to have sex until I was twenty-one," she replied firmly.

"Hold everything! Annie, did you want me to tell you that too?"

"Yes."

"But do you know what you would have said to me?"

"Yes. I would have said that you were out of touch, didn't understand, and, besides, I would have it my way anyway." Eve wondered if that was why she hadn't said what Annie wanted to hear. Was she afraid to hear Annie's response?

Eve had listened to the advice that adolescents should not be given messages that sex was bad. She had also heard that the best thing to do was give teenagers information on pregnancy and sexually transmitted diseases, especially AIDS, and then to say the decision was theirs, making sure, at the same time, they had access to birth control.

"So, in spite of what you'd say to me," said Eve, "you wanted me to tell you to wait?"

Corky answered for Annie. "I needed the voice of someone who loved me, my mother's voice, in my head when I stood toe to mushy toe with a panting ninth-grade boy who was telling me he loved me, telling me I wanted to 'do it' and moving right ahead. I wanted to have a reason to say no and feel that I hadn't signed some social death warrant by refusing to have sex."

"Me too," added Annie.

Eve thought for the first time about how parents' rules "in the head and heart" can set important boundaries for growing up. Telling her daughter to refrain from having sex until age twenty-one would have been a rule that Eve could not enforce. Eve thought about the possible natural consequences of early sexual intercourse:

- Annie might have regrets about feeling used.
- She might get a sexually transmitted disease; she could die of AIDS.
- Too early sex can be so titillating and preoccupying that the

energy for personal growth and learning relationship skills can be subsumed by the sexual excitement.

- Easy sex and the game-playing that immature sexual relationships involve may infringe on Annie's job of finding out who she is.
- She may become so busy taking care of others she forgets to do her job of finding out what *her* needs are, what *her* gifts are, what *her* goals are.
- Annie may have an untimely pregnancy.
- Normal adolescent behaviors and tasks may be postponed until later, and then the wish to recapture teenage experiences may interfere with adult tasks.

These consequences are definitely not okay with a responsible parent. The moral of the story: It's necessary for parents to set "rules" expressed as wishes, hopes, or expectations for the health, safety, and sound development of sons and daughters. To omit expressing these hopes is to leave a big hole in the defenses we want our children to have—defenses that help them protect their health and safety whenever they need that help. Although this story is about a girl, it applies absolutely equally to boys.

chapter 11

Life Examples of the Structure Chart

The Structure Highway

As with nurturing, it is helpful to think of providing structure and the Structure Chart as a highway. Nonnegotiable and negotiable rules are the two safe driving lanes, criticism and marshmallowing are the shoulders, and rigidity and abandonment are the ditches. If your parenting car slips onto the shoulder, come back onto the highway without overcorrecting and ending up on the opposite shoulder. If you realize you are in the ditch, try to swing back onto the highway yourself. If you need help, call the parenting tow truck—a friend, a parenting class or support group, or a counselor. Just don't stay stuck in the ditch. As much as you can, live life in the driving lanes.

Using the Structure Chart

Use the following examples to practice identifying where you are already providing clear structure.

Here are examples of several situations that involve providing structure for children. As you read them ask yourself: *Am I using nonnegotiable and negotiable rules in my parenting or do I use one of the four nonsupportive responses?* If you do the latter, decide if the nonnegotiable and negotiable rules suggested here would fit for your home situation. If they do not fit, revise them to be more appropriate for you.

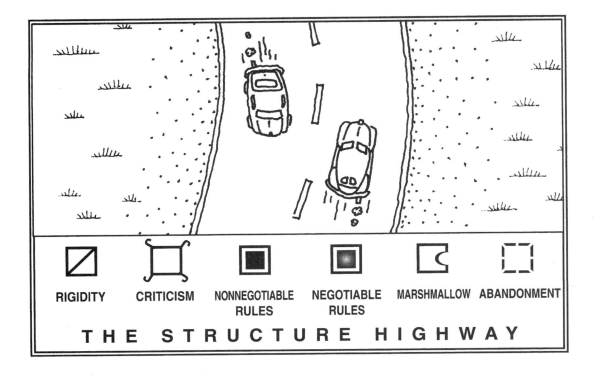

THE STRUCTURE HIGHWAY

EXAMPLE 1

Situation: Four-year-old child is attempting to cross street by herself.

The parent:

Rigidity: Yanks child by arm and says, "If you put one foot into the street, I'll spank you."

Criticism: Screams at child, "Stay out of the street, stupid! What's wrong with you? Haven't I told you a thousand times, you're gonna get killed!"

Nonnegotiable Rules: Says seriously, "Come and get me when you want to cross the street. You can only cross with a grown-up or your older brother."

Negotiable Rules: None. Street safety is not negotiable.

Marshmallowing: Says pleadingly, "Try to remember not to run into the street."

Abandonment: Doesn't notice.

Life Examples of the Structure Chart

EXAMPLE 2
Situation: Three-to-six-year-old child is eating candy.
The parent:

Rigidity: Grabs candy from child and says, "You may never have candy. It's bad for you."

Criticism: Frowns and says, "You little sneak. Where did you get the candy?"

Nonnegotiable Rules: Gently takes candy from child. Says lovingly, "I will offer you candy twice a week."

Negotiable Rules: Says, "Grandpa always brings candy. Let's decide when and how much of it you get to eat. I'll help you store it. You may choose to give some to other people."

Marshmallowing: Says, "I can't keep you out of the candy, can I? You're my little Sweet Tooth."

Abandonment: No rules. Sweets always available. Parents don't notice what child eats. Parents eat sweets instead of nutritious food.

EXAMPLE 3
Situation: Nine-year-old has been getting poor grades on schoolwork.
The parent:

Rigidity: Says, "If your homework is late one time, you are grounded for a month."

Criticism: Says angrily, "You are lazy and stupid and you just don't care."

Nonnegotiable Rules: Says, "You must spend an hour on homework after dinner when the whole family reads or studies."

Negotiable Rules: Discusses with child, "Shall we talk to your teacher about how much help parents should give?"

Marshmallowing: Says, "I know you don't enjoy homework, but try to get it done, will you?"

Abandonment: Doesn't notice. Doesn't respond to report cards or calls from school.

EXAMPLE 4
Situation: Seven-year-old child resists going to bed.
The parent:

Rigidity: Says, "You must be in bed at eight o'clock no matter what day it is or what is going on. No exceptions."

Criticism: Says, "You never go to bed when I tell you to. Don't you dare get out of bed and don't turn your light back on."

Nonnegotiable Rules: Says, "We will find a bedtime that allows you to get enough sleep so you wake on your own in time to get ready for school."

Negotiable Rules: Says, "On weekends and vacation days we can have flexible bedtimes."

Marshmallowing: Says, "Try to get to bed earlier tonight. I'll finish your chores for you."

Abandonment: Pays zero attention to bedtime or keeps child up late on a whim.

EXAMPLE 5
Situation: Twelve-year-old child is late for dinner.
The parent:

Rigidity: Says, "We always eat together at eight, twelve, and six o'clock. No food between meals. If you are not here at mealtime, you don't eat."

Criticism: Says harshly, "You forgot to be home in time for dinner again. You'd lose your head if it weren't fastened on! No dinner for you, stupid!"

Nonnegotiable Rules: Says, "If you are not here for mealtime, you may have the leftovers from dinner."

Negotiable Rules: Says, "If family or individual activities conflict with mealtime, we'll negotiate times to suit us all."

Marshmallowing: Says, "What do you feel like eating, Honey? I'll fix something for you at any time of the day or night."

Abandonment: Does not care if child is present at mealtime. Does not notice what child eats.

EXAMPLE 6
Situation: Ten-year-old boy is always running home and hiding or else getting into fights.
The parent:

Rigidity: Doesn't let child in the house. Tells him to stand up for himself. If he does fight, he is to win.

Criticism: Lets him know that parent has no tolerance for either a wuss or a bully.

Nonnegotiable Rules: Teaches child how to assess his safety accurately and when it is important to get away from a situation. Finds out about the safety of child's world and does whatever possible to make it safer.

Negotiable Rules: Teaches child about fight, flee, and flow with stories from own life or other people's lives. Makes up situations from child's world and has child tell what might happen if he ran, if he stayed to fight, or if he flowed. Helps child generate ways to flow in each situation.

Marshmallowing: Doesn't let child out unless accompanied by parent.

Abandonment: Doesn't notice child is having problems.

EXAMPLE 7
Situation: Eighth-grade girl wants to go to a boy-girl party at a friend's house.
The parent:

Rigidity: Says, "You cannot go to parties at houses, only at school."

Criticism: "Those friends of yours are trouble. I bet there will be drugs and who knows what else. I don't trust you. Of course, you can't go."

Nonnegotiable Rules: Says, "You may go to any school party. You can only go to parties at houses when the parents are home and are supervising the parties. Parents being upstairs is not enough. You are to call us anytime you feel unsafe and we will come and get you."

Negotiable Rules: Says, "I must know where you are when you are out. Together we will think of ways you can have fun, take care of yourself, and be safe."

Marshmallowing: Says, "I want you to be popular, so go to all the parties you are invited to. Do you need some new clothes?"

Abandonment: Says, "I'm going to a party myself. Do whatever you want."

EXAMPLE 8
Situation: Thirteen-year-old daughter is pressured by boy to have sex.
The parent:

Rigidity: Says, "No daughter of mine has sex until she is married if she wants to stay part of this family."

Criticism: Says, "You dress like a hooker; what do you expect?" or "You are a slut if you have sex before you are married."

Nonnegotiable Rules: Says, "You are too young to have sexual intercourse. You have other things to learn now. Save that for later."

Negotiable Rules: Says, "Even if you want to, remember that this is not the time. Let's think of things a girl can say to a boy who is pressuring." (I have decided to wait until I'm older. Go home and take a shower. You are getting in my way. You asked me before. Do you have a memory problem or something? Sorry, I'm busy. Nope, I have other plans.)

Marshmallowing: Says, "Oh, dear, young people are growing up so fast these days."

Abandonment: Says, "I have no control over you; you will do what you want anyway."

Test Your Knowledge

Test how well you are identifying the structure positions. For the following examples, after each response, write "Rigidity," "Criticism," "Nonnegotiable," "Negotiable," "Marshmallowing," or "Abandonment" as the structure position you think fits most closely. Remember that tone of voice, body language, and context can move some responses from one position to another. Compare your answers with those provided and think about ones that differ and what might account for this.

EXAMPLE 9
Situation: Teenager has just reached legal driving age and passed licensing examination.
The parent:

1. Says, "Do as you like." Parent is gone, drunk, or preoccupied or teases instead of setting limits. _____
2. Says, "When you have driven with us enough for us to be satisfied with your skill level, then you can drive farther and give more kids rides." _____
3. Says, "Don't ask for the car. I'll decide when you need it and when you don't." _____
4. Says, "You must observe the traffic laws. For now, you are not to have more than two other kids in the car, and not to go beyond the city limits." _____
5. Laughs, "Take the car? Ha! Are you kidding? I don't want my car wrecked." _____
6. Sighs, "I know you want the car. I need it too, but I'll take the bus." _____

Answers: (1) Abandonment (2) Negotiable (3) Rigidity (4) Nonnegotiable (5) Criticism (6) Marshmallowing

Life Examples of the Structure Chart

EXAMPLE 10

Situation: Sixteen-year-old daughter tells mother about being sexually molested by a friend of the family.

The mother:

1. Says, "That's just awful, but I'm sure you will forget about it soon. He's from a good family so we won't tell."

   _____

2. Looks at daughter with disgust. Asks, "What did you do to bring it on?" _____

3. Sighs and says, "That happened to me too." _____

4. Says, "He must be stopped from molesting you or anyone else. Let's think of all the things we could do and then decide which one to do first." _____

5. Says, "There must be no scandal about our family. Do not mention it again." _____

6. Says firmly, "No one should be sexually abused. I will call a child protection agency. I will see to it that you are safe. We will get this abuse stopped now." _____

Answers: (1) Marshmallowing (2) Criticism (3) Abandonment (4) Negotiable (5) Rigidity (6) Nonnegotiable

EXAMPLE 11

Situation: Parent is frustrated because six-year-old Sally argues about everything. To make peace, the parent gives in, but she feels rotten about it.

The friend:

1. Says, "You can use your good sense to know when to stop responding to her arguments. Make a decision and stick to it."

   _____

2. Says, "You're too easy on her. I'd see to it she knew who was boss. It would be my way or the highway." _____

3. Shrugs shoulders and says, "So, what else is new?"

   _____

4. There is no response at this position. Parents are in charge of whether or not they argue with a child, they do not negotiate about it. _____

5. Says, "What's wrong with you? Afraid to stand up to a six-year-old child?" _____

6. Commiserates and says, "I know. Don't you hate that?"

   _____

Answers: (1) Nonnegotiable (2) Rigidity (3) Abandonment (4) Negotiable (5) Criticism (6) Marshmallowing

Using the Structure Chart
to Care for Yourself and Other Adults

Children are not the only ones who need structure. Since certainty is a human hunger, we all need the structure that provides it throughout our lives. When we find ourselves in unsafe structures, we respond in many ways. Some of us leave the scene. Some stay and try to create a safe structure. Others withdraw into a corner. Still others turn to recognition hunger and try to feel safer by making themselves known. You may be able to think of times when you have done each of these.

The external world imposes many structures on adults—how to drive, how to pay taxes, what we may and may not do in the workplace and in public areas. But probably the most freeing *and* the most limiting are the structures we put on ourselves.

To improve your own internal structures, reread the examples of healthy nonnegotiable and negotiable rules included in this book. Remember that you *deserved* to hear such rules when you were a child and that you can and should hear and incorporate them now. When you use them with your children, take them to heart for yourself.

As you read the following example of an adult situation, think of the words as coming from somewhere within yourself—as messages you give to yourself telling you what to do. Remember that you are no longer a child but an adult who is in charge of selecting your own structure that works best for you.

EXAMPLE 12
Situation: You have been told by people who care about you that you should be taking better care of yourself.
You say:

Rigidity: "Only after everyone else's needs are met."

Criticism: "I'm a grown-up. Only weaklings need that self-care stuff."

Nonnegotiable Rules: "I will choose one specific way to care for myself each day and do it."

Negotiable Rules: "I will try out several ways to care for myself and decide if they are helpful."

Marshmallowing: "I need so much there is no point in even starting."

Abandonment: "I do not believe my needs are important."

Using the Structure Chart
to Set Boundaries with Other Adults

Other people constantly ask us to do things. When you feel unsure about whether to say yes or no to a request, try thinking of the request in this way. Ask yourself what boundary (nonnegotiable rule) would provide for your safety or for your health. For example, while responding to a friend's request, your thought process might be something like the following.

Friend: "Will you have breakfast with me tomorrow?"

You ask yourself: "What does my day's schedule demand of me tomorrow? My meetings start at 11 o'clock in the morning and continue through an evening dinner meeting. The next day I'm teaching an all-day workshop." You ask yourself: "Is getting up earlier to go out for breakfast good for my health? I need the extra hour of sleep. I will say no because I don't want to say yes and then resent my friend."

You say to friend: "Sorry, I need to sleep late. We can have breakfast another day."

Use the structure positions to identify areas where you are setting healthy boundaries with other adults. When you set healthy boundaries for yourself, you are better able to take good care of other people. If you don't believe this, think of the times you have neglected yourself and, as a result, others took advantage of you or were angry with you or you were angry with them.

Read the following five examples and decide if you would use one of the four nonsupportive responses in each example. If so, decide if the nonnegotiable and negotiable rules suggested would fit your situation. If not, revise them so you can successfully set boundaries. Look through all of the examples. If some seem more difficult than others, skip them until you have studied the easier ones. The difficult ones may be close to a problem you need to address courageously.

> *Use the structure positions to identify areas where you are setting healthy boundaries with other adults.*

EXAMPLE 13

Situation: A colleague is in trouble with the boss and asks you to lie for her.

You:

   Rigidity: Say to yourself, "Never tell a lie, no matter what."

   Criticism: Say to yourself, "You're a fool if you lie for her. You let people use you all of the time."

   Nonnegotiable Boundary: Say to yourself, "Other people are responsible for their behavior and choices and you are responsible for yourself."

   Negotiable Boundary: Weigh this request against your own value system. Get more information if you need to.

   Marshmallowing: Say to yourself, "Help her out. You don't want to get on her bad side."

   Abandonment: Avoid thinking about it.

EXAMPLE 14

Situation: Your best friend is telling racist jokes.

You:

   Rigidity: Say to yourself, "You must always laugh at jokes that a friend tells."

   Criticism: Say to yourself, "He's a bigot and you are dumb for listening."

   Nonnegotiable Boundary: Say to yourself, "Telling racist jokes is not okay" and then tell your friend to stop.

   Negotiable Boundary: Consider the most effective response you can think of.

   Marshmallowing: Tell yourself that your friend doesn't mean any harm. Laugh to make him feel good.

   Abandonment: Laugh and forget about it.

EXAMPLE 15

Situation: You've been asked to accept a volunteer job on the church fund-raising committee and you are already very busy.

You say to yourself:

   Rigidity: "If the church asks, I must do it."

   Criticism: "I am always so selfish. It wouldn't hurt me to extend myself a little."

   Nonnegotiable Boundary: "If accepting the job would overextend me physically and emotionally, I won't do it."

Negotiable Boundary: "I can turn down any job that is offered. Think! Do I want to accept it, or can I fulfill my obligation in another way that suits me better?"

Marshmallowing: "I'll go ahead and do it. I can squeeze it into my schedule somewhere. Miss some sleep if I need to."

Abandonment: "I won't think about it."

EXAMPLE 16

Situation: Your partner's drinking is interfering with family and job.
You:

Rigidity: Say to your partner, "Get out!"

Criticism: Say to your partner, "You good-for-nothing! What's the matter with you?"

Nonnegotiable Boundary: Say to your partner, "Get help with your problem. I will get help too. If you do not get help, I will make whatever change I need to make for my own welfare and the welfare of the children."

Negotiable Boundary: Decide that continued support of problem drinking is not negotiable.

Marshmallowing: Say to your partner, "If you want to sleep off last night, I'll call your boss and say you have the flu."

Abandonment: Observe partner drinking destructively without comment.

EXAMPLE 17

Situation: Your spouse is to pay household bills but lets them run overdue.
You say to spouse:

Rigidity: "You must always pay the bills the day they come in. If you let them go overdue one more time, I'll take the household money away from you and I'll make all the household spending decisions."

Criticism: "What? Again? You are not fit to be trusted with money!"

Nonnegotiable Boundary: "Our agreement is that we both contribute to the household account and you manage it. I don't want to spend money on interest, so pay the bills on time or you pay the interest from your personal allowance."

Negotiable Boundary: "Let's review and possibly renegotiate our agreement after we have both calmed down."

Marshmallowing: "Tell me how much money you need." Laughs.

Abandonment: "I don't care what you do. You handle all of the money so I don't have to think about it."

Test Your Knowledge

For examples 18 and 19, write the structure position you think fits each response. Compare your answers with those provided.

EXAMPLE 18

Situation: A friend complains of his spouse's drinking problem and asks for advice.

You say to your friend:

1. "I am willing to support you in finding help. How can I do that?" _____
2. "There's nothing to be done. Drunks are all alike. She'll hit bottom." _____
3. "I have troubles of my own." _____
4. "Why do you tolerate it? She is dumb for drinking and you are just as dumb for putting up with it." _____
5. "Get outside help for yourself. Until you do, I will not continue to listen to you complain." (If your friend starts to talk about his spouse's drinking, you remind him of your position and end the conversation or change the subject.)

   _____

6. "You poor thing. It must be miserable. You can talk to me as often as you need to. Feel free to call anytime." _____

Answers: (1) Negotiable (2) Rigidity (3) Abandonment (4) Criticism (5) Nonnegotiable (6) Marshmallowing

EXAMPLE 19

Situation: Your counselor and support group point out ways you support addictive behavior in your family.

You say to yourself:

1. "Each day, I will pick a way I support addictive behavior and hold myself accountable. I will get a friend or counselor to monitor me lovingly, and we'll celebrate my successes."

   _____

2. "I don't want to upset my family or rock the boat." _____

3. "I can't change." _____
4. "I'll listen to the feedback, and I agree to look closely at my behavior and what I might want to change." _____
5. "I'm too old to change. I hope she gives up her addiction." _____

6. "I have botched everything I've tried. I can't do anything right." _____

Answers: (1) Nonnegotiable (2) Marshmallowing (3) Rigidity (4) Negotiable (5) Abandonment (6) Criticism

EXAMPLE 20

Situation: Your eleven-year-old has saved enough money to buy a cellular phone. He says it's his money and he can spend it as he wants. You think cellular phones are only for adults.

For each structure position, answer the question What would I do if I were to be rigid, criticize, set nonnegotiable rules, etc.?

Rigidity: _____

Criticism: _____

Nonnegotiable Rules: _____

Negotiable Rules: _____

Marshmallowing: _____

Abandonment: _____

Write an example for a problem of your own. Identify the situation. Then ask yourself, "If I were to be rigid about this, what would I do? If I were to criticize, what would I say?" In this manner, identify all structure positions. Notice what would be easy to do and then think what you need in order to stay in the driving lanes of the Structure Highway (see page 90).

chapter 12

The Nurture / Structure Highway

We offer stimulation and recognition through nurture. We touch, we support, we recognize by affirming both being and doing. The ways we offer stimulation and recognition are arranged on a continuum from hard to soft interactions.

ABUSE CONDITIONAL CARE ASSERTIVE CARE SUPPORTIVE CARE OVERINDULGENCE NEGLECT

We examined each of these in the Nurture section.

We offer certainty by providing structure. The ways we teach the rules for safety, responsibility, and respect are also on a continuum.

RIGIDITY CRITICISM NONNEGOTIABLE RULES NEGOTIABLE RULES MARSHMALLOW ABANDONMENT

We examined each of these in the Structure section.

As we know however, children do not live by either nurture or structure alone. Adequate parenting combines nurture and structure to support the growth of body, mind, and soul. We are now ready to combine the Nurture Highway and Structure Highway into one graphic representation—the Nurture/Structure Highway. We think of the extreme ends of each continuum as the ditches along the highway, the next two positions as shoulders, and the middle two positions as the safe lanes where traffic generally moves smoothly.

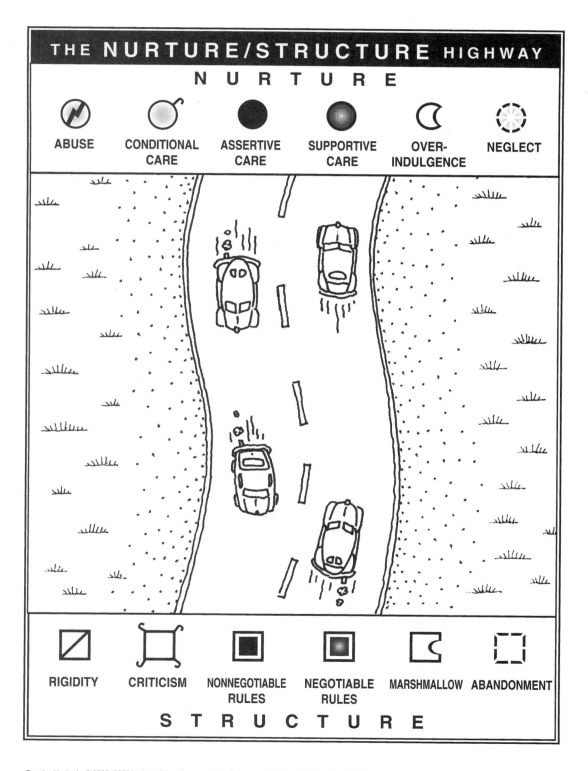

THE **NURTURE/STRUCTURE** HIGHWAY

NURTURE

ABUSE | CONDITIONAL CARE | ASSERTIVE CARE | SUPPORTIVE CARE | OVER-INDULGENCE | NEGLECT

RIGIDITY | CRITICISM | NONNEGOTIABLE RULES | NEGOTIABLE RULES | MARSHMALLOW | ABANDONMENT

STRUCTURE

You can make a copy of the Nurture/Structure Highway and use it to help you with your parenting. Make a small copy for your wallet. Put a large copy on the refrigerator or bulletin board. Get a copy blown up and run tiny toy cars on it. Many parents have discovered that moving toy cars on the Nurture/Structure Highway is a playful way to gain insights into their parenting.

- Fred borrowed his children's Hot Wheels cars. He explained to his children that he had been driving on the Marshmallow shoulder and that from now on he intended to be more clear about rules.
- Daryl found a tiny tow truck to remind him to use the support of his Parents Anonymous group if he got in the ditch.
- Bonnie noticed that if she drove his sports car too fast on the Nonnegotiable Rules lane she swerved into the Rigidity ditch.
- Saturday night, Ian placed a lot of cars on the highway to indicate how he had parented that week. He was surprised to see how many cars were in the driving lanes and he celebrated his successes.
- Teresa felt tired as she pushed her station wagon along. She stayed mostly in the driving lanes, but it was a trudging, grudging journey. A friend helped her realize that she was low on gas. She had been taking good care of the kids, but neglecting herself.
- Peter positioned red cars at the "starting gates" of Assertive Care, Supportive Care, Nonnegotiable Rules, and Negotiable Rules to remind him of his goals. On a day when he had parented in the driving lanes, he moved the red cars out of the starting gate and onto the highway.
- Barney had been raised with Conditional Care so it was easy for him to love his kids when they pleased him and Criticize them when they didn't. Barney realized his car had broken down on the Conditional Care/Criticism shoulder. He decided to get some help for himself and do some growing up again.
- When Kelly positioned a car to represent each of her friends, she saw that she was running with a crowd of shoulder and ditch drivers. It was time to find some new road friends.

You can use the Nurture/Structure Highway to help you remember that you are in charge of where you drive your parenting car and you can choose your lanes. If you hit a shoulder now and then, keep the big picture in mind and head back to the road.[1]

The Nurture / Structure Highway

Although we expect and intend to stay in the driving lanes, what automobile driver has not pulled over onto a shoulder now and then or even ended up in a ditch when conditions became slippery or when there were too many distractions?

The goal is to

- stay in the driving lanes of the highway
- use a balance of nurture and structure
- drive off the shoulders back onto the highway without overcorrecting
- drive out of the ditch when possible and get help when it is needed

chapter 13

When Parents Disagree about Rules

When Parents Disagree about Rules

When parents disagree about minor rules, they may decide to have Mom's rule and Dad's rule and let the children learn about handling differences. For example, if the kids miss the bus when they are with Dad, he takes them to school because he believes attendance is important. If they miss the bus when they are with Mom, they walk to school or stay home and study all day because it is important to her that children learn to be responsible for themselves.

Finding Agreement on Major Rules

If parents disagree on an important rule, however, they will have to come to an agreement, even if this means "fighting it out." In *The Family*,[1] John Bradshaw lists ten rules for fair fighting. You may want to study them in more detail. Here is a shortened version:

1. Be assertive, not aggressive.
2. Stay in the now.
3. Avoid lecture; stay with concrete, specific behavioral details.
4. Use "I" messages; avoid judgments.
5. Be rigorously honest.
6. Don't argue over details.
7. Don't assign blame.
8. Use active listening.
9. Fight about one thing at a time.
10. Go for a solution, not for being right, and hang in there unless you are being abused.

Protecting the Children

Sometimes "fighting it out" doesn't bring agreement, especially if the parents bring very different attitudes about rules from their own growing-up years. If one parent believes that rules are made to be broken, finessed, or ignored; or if one or both adults take a hard-line "I-am-right" position, it is time for outside help. A friend, a clergy person, a counselor, or parenting class can help parents achieve agreement. (See Where to Go for Additional Help in appendix B.) Sometimes parents have to assess their own rigidity and become more flexible. Sometimes one parent has to take action when the other parent's hard line involves psychological, physical, or sexual abuse of a child.

Sometimes parents need to provide safety for children by intervening with other adults, as we do when we dismiss a careless babysitter or keep children away from a punitive adult. The following four structure examples represent areas that are often more challenging for parents to handle: ridicule by a family member, compulsive caretaking, religious rigidity, and incest. Read each example and think about the possible effect on the children and the adults if each position were used. Remember that as we offer better structure for our children, we also develop stronger structure in ourselves.

EXAMPLE 21

Situation: Mom hears Dad laugh and say to three-year-old son, "Your ears stick out. You look like Dumbo the Elephant!"
Mom says to Dad:

Rigidity: "If you ever say that again, the boy and I are leaving."

Criticism: "Henry, you are always calling names. You're the dumbo."

Nonnegotiable Rules: "Ridicule is damaging. You must find other ways to talk to him."

Negotiable Rules: "It is not okay to talk to our son like that. Is there some way I can help you stop ridiculing and start affirming?"

Marshmallowing: "Henry, you are such a tease!"

Abandonment: Doesn't say anything to father or son.

EXAMPLE 22

Situation: Mother is depressed and threatening suicide.

Dad says to child, age nine:

Rigidity: "You must take care of your mother now." Tone of voice implies that what child wants or needs is not important.

Criticism: "Now what did you do to make her feel so bad? Don't do anything that will worry her."

Nonnegotiable Rules: "It is not your job to keep your mother from hurting herself. I will see that she gets the help she needs." Finds professional help for the mother, adequate care for the child, and support for himself.

Negotiable Rules: Not applicable for situation. Getting help for Mom and child is not negotiable.

Marshmallowing: "I'm sorry you have to ignore your friends to keep an eye on your mother. If we give her lots of attention, she'll be better soon."

Abandonment: Spends all his time at work and ignores child.

EXAMPLE 23

Situation: Frank's religious group has a rigid rule or practice for every situation. The members believe in disciplining children by using fear and the paddle.

Frank says to himself:

Rigidity: "I will adhere to the teachings of my church and my religion even if I have to abuse my children to do so."

Criticism: "If I don't follow the rules, I am a bad person."

Nonnegotiable Rules: "Beatings harm children and scaring kids makes them fearful, not strong. I will learn how to structure without abuse or intimidation."

Negotiable Rules: "I will learn other ways to set rules and enforce them, and then I will decide what will be helpful for my children."

Marshmallowing: "I'm uneasy with what my religion says about punishing children, but the leader must be right."

Abandonment: "I will follow my church's teachings and ignore my children's feelings, needs, and reactions."

EXAMPLE 24
Situation: I saw my spouse touch our child in a sexually stimulating way.
I say to spouse:

Rigidity: "I will never let you see the child again as long as you live."

Criticism: "You pervert! You never do anything decent."

Nonnegotiable Rules: "You cannot be with any of our children until experts decide it's safe for all of us to be together again. Either you leave temporarily now or I will leave with the child now."

Negotiable Rules: Not applicable for situation. Sexual touching of a child by any adult is not negotiable.

Marshmallowing: "Honey, when you do that, it makes me feel anxious."

Abandonment: Pretends not to notice.

When Divorced Parents Disagree about Rules and Consequences[2]

Structure and consistency are especially important for children of divorced parents. These children may be forced to adapt to irregular schedules, two homes, the addition of stepparents or stepsiblings, different schools, and many other disquieting factors over which they have no control. Especially during transitions, a lack of parental structure may leave children feeling insecure about the world around them.

Expectations that are clear and consistent help provide certainty. Healthy structure offers children a sense of safety, security, and love. But, when there are two households, how can parents maintain control in the midst of emotional chaos?

> *A lack of parental structure may leave children feeling insecure about the world around them.*

- It is critical to help your children process their feelings and grief about the divorce. Get outside help for them if they need it.
- It is also critical for both parents to grieve the divorce without expecting support from the children.
- Explain to the child that even though the adults weren't able to reconcile their differences, neither parent wants to "divorce" the child.
- Assure your children that they do not cause the disagreements between you and your ex-spouse. Adults are responsible for their own behavior.

- Keep the welfare of the children paramount. Figure out which issues directly involve the children, which are about you, and which are about your relationship with your ex-spouse.
- Remember that being consistent about rules is one way of showing children you love them.
- If possible, establish regular communication with your ex-spouse to discuss what's happening in the children's lives.
- Never use children as messengers between you and your ex-spouse or involve them in disagreements between you and your ex-spouse.
- Do not criticize the other parent in front of the children, but speak the truth when children ask questions.
- Explain that the children will have to learn to live by two sets of rules—Mommy's rules and Daddy's rules—but parents should make every effort to agree on big rules.
- Be sure to explain the rationale for the rules and consequences you choose to use in your household in terms that are easy to understand.
- Never make children choose between you and your ex-spouse.
- Do not allow your children to use guilt about the divorce to convince you to ease up on your structure.
- Remember that you have control over the structure for your children only in your own home.
- Use only consequences that can be enforced in your home; then do follow through.
- In situations that call for discipline, be sure to gather facts for yourself and don't rely on the word of the child or the ex-spouse alone. Divorced parents often don't communicate well with each other and children may take advantage of this situation.
- Do not attempt to control what happens at your ex-spouse's home unless you perceive that something going on there is emotionally or physically abusive to your child. If this is the case, contact child protective services immediately.
- Check to see if the child is attempting to stir things up between you and your ex-spouse and refuse to be stirred.
- Remember, your main responsibility is to rear and love your children the best way you can. Stay true to this goal and trust your children to make well-informed decisions.
- Whether or not you are considering adoption, use the affirmations on page 269.

chapter 14

Structure, Shame, and Victim Blame

Messages That Support Structure

Two types of messages support the development of healthy structure in people of all ages: *credit and approval for jobs well done* and *offers to help you do better* when you are doing poorly.

Let's take the first message, the one involving credit and approval. Listen to some examples: "I admire how you do that!" "You wrote a great paper." "Wow! Good job!" "I liked the way you combined colors in that painting."

The other message that supports structuring tells people what they are doing poorly and how they can do better. This one is particularly challenging to give if we have learned to assume responsibility for other people's feelings. But this message is not about "making people feel bad," it is about caring enough about others to show them how to do better.

The message is most helpful if offered in this way: "Don't do that because . . . do this instead." For example: "Don't use that saw to cut with the grain of the wood. It is for crosscuts. Use the ripping saw instead. I'll show you how." Or, "When you criticize me, I don't like it and I get mad at you. Tell me what behavior you don't like and what to do instead."

Any "stop-that" message that does not also say what to do instead is criticism, not structure. The overriding consideration when using a do-better message with children is to deliver it in a steady, clear, and caring way. The words, the voice, and the demeanor must be firm and loving.

Hearing Structure as Criticism

Sometimes people will choose to hear these messages not as structure, but as criticism. Then they may avoid you, accuse you of "yelling," or do something that lets you suspect they feel ashamed.

When you notice that a child seems to be converting either an "I-like-what-you-do" or a "You-can-do-better" message into criticism or shame, you can intervene. For example, if your child rejects compliments, you can

- Kindly say, "You need more practice at accepting compliments."
- Ask your child to listen for the caring in your compliment or your "do better" as you repeat the message. Use a quiet voice. Say, "I'm not sure you heard me. Please listen again. Listen for my love. Listen and believe what I'm saying."
- Give your child a very gentle, loving, playful nudge on the arm and say, "I expect you to listen to me."
- Say, "I don't like that you don't accept what I say in the spirit in which I give it. How come you made it critical when I didn't mean it that way?"
- Touch the child gently, even shoe to shoe, and repeat the message.

These challenges can help adults too. Maybe your parents used rigidity, criticism, marshmallowing, or abandonment. If they used lots of less helpful structure, you may need to grieve not getting the helpful structuring you deserved. You can decide now how to get and begin taking in new structure messages without feeling criticized or ashamed.

> *Sometimes people will choose to hear these messages not as structure, but as criticism.*

Some of the most powerful negative messages we carry are old criticism or marshmallow messages we heard from adults when we were children. If we internalized these old messages, and voices, they become our own worst enemy. They encourage us to confuse guilt about our behavior with shame about our being. Think about messages from your childhood and notice if you are using old, destructive language when you talk to yourself.

If your parents used marshmallowing, you learned the language of caretaking—those who take care of others' needs at the expense of their own—and you may be neglecting to hold yourself and others accountable in healthy ways now. It is important to notice if you are blaming others when you should be accepting more responsibility for your own attitudes, feelings, and behaviors.

From Blame to Shame to Blame

Sometimes people create destructive messages where none were intended; they convert structure messages into criticism and feel blamed. People who grew up without enough healthy structure had to use criticism as structure. They are so accustomed to hearing structure in a critical tone that when they hear straight structure, they automatically assume it is critical, feel blamed, then shamed, and then turn the feelings outward and blame others. They

- reject the structure because they hear it as blaming and shaming,
- sabotage the project or activity, or
- blame the sender: start an argument, bad-mouth the sender, or hang on to bad feelings until they have enough piled up to warrant lashing out.

Instead of blaming others, some people raised with criticism, abuse, or neglect learn to cope by blaming themselves. When these people are given criticism, or structure that they perceive as criticism, they

- feel hurt but comply,
- feel ashamed and comply, or
- feel ashamed and hide, run away, or forget.

When children who tend to blame themselves are told to do something, they say, "I should have known how to do that. . . . I should be able to figure everything out on my own. . . . If I have to be told to do something, it means I am in trouble." As adults, when a teacher, employer, or mentor tells them they are doing a job poorly or behaving inappropriately, they translate the message into "What's wrong with you?"

People who blame themselves for the criticism, marshmallowing, abuse, or neglect they receive from others suffer from internalized victim blame.

Victim Blame

Victim blame is the process of using words or actions that blame victims for what happened to them. It is also blaming others for something that is natural for their stage of development. Here are some examples of victim blame:

- Hitting a one-year-old girl for touching things and telling her it is her fault. (The job of a child that age is to explore everything. Her parents should offer her a safe place and distract her when she approaches something unsafe.)
- Calling a two-year-old boy terrible when he says no. (The job of a two-year-old is to practice thinking separately from his parents. His parents could call him "terrific" for practicing saying no because he will need to know how to say no to many things during his life.)
- Making fun of a six-year-old girl who is afraid to start a new school. (A six-year-old is learning that the world is a big place. Her parents need to accept her fear, take her to school to see the place, explain the rules to her, and reassure her.)
- Ridiculing a teenage boy whose voice is changing. (His parents need to find a complimentary way to celebrate the onset of puberty.)
- Touching a young girl sexually or making suggestive comments and then telling her it is because she is flirting or pretty. (Grown-ups are always responsible to offer children and young people only respectful, nurturing interactions.)

People who have experienced a great deal of victim blame—as abused or neglected children; victims of sexual abuse; recipients of racial and other prejudices; or victims of institutionalized violence, such as being spanked at school, beaten by police, or hazed in the Marines—often internalize the messages and blame themselves. Here are some examples of internalized victim blame:

- "Mom would have loved me if I hadn't been such an active kid." (Instead of, "I deserve parents who love me and are willing to handle me as I am.")
- "My beauty is a mixed blessing. Because of it, my sister's boyfriend started having intercourse with me when I was eight." (Instead of, "My sister's boyfriend raped me when I was eight.")

- "My spouse wouldn't drink so much if it weren't for me." (Instead of, "My spouse drinks too much.")
- "If I am quiet/good/clean the house/get good grades/make jokes/keep their attention on me, they won't drink." (Instead of, "My parents drink too much and I need help.")
- "If anyone finds out I had sex with my parent, they won't like me so I won't tell." (Instead of, "I am the child of a parent who committed incest. I expect you to know this crime is very hard on victims, whatever their age, and I need help and support.")
- "My parent is in jail. I suppose you won't like me." (Instead of, "My parent is in jail. *She* did something wrong. And I expect you to see *me* for myself.")

Time to Change

Some people convert "Do this" or "You can do better" messages into victim blame and feel ashamed or vulnerable. Others resist or want to blame other people or circumstances when they receive reasonable direction. If we find ourselves doing this, we can use these cues to decide to believe differently about ourselves. We can learn to hear a message of "That is incorrect; here's how to do it better" as helpful. We can practice hearing these messages as support rather than criticism. We can decide to be competent, thriving people instead of victims. Also, we can remember that *we* can decide how to use the other person's information to improve our behavior or skills.

> *We can decide to be competent, thriving people instead of victims.*

It is true that sometimes other people don't give a "You can do better" message well. They use words or tones that sound critical to us. But even when they really are critical, we can still listen for the helpful part of their message. We can choose to ignore the critical part and not take that in. *We deserve helpful structure, not criticism.* We can take the helpful part of the message and use it to improve our lives and our skills.

chapter 15

Growing Up Again—A Story of Change

Martin's Story

Martin was abused as a child. What structure he received from his parents was critical. The rules changed from day to day, and when he broke the rule of the day, the punishment was harsh. He learned to stay low and not make waves.

Since Martin disliked the hurtful parenting he had received, he decided to parent differently. He gave in to his children in order to please them. He sacrificed himself for them and didn't make and enforce rules because he was afraid if he did his children wouldn't love him. He continued his marshmallow parenting and became an impotent martyr, his children were left as he was in his childhood, without the protection, security, and freedom that only firm, consistent structure can give.

> *He gave in to his children in order to please them.*

When his children began to have troubles at school and with friends, Martin decided to do some things differently. He was tired of feeling powerless and ineffective. He found a parent support group that helped him identify some affirmations and new rules he could use to care for himself and his children. Martin was "growing up again." His messages, which he repeated daily and gradually came to believe, were *I am important; I deserve love and respect; I can learn to be a firm, loving, respectful parent.* Martin accepted that his job as a parent was to set the rules and enforce them, that he would keep getting support, and that he would stop trying to please the kids when they disagreed with him.

Here are the twelve aspects of structure that Martin's parenting group studied:

1. All behavior has consequences—positive or negative.
2. Penalties and rewards must be related to behavior to be effective. It's the parents' job to decide what consequences are appropriate for misbehavior.
3. Children must know the consequences of breaking rules ahead of time and are often good at helping to decide on the consequences.
4. Setting, negotiating, and enforcing rules is an act of love and is the job of the parent. Whether the kids thank, fuss, hassle, pout, or threaten to leave is up to them. Parents may choose to hassle or not, but they must provide structure.
5. Discipline is the process of teaching children skills and attitudes for taking care of themselves and others. Discipline is based on self-esteem; fear, shame, and ridicule have no place in that teaching. Parents who use shame and ridicule because they need to control their children find that it is an effective control because it brings children to their knees and stops unwanted behavior. Parents don't realize how hard it is for children who have been ridiculed to stand up again.
6. Punishment is hurtful stuff parents do when they feel scared, vindictive, or tired, and it indicates that they need new structure, stronger boundaries, and new rules to protect and care for themselves and their children. Penalties are effective for children only if they motivate healthy growth in the child.

> *Punishment is hurtful stuff parents do when they feel scared, vindictive, or tired.*

7. Few rules are better than many. Martin started with thirty-seven, cut back to twenty, and finally got to six.
8. It is a good idea to write the rules out and to post them. (See Sample Rules Charts in appendix A.)
9. It is okay, important, and essential to get help when you don't know what to do or if you have tried all the things you know and the problem remains unsolved. (See Where to Go for Additional Help in appendix B.)
10. It is okay to make mistakes and to keep working at correcting them until you succeed.
11. It is okay to apologize, to say, "I'm sorry I did that and I won't do it again."
12. It is important to be true to the best that is in you.

Listen to Martin now:

"Nat is just beginning to use the car and has permission to take it on short runs around town. I pay for the gas, but he is not to let the gas level fall below a quarter of a tank. If I go to use the car after he has used it and find less than a quarter of a tank, he doesn't use it again until he pays for a tank of gas out of his own pocket. This is nonnegotiable. I do negotiate with him about when he will use the car, where he is going, for how long, and with whom; and what he'll be doing."

Martin has a lot of support and he borrows ways to structure from other people who already do it well. As he gets better at setting positive rules for his son, he realizes it is getting easier to set healthy boundaries for himself.

You, like Martin, may realize that your parents used some not-so-helpful methods of providing structure. If this is true, you now have the challenge of changing the parenting legacy you inherited. You can. You can learn helpful structure for yourself and you can teach it to your children. You *can* learn to drive on the Nurture/Structure Highway.

Structure with Love

Cindy was thoughtful. She stared at the Structure/Nurture Highway and then sighed, *When I think the children's father is overindulging, I get rigid. We both miss the safe driving lanes and where is love?*

Paul made a three-generation connection as he traced a triangle across the board. *I was neglected as a child. As an adult I abused my body by overworking. But I was determined not to abuse my children, so I became rigid. That was good because it kept me from abusing, but bad because rigidity neglects children so I brought it full circle. I'm going to stop this cycle and balance structure and nurture.*

> Structure is believable and acceptable to a child when the child feels loved.

Structure is believable and acceptable to a child when the child feels loved. Structure without love and nurture is harsh and constitutes only half of what children and adults need.

Usually, if we keep ourselves from knowing or getting the nurture and structure that we need, "the good stuff in life," we are using denial. The process that supports denial is called *discounting* and we will pursue that in section 5.

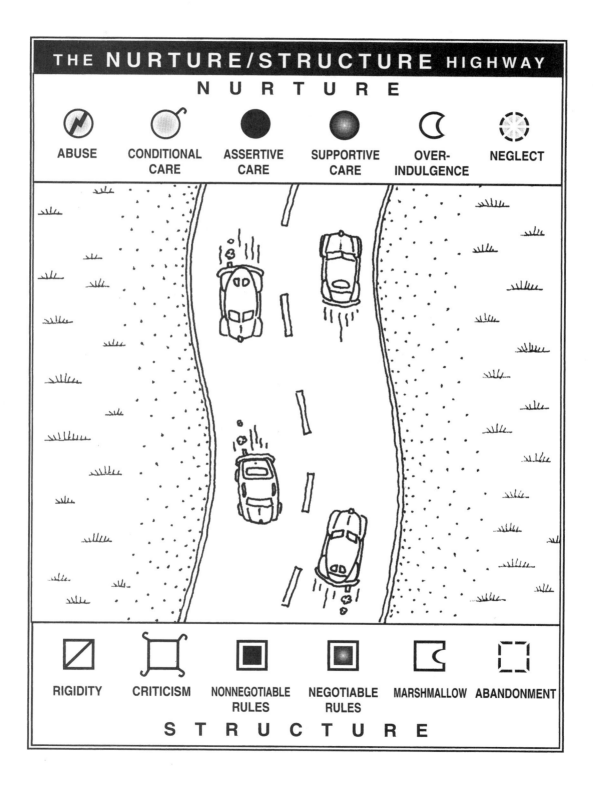

SECTION IV

Overindulgence

Misguided Nurture,
Inadequate Structure

I am not enough:
I will never be enough

ANONYMOUS OVERINDULGED RESEARCH RESPONDENT

chapter 16

Overindulgence

Misguided Nurture, Inadequate Structure

Who among us does not wish to give our children all that will be helpful to them? And who among us does not consider from time to time that we may have given too little or too much? This chapter is about giving too much: what we give too much of, how that affects children when they become grown-ups, and what to do about it. This giving too much is called *overindulgence*.

William, the father of three, recently said, "I don't need to hear about overindulgence. I know about it. It's the clothes and toys and expensive trips and camps that rich people give their kids. Some grandparents do it too. They shower grandchildren with stuff that is too old for the kids and that the kids don't need or even want. Don't talk to me about overindulgence. I buy a few toys now and then, but my kids aren't spoiled."

Overindulgence is not quite the same as spoiling. When we refer to a child as spoiled, we usually are referring to child behaviors that annoy adults. While an overindulged child may act spoiled, the results of overindulgence are more far-reaching than that.

William's response indicates that he is comfortable accepting the cultural myths about overindulgence. Conventional wisdom that lets us believe that only "other people" are overindulging has not been satisfying to many readers of the first edition of *Growing Up Again*. They said

- *Tell us more about overindulgence.*
- *How do we know if we are doing it?*

- *Does it really harm children?*
- *If we have been overindulging, can we do something about it?*
- *Is it only about poor nurturing, or does it involve structure and discounting too?*

In response to these challenges, author Jean Clarke enlisted the aid of her research partner, David Bredehoft.[1] His search of the literature did not reveal any research on overindulgence so they launched a research project of their own. It exploded many of the cultural myths about overindulgence. The information in section 4 is based on this research.

What Is Overindulgence?

This section will include

- A definition of overindulgence
- Who did the overindulging
- Ways overindulging was done
- The effects in adult life of being overindulged as a child
- Why parents overindulge
- What to do instead

Probably every adult has a definition of overindulgence based on personal observation or experience. But what one parent thinks is overindulgence another thinks is just fine. Before we look at a formal definition, write your own description for each of the following four concepts. You may think about them in reference to economics, love, attention, comfort, food, toys, or any other topic you wish to focus on.

Too little	What is too little or scarcity?
Enough	What is enough?
Abundance	What is abundance?
Too much	What is too much or overindulgence?

If you do this exercise with other people, you will notice that concepts of *too little* vary from abject poverty to barely enough to meet developmental needs. Either way, the person feels deprived. *Enough* may seem to one person to be the minimum quantity required to meet basic needs while to another person it is the amount needed to feel satisfied. *Abundance* for some people produces a feeling of extreme well-being or joy and to others signals that they have enough to share with others. *Too much* for some people is the amount that takes the edge off the joy that abundance brings. Others describe *too much* as smothering, stopping, debilitating.

When parents give *too much*, they are overindulging. That is the focus of this chapter. Pay special attention to what *too much* means to you as you interpret the information presented, either to help you assess the parenting you are doing or to think about the parenting you received.

Definition of Overindulgence

Dictionary definitions of indulgence range all the way from tolerance to dissipation to excess. Not much help there, so Bredehoft and Clarke determined to identify a definition of overindulgent parenting by finding out what it means to adults who were overindulged as children.

Through a newsletter and at workshops adults who had been overindulged as children were invited to volunteer for in-depth interviews about their experiences. The composite definition of overindulgence that follows and the research survey questions were built directly from the information given by those adults.

Overindulging children means giving them too much of what looks good, too soon, too long; giving them things or experiences that are not appropriate for their age or their interests and talents. Overindulging is the process of giving things to children to meet the adult's needs, not the children's needs.

Parents who overindulge give a disproportionate amount of family resources to one or more children in a way that appears to meet the children's needs but does not. Overindulged children experience scarcity in the midst of plenty. They have so much of something that it does active harm or at least stagnates them and deprives them of achieving their full potential.

Overindulgence is a form of child neglect. It hinders children from doing their developmental tasks and from learning necessary life lessons.

The Research Sample

The questionnaire was distributed through the newsletter *WE²*, at workshops and meetings, and in some college classes. A total of 730 people returned the eleven-page survey. Based on the definitions, 124 of the 730 indicated that they had been overindulged as children.[3] The information reported here is drawn from the 124 who were overindulged. The difference in perception between those who were overindulged and those who were not can be summed up in the statement, "Those who were not overindulged underestimate our pain." The 124 overindulged respondents were mostly female, most grew up in two-parent families, and most were highly educated. Most were American, a few were Canadian, English, or Australian. Since this was not a random sample representative of the U.S. population, it does not tell us how frequently overindulgence occurs in the general population or that females are more frequently overindulged than males, or that most overindulged children grow up in two-parent families. It also does not tell us what level of education we can expect of overindulged persons. It does not even tell us that only highly educated people are interested in overindulgence. It only tells us that these were the characteristics of the people who cared enough about overindulgence to respond to the invitation to be part of the research. As you look at the results of the questionnaire, keep the sample in mind.[4]

> *Overindulgence is a form of child neglect. It hinders children from doing their developmental tasks and from learning necessary life lessons.*

Cultural Myths about Overindulgence

Like our example of William in the beginning of this chapter, we all have an idea about what it means to overindulge a child. We usually think of an only child, the apple of his parents' eye, the pride of his grandparents. From infancy, the overindulged child is showered with gifts at every turn and has no responsibilities because his parents and grandparents do everything for him. No family sacrifice is too much for the little angel, who comes to expect the rest of the world to provide for him in the same way.

According to the Bredehoft-Clarke research, however, this picture is not accurate. Let's look at these myths one at a time:

Myth 1: The typical overindulged child is an only child.
Reality: Most respondents had two or more siblings, and three-fourths of them reported that their siblings were also overindulged.

Myth 2: Parents who overindulge are well-off economically.

Reality: Asked, "When you were growing up how much money did your family have compared to other families?" respondents answered:

A lot more	6%
More	27%
Same	43%
Less	16%
A lot less	5%

Most respondents, then—64 percent—were no better off economically or were worse off than most people they knew.

Myth 3: Grandparents are the most notorious overindulgers.

Reality: In the survey, **parents were the indulgers 96 percent of the time.** Both parents were the indulgers in 43 percent of the homes, Mom alone in 42 percent, and Dad alone in 11 percent. Only 4 percent of respondents named Grandma as the overindulger, and Grandpa didn't even make the list. We parents have to stop blaming others for overindulging and look at our own behaviors.

Myth 4: Overindulgence occurs mainly with young children.

Reality: In the survey, 21 percent of respondents reported being overindulged during childhood, **38 percent as adolescents**, and 22 percent over their entire lifespan. Many parents continue to overindulge their adult children, for example, paying off their credit cards or saying, "Bring the kids over *any* time."

Myth 5: Parents who overindulge just want their children to be happy and go to extremes to avoid abuse.

Reality: Nineteen percent of the respondents reported that they had been physically abused. Over half of these same individuals reported being hit with belts or other objects from time to time.

- *My mother would lose control and hit us with objects such as a vacuum cleaner hose, shoes, hairbrushes, and a yardstick.*
- *I was spanked with the hand, belts, and sticks.*
- *My father was unpredictable and would hit my mother and us kids.*

Psychological abuse was even more prevalent in the sample, with 70 percent reporting that they had been ridiculed, shamed, and discounted, and that they had experienced the withholding of love.

Examples:

- *My body wasn't good enough.*
- *I wasn't smart enough.*
- *I got material things but no closeness.*
- *My dad would make fun of me when I made a mistake and called me stupid. I felt shamed.*

What a strange experience for a child—to have too much freedom or too many things and too little love. How can a child make sense of this withholding of love without deciding, at some level, that he or she must be defective?

And 14 percent reported that they had been sexually abused by a family member. The boundary dilemma this form of abuse creates— you can expect no limits in some areas, but you can't have your sexuality or your body to yourself—is profound.

Almost half—49 percent—of respondents also reported addiction in their families, including (in order of prevalence) alcoholism, other drug addiction, and workaholism. This situation creates incredible double binds for children: The parent overindulges yet is unavailable; the parent overindulges and yet the child must care for the parent. The parent may overindulge in part because of the addiction, a lack of energy to set limits, or a need to assuage guilt or try to make amends.

Myth 6: Parents overindulge mainly by showering their children with gifts, expensive clothes and toys, vacations, and educational opportunities.

Reality: Over half of the respondents reported that they were overindulged by having things done for them and by not having the responsibility of learning life skills such as organizing, budgeting, carrying projects through to completion, cleaning, and social skills. We will have to give up the myth that the main area of overindulgence is buying things. The main area is, in fact, not teaching skills.

In summary, according to this survey, parents were the main overindulgers and the major area of indulgence was not requiring the child to be a contributing family member: being done for, not having to learn skills and follow rules, having too much freedom and too many privileges.

Let us go on and look at the reported effects of this overindulgence.

chapter 17

The Hazards of Overindulgence

If It Is Supposed to Feel Good, How Come I End Up Feeling Bad?

The unfortunate effects of overindulgence are widespread and long lasting. They fall into six general areas:

- Mistaken decisions
- Missing skills
- Difficulty knowing what is enough or normal
- Difficulty with boundaries
- Being stuck in double binds
- Pain

The Bredehoft-Clarke research did not identify a "profile" of adult children of overindulgers because the mistaken decisions vary so dramatically and the lack of skills depends on the age and situation in which the overindulgence occurred.

Some people dismiss the uniqueness of overindulgence by equating it with narcissism. "Overindulged people are narcissists. They are self-centered." Are overindulged people narcissistic? They could be. But, if narcissism is the result of preverbal problems that result in the adult needing to control the situation in order to see himself as he wants to be seen, this phenomenon does not fit for many of the overindulged. They are often unaware of the results of their behavior rather than using those behaviors to control others. Whereas narcissism may require extensive therapy to be overcome, many overindulged persons can identify the skills they need, learn them, and

> *Some people dismiss the uniqueness of overindulgence by equating it with narcissism.*

deliberately replace old decisions with more useful ones. Some people find this hard to do. Others are so relieved to have a name for what was holding them back and so hopeful of seeing another way of being that they tackle the growing up again with relish.

Let us look at typical answers to the Bredehoft-Clarke survey questions that illustrate the six general outcomes of overindulgence: mistaken decisions, missing skills, not knowing what is enough, boundary difficulties, double binds, and pain.

Mistaken Decisions

Some children decided that they were entitled to privileges and not responsible for their actions.

- *I deserve to be valued by others even if I am self-centered. I failed to develop excellent social skills.*
- *If I don't feel capable, I don't have to try. If someone doesn't see it my way, they don't like me. People will bail me out and understand if I goof up, and if they don't, they don't like me.*
- *I don't have to grow up.*

Others decided the opposite—that they were totally responsible.

- *If you work hard enough, you can fix it. The situation isn't wrong, I am. I'll change.*
- *I can never do enough. I don't truly deserve what I get. It's hard to make my own decisions.*
- *Be independent! Don't let anyone control you.*
- *I felt overwhelmed because I perceived that I was expected to parent me and my siblings when we were overindulged. I felt I needed to provide the structure; i.e., clean the whole house when no one was expected to do chores. I felt embarrassed in front of my friends because we were never expected to help out, so I self-imposed that structure.*

Still others resented the overindulgence.

- *I always felt angry. I was the maverick that received all the attention and I hated it. I just wanted to be left alone.*
- *I fabricated stories to friends about having to do chores as I wanted to be like them; i.e., "Can't meet you until 6:30 'cause I have to do the dishes first." (Even though I had no such thing to do.)*

Think of the results of these mistaken decisions when these persons get into the workforce. The entitled ones don't have to do their share and blame you if you expect them to. The totally responsible workers make poor team players, and the resentful ones can vent their anger whenever you innocently touch that old sore spot.

Missing Skills

Some of the people reported missing general skills: *I don't have social skills.* Others reported missing specific skills: *I never learned to use the telephone. My mom always made all of the arrangements and took all of the calls. I don't know what to say on the phone, so I won't answer it and my wife gets mad at me.* This information came in an interview. When asked if he had told his wife, the man replied, *No, I'm too embarrassed. How can you tell someone you are forty-six years old and you don't know how to talk on the phone? I can't even hold a job unless I have a secretary.*

Think for a moment about how parents teach telephone skills to a child. Nine-month-olds have a toy phone. Eight-year-olds are expected to be able to identify themselves clearly and take messages. How many steps are in between? And how many more missing skills are too embarrassing to talk about?

Healthy structure includes learning skills. Here are more examples of missing skills that the respondents were expected to have learned as children:

- *Delayed gratification is the main skill I lacked. I was always given things when I asked for them. It's hard now not to buy things I want or need immediately. I have a very hard time saving money.*
- *The ability to be a decision maker. I've always waffled on major decisions.*
- *I don't know how to behave in a group unless I have a role that makes me the center of attention.*
- *I missed learning spontaneity, being able to let go and not feel guilty.*

Some children were overcared for and developed "learned helplessness." You cannot teach a child how to strive by striving for your child. Other children did strive but were overindulged by lessons and tutors and constant opportunities to learn skills. In this case, the deprivation of overindulgence happens when children are so busy learning to play sports, make music, dance, do art or drama, become a computer expert,

> *Some children were overcared for and developed "learned helplessness."*

and so on, that they don't have time to learn everyday socialization and self-management skills.

Not Knowing What Is Enough

Of the survey respondents, 71 percent indicated that one pressing problem they face is not knowing what is enough or normal. For example:

- *I am not enough.*
- *I'm afraid I'll never have enough of what I need.*
- *When is there enough money?*
- *I don't know how much time and things to do for my kids.*
- *In reference to food, clothes, choices, anything I buy—how many is too much?*
- *I constantly need outside affirmations from my friends on what's enough. I'm slowly learning to be mindful of what's enough for me. I've given up on normal and go for healthy instead.*
- *I can't tell the difference between generosity and overindulgence.*
- *I have to read books to find out what might be normal.*

During an interview one woman said, "I live in fear that I will go to my grave without having even one day when I knew how much was enough." No loving parent would wish this situation on a child. Parents need to teach the *concept* of enough, "Let me know when I have pushed you high enough on the swing." Parents also need to teach by modeling and by being in charge of how much is enough in many areas. "That is enough!"

> *"I live in fear that I will go to my grave without having even one day when I knew how much was enough."*

How we teach about enough will vary with the child's personality type; some children need more leeway than others. Also consider the child's learning style. Some children will respond to a verbal "You have had enough." Others need an action reminder: "You may fill this bucket with toys to take in the car. No more." Other children like a visual reminder: The note on the ice-cream tub says, "Leave some ice cream for other people."

Consider how we teach about enough at each developmental stage. Here is a list to get you started:

Stage 1 Birth to Six Months—"Baby, I'm taking you home now. You have had enough stimulation and I see signs you are starting to get overtired."

Stage 2 Six Months to Eighteen Months—"I'm getting you ready for bed now. You have been up long enough."

Stage 3 Eighteen Months to Three Years—"I'm putting some of your books away for a while. There are enough here for you to be able to find one you want me to read."

Stage 4 Three Years to Six Years—"Come in the house now. You have been in the sun long enough."

Stage 5 Six Years to Twelve Years—"Let's figure out what is enough food and water for you to carry on your hike."

Stage 6 Twelve Years to Nineteen Years—"How well are you balancing enough time for friends with time for study and household chores?"

Remember, knowing what is enough and being able to delay gratification are not only important life skills, they are also potent factors in the prevention of the abuse of drugs, food, sports, sex, and work.

Two well-illustrated books that can help children grasp the concept of enough and sharing are *Just Enough Is Plenty: A Hanukkah Tale*[1] and *Too Many Toys: A Christmas Story*.[2]

Boundary Difficulties

One part of structure is learning skills. Another part of structure is setting rules and teaching about boundaries. The Bredehoft-Clarke survey asked if there had been rules in the home. Of the respondents 88 percent said yes, 75 percent said the rules were enforced, but 56 percent reported no consistent consequences if rules were broken. In general, the rules covered areas such as curfew, grades, and looking good to other people. **Only 16 percent indicated that there were rules about household tasks.** One person said, *There were no rules. Only worries.*

Respondents also indicated persistent difficulties setting and respecting boundaries in adult life. Overindulging, which pushes in upon the child, makes it difficult for the child to learn about personal boundaries—where he or she ends and other people begin. Listen to the words of the overindulged.

- *Boundaries are a dilemma. I take things personally that have nothing to do with me.*
- *The skill I didn't learn that has affected me all my life is to set boundaries. I often find myself in a triangle situation.*
- *Boundaries (saying no), socializing, intimacy, communication.*

Setting boundaries is not the only problem. The pain resulting from invading other people's boundaries becomes apparent. During the interviews, people offered many stories of both their confusion when others were angry at them for bursting in and their feelings of reticence to move in, not knowing when and how to do so without offending.

CERTAINTY

Children do not learn about boundaries in one afternoon when we have "our boundaries chat." They learn to set and respect boundaries from the structure they experience at every age. They get messages about becoming differentiated, separating their needs from the needs of others, at every developmental stage.

When Heidi Caglayan and Sandy Agajanian read the developmental affirmations in the Ages and Stages chapter (page 211), they said, "These are not the messages overindulging parents give. Let's rewrite them to show you what may be heard instead."

A sample is on the next page.

> *Surprised when the child has not developed important life skills, the parents may blame the child.*

One way to check if we are overindulging is to notice if we are giving healthy developmental affirmations, or messages that invite dependence. Children may get a few or many overindulgent messages, but all of them put children in a double-bind position as they try to grow up.

Double Binds

An area not questioned directly in the survey but one that emerged from responses to other questions was the prevalence of double binds. A *double bind* is a set of two or more messages or experiences that contradict each other. Often parents overindulge from a good heart with high hopes of making the child's life easy, not realizing they are making the child's life difficult by keeping the child from becoming competent. Surprised when the child has not developed important life skills, the

Developmental Affirmation	*Overindulgent Message*
STAGE 1	
What you need is important to me. I love you and I care for you willingly.	What you need is expensive. I love you and I care for you too much.
STAGE 2	
I like to watch you initiate and grow and learn. You can be interested in everything.	I like to watch you stay young and under my thumb. You can have everything.
STAGE 3	
I'm glad you are starting to think for yourself. You can become separate from me and I will continue to love you.	I'm glad you are starting to think my way. If you become separate from me, I will lose my identity.
STAGE 4	
You can be powerful and ask for help at the same time. You can try out different roles and ways of being powerful.	You can be powerless and then I will help you. You can try out different roles and ways of being powerless.
STAGE 5	
I love you even when we differ; I love growing with you. You can learn the rules that help you live with others.	I love you when we agree; I love buying for you. You can learn my rules that help you live with me.
STAGE 6	
You can know who you are and learn and practice skills for independence. My love is always with you. I trust you to ask for my support.	You can know who I am and learn and practice skills for dependence. My love is always with you. I trust you to ask for more money.

parents may blame the child. The child ends up being stuck in a double bind, often confused and sometimes deeply angry. (See the discussion of double binds in chapter 22, page 174).

Here are common double binds resulting from overindulgence.

- Stay dependent. / Why don't you grow up?
- I've given you everything. / Why don't you get things for yourself?
- I give you money anytime you ask. / Why don't you know how to handle money?
- I'll do it for you. / Why can't you do it for yourself?
- I bail you out. / Why don't you take care of yourself?
- You don't need to learn this. / How come you don't know it?
- I anticipate your needs. / How come you don't know what you need?
- I respond to all of your demands. / Why don't you appreciate me?
- I've given you more than enough. / How come you don't know when you have enough?

Explore the Double-Bind Chart (page 176–177) to get ideas about how double binds may be put on children of different ages. If you have been putting a child in a double bind, endeavor to send only one message. If you recognize that you or your children get double-bind messages, use the Getting Free of Double Binds section of appendix A to help you cope with them.

Pain

The pain—there is a plaque that says *Too much of a good thing is wonderful.* Not so! Not according to the overindulged people who participated in the research project. First there are the stressful results of the mistaken decisions, the lack of skills, the difficulties with enough, the problematic boundaries and the double binds.

Second, there is the pain of ridicule and the resulting secrecy. Overindulged people who agreed to be interviewed seemed very eager to talk, but very secretive about it. Some waited until no one was watching and then asked, "Can we go somewhere alone?" They all spoke of ridicule. Some said it was the first time anyone had been willing to listen to the pain. They expressed relief to finally have a name for it and to talk about it. Think about this situation. If someone tells us they were beaten, burned, experienced incest, neglected we say, "I'm sorry. That shouldn't have happened." But think of the usual responses if someone says, "I got to play whenever I wanted to. I didn't have to do chores" or "I got a red convertible before I got my driver's license" or "When I was in high school and I wanted a new cashmere sweater, all I had to do was tell my dad what color. I must have had forty." The usual responses are "Lucky you" or "I wish I'd had that" or "What do you have to complain about?" or "Spoiled brat!"

Ridicule and envy are not helpful to overindulged persons attempting to share pain or to find out what is normal. So they learn to be silent about it, to make the overindulgence a secret.

When the people in the research study did try to talk about their overindulgence, they seldom got help or sympathy. Several said they could not talk with their parents about the overindulgence because it came from love.

Three-fourths said they had tried to discuss the overindulgence. Half of them approached their mothers, the rest talked with a sibling, friend, spouse, or counselor. What were the responses? Of the people they approached, 47 percent got mad, 41 percent sulked, 35 percent downplayed it, 21 percent denied it, 11 percent ridiculed them, 2 percent listened, and almost none empathized. (This is more than a 100 percent response because people could indicate more than one choice.)

> *They learn to be silent about it, to make the overindulgence a secret.*

This is a clear call to all of us to rethink how we respond to stories of overindulgence. Instead of, "You were lucky," we can say, "I'm sorry to hear that you were overindulged. I know that has made it hard for some people. How are you dealing with it?"

Three-fourths also said they had tried to stop the overindulgence by such methods as refusing, confronting, arguing, and withdrawing. "Yes, I tried to stop it. When I was in sixth grade, I vowed to hang up my own coat."

When asked if, as children, they had contributed to the overindulgence by pushing, about half indicated that they had. Of the respondents, 82 percent said they learned to manipulate to get what they wanted. We shouldn't be surprised—children learn within the environment we set up. Skills in pressure and manipulation, however, were probably not what the parents intended to teach and can certainly cause pain in later relationships. The theme of pain appeared consistently throughout the research data. Here's a sample:

- *I feel insecure because my parents didn't seem to have things under control or didn't seem to know as much as other parents about how to raise their children.*
- *I felt it was my duty to never express any real feelings at home being fearful of losing my parents' love.*
- *I learned to fake it, bluff, act tough, know-everything attitude, even if I didn't. Don't listen to my heart—I need Mom to take care of me.*
- *I have unfair expectations of others. They let me down. I overdo for others and am not sure when enough is enough.*
- *My Prince will come. I need to be taken care of. I'm not really all that capable of making a lot of money and besides I don't need to because of my "Prince."*
- *I tend to overdo everything—working, spending, acquiring things, talking, eating.*

Since the effects of overindulgence are so painful and have such a debilitating impact on later life, it is imperative that we find clearer ways to offer nurture and structure to children as they grow.

chapter 18

Why Parents Overindulge

Since overindulgence is a form of neglect and causes such pain, inconvenience, and distress later in life, why would parents overindulge their children? Before you answer that question, take the following true-false quiz and guess which reasons were reported in the Bredehoft-Clarke research.

Why Parents Overindulge

Circle T if you believe the statement is true or F if you believe the statement is false.

Parents overindulge their children

1. T F   To relieve feelings of guilt—a little guilt/a little gift
2. T F   Because they themselves were overindulged as children
3. T F   Because they come from a position of scarcity
4. T F   To mask favoritism
5. T F   To compete with spouse, partner, grandparents
6. T F   As a way of controlling children
7. T F   Because they fear confrontation or rejection; they want to "make smooths"
8. T F   Because they want to project a certain image of their children
9. T F   To feel like they are good parents
10. T F   Because they lack skills to set limits
11. T F   To be fair
12. T F   As a way of competing with their spouse over control of a child
13. T F   Because it is the path of least resistance

14. T F   Because it is a quick fix for whining
15. T F   To cover conflicting goals
16. T F   To be popular with children
17. T F   To compensate for an abusive parent
18. T F   To compensate for an absent parent
19. T F   As a way of buying love by an absent parent
20. T F   To buy favors from children
21. T F   Because parents idolize children
22. T F   To build parents' own self-esteem—"What a good parent I am"
23. T F   Because of the influence of media programming
24. T F   Make the children happy
25. T F   To set up peer-group competition among children
26. T F   To compete with a parent peer group
27. T F   Because they are afraid of their child's anger
28. T F   Because they feel sorry for a child who is too limited
29. T F   To give love without balancing it with rules
30. T F   Because they project their needs onto their children; the parents want child to have clothes with expensive price tags, be a team captain, go to hockey camp, etc.
31. T F   To oppose spouse or grandparents—contrary parenting
32. T F   Because they want child to have what they didn't have
33. T F   Because they don't know child development
34. T F   Because they can't withstand the pressure of media advertising or pressure from other children
35. T F   Because they are habitually codependent with everyone
36. T F   To please the grandparents or other adults
37. T F   To compensate for illness in the family
38. T F   Because they lack time and energy to teach children skills

If you circled True for all 38 reasons, you are correct. All of these reasons have been reported and you may know of others.

What did the research tell us?

Question: Why did parents overindulge? Was it for the welfare of the children?

Answer: No. Of those who were overindulged, 67 percent felt that the overindulgence related to parental problems, not to the children's welfare.

EXAMPLES:
- *My father's work-related absences.*
- *My mom felt guilty due to my dad's emotional neglect and physical abuse.*

- *One sibling is deaf, and my mother felt responsible.*
- *Mother's job out of the home and her poverty as a child.*
- *The death of my father when I was four.*

While parents may think they are acting for their child's welfare, most of the adults who were overindulged as children saw the overindulging as something done to meet their parents' needs. This gives us a direct clue about **how to avoid overindulging—recognize our own needs and get them met directly, not through our children.**

chapter 19

What to Do Instead of Overindulging

You may ask, How do we know if we have been overindulging and can we do something about it?

<blockquote>
How do we know if we have been overindulging and can we do something about it?
</blockquote>

How Do We Know?

Overindulged children do the same things all children do, but they exhibit certain behaviors in excess or behaviors inappropriate for their age. Overindulged children often

- are whiny and clinging
- demand what they want without regard for others
- ignore directions in order to push limits
- ignore rules
- interrupt often and inappropriately
- are insensitive to others' feelings
- behave with other children or adults in ways that seem inappropriate to the social setting
- expect others to do for them what they can do for themselves
- are extremely fearful or fearless
- act confused or angry
- act older or younger than their age

Not all overindulged children exhibit all of these behaviors. However, if a child fits three or more of these descriptions, overindulgence could be an underlying cause.

Can We Do Something about Overindulgence?

Yes, indeed.

- The first and perhaps most important thing we can do is to identify the reason we are overindulging and change that position, belief, or habit.
- We can also stop, *right now stop*, thinking we know why other people overindulge. We don't know unless they identify that reason or need within themselves and then tell us.
- We can learn what children need at each stage and meet those needs.
- We can look at the Nurture/Structure Highway and see what we have been doing. If we have been driving on the shoulders or in the ditches, we can get back onto the highway and replace overindulgent, misguided nurture with assertive and supportive care.
- We can devote the time and energy necessary to provide helpful, clear structure.
- We can stop saying, "It doesn't matter. You didn't mean it. I'll take care of it. Don't worry about it."
- We can say, "It does matter. Even if you didn't mean it, you need to make amends. How are you going to take care of it? Do you need help?"
- We can be vigilant about teaching children what is enough.
- We can do whatever we need to do to take care of ourselves so we don't need to overindulge.
- We can remember that if we were not overindulged, we may underestimate the pain overindulgence causes. The 606 research respondents who indicated they had not been overindulged *did not view* overindulgence as resulting in a painful, secretive, shameful, and difficult to recover from experience.
- If we were overindulged, we can stop overindulging ourselves and our children. We can remember that it probably came from a good heart, yet recognize that overindulgence is not okay. The lines between love and overindulgence can be thin. We can find the structure and love that we need and start right now growing up again.
- A place where the structure is both clear and consistent—such as a strict school or workplace, the military, or a religious order— can help some adults who were overindulged as children.

- If we live or work with someone who was overindulged, we can remember that the person's self-centeredness is not directed at us. When overindulged people switch the television channel, they may be totally unaware that we were watching. Dismissing their behavior continues the overindulgence. Continually setting boundaries is a way we can support both their and our growing up again.

Our current culture urges us to overindulge[1] and good parenting has become a counterculture activity.

> *Our current culture urges us to overindulge and good parenting has become a counterculture activity.*

Alternatives to Overindulging at Each Developmental Stage

Job of Child at Developmental Stage	Examples of Overindulging	Decisions a Child May Make	Examples of Helpful Parenting	Decisions a Child May Make
Birth to 6 Months To decide to be, to live, to bond with caretakers, to call out to have needs met.	Mom offers the breast or bottle to baby Zach every time he squeals or just when he "looks hungry" or when she thinks he should be hungry.	*I don't know when I am hungry. I don't need to ask for what I need. The world will supply it.*	Mom waits until baby Zach calls her or rustles loudly or however he communicates. Then she checks to see if he needs dry clothes, soothing stimulation, loving, or food.	*I can know what I need and ask for it.*
6 to 18 Months To reach out and explore her world and learn to trust her senses. To attach to her caretakers.	Every time little Stephanie reaches for a toy, parent hands it to her or plays with the toy for her. Parent surrounds child with toys too mature for her.	*I don't need to reach out for what I want. I don't know how to explore my world.*	Parent provides a safe area with safe objects for Stephanie to explore and lets her do that in her own way. Lets child play with pots and pans. Parent provides a few toys at a time.	*It is safe for me to learn about my world. I can trust my senses.*
18 Months to 3 Years To start cause and effect thinking, to give up belief he is the center of the universe. To start to follow simple commands: come, stop, go, wait.	Every time Charlie says no, the adults give in. Charlie gets what he wants and more than he asks for.	*I am the center of the universe. I can have whatever I want. I don't have to consider other people.*	Sometimes Charlie gets what he wants and sometimes he doesn't. Adults carry this out in a matter-of-fact way with no criticism. Adults expect Charlie to follow simple commands: come, stop, go, wait.	*I have to take others' needs into account. I can say no and be angry and still be loved. I can learn to follow directions.*
3 to 6 Years To assert an identity separate from others. To learn ways of exerting power and to learn that behaviors have consequences.	Julie whines for a candy bar in the check-out line at the grocery store. Dad says no three times and then buys two bars for her.	*Only my wants count. I don't have to take other people's needs, wishes, or feelings into account. I can have whatever I want.*	Julie is told before entering the grocery store if she may or may not have candy and that directive is followed without criticism or apology.	*I can ask for what I want and expect parents and rules to be dependable.*
6 to 12 Years To learn what is one's own responsibility and what is others' responsibility. To learn skills and about rules and structure.	Jerrod is often late for the school bus so his dad packs Jerrod's lunch and waits for him and takes him to school.	*I am not competent. I don't need to learn how to take care of myself. I don't need to care for others.*	Father asks Jerrod if he needs ideas of how to get himself ready for the school bus. Parents do not make excuses to the school when Jerrod is tardy.	*I need to learn to be responsible for myself and to others.*
13 to 19 Years To emerge gradually as a separate independent person, responsive to others and responsible for own needs, feelings, and behavior.	Rosa has many school activities so her parents do her household chores for her. Parents change their schedules to drive whenever Rosa wants a ride.	*I don't need to be competent. I am not competent enough or valued enough to be a contributing member of my primary group.*	Parents negotiate with Rosa what she can reasonably be expected to do and when and how she can get where she needs or wants to go.	*I am responsible for myself and to others.*

SECTION V

Denial

The Glue
That Keeps Us Stuck

god save the children
trapped in the game
living in fear
hiding the pain
battered by devils
screaming in vain
feeling the wrath
then doing the same

STEVE LYNCH, *THE CARLETON VOICE*

chapter 20

How We Deny

The Four Levels of Discounting

"Yes, my work does keep me from being with my family, but I am not a compulsive worker. I just find my job interesting and my contribution is essential right now."

"My son has been given three citations for driving while intoxicated, but he really wasn't. He doesn't have an alcohol problem. He drinks socially, but he doesn't drink any more than his friends. Kids will be kids."

"My family has so many things going on that I am too tired and I don't have the time or energy to stay with a fitness program."

These are some of the many faces of denial.

Once a person has made conclusions about life, especially if those conclusions were made early and under duress, he or she tends to defend them. Often, old decisions, once made, were pushed outside of awareness, where they are followed automatically and not thoughtfully. When behaviors resulting from those decisions lose their usefulness or become downright harmful, the person may still defend them vigorously. That position is called *denial*. When harmful, unuseful behaviors based on present decisions or illusions are stubbornly held to in the face of compelling reasons to change, this too is denial. The process of protecting and maintaining denial is called *discounting*.

This section will cover these questions:

> *Old decisions, once made, were pushed outside of awareness, where they are followed automatically and not thoughtfully.*

- What is discounting and how do people do it?
- What are the effects of discounting on children?
- What are examples of the four levels of discounting?
- How can people recognize and stop the many ways of discounting?
- How can people combine nurture, structure, and discounting information to solve problems?

What Is Discounting?

Discounting is making something more, less, or different than it really is. It is what we do to protect a denial and to keep from solving a problem. Discounting is a distorted thought process. When we discount, we deny our responsibility for responding appropriately to a current reality. We react in a way that attempts to alter the reality to make it fit some previous decision or perception. By discounting, people can redefine a problem, situation, or need, so they believe they don't have to do anything about it or so they can do less than is needed. By discounting, we keep ourselves from acting responsibly. We keep ourselves powerless.

> *Our perceived inability to do something or understand what is going on is usually based on some old personal decision about our* lack of power.

Our perceived inability to do something or understand what is going on is usually based on some old personal decision about our *lack of power*. For example, Dana decided when he was young that it was not safe for him to think for himself. As an adult, he stays in a job that is toxic for him and lives in fear of being fired.

Power is the ability to recognize what we and other people need and to take action on that information. Power misused is exploitative. Positive power is action taken to care for our own needs and the needs of others. But, for some of us, at an early age, it was not safe to act in a way that looked powerful or wise, or to be honest about what we saw in our families. It was safer to accept the big people's definition of the world, to let them tell us what to say, what to think, even how to feel. Perhaps the family had some secret that children had to deny, even to themselves. So we learned to give away our power by discounting.

Probably all people use denial at times and do some discounting out of habit to protect old perceptions. Some discounts have only small negative effects, but some are deeply serious. Since when we discount we may not be aware we are doing it, we can use the information in this chapter to help us get a clearer picture of what discounting is and to recognize our own habits of discounting. If we find areas where we are discounting, we can decide what changes we want to make to improve the ways we care for ourselves and the ways we parent.

What Do People Discount?

People discount themselves, other people, and situations. Look at the following ways John discounts and at the decisions and beliefs that the discounting protects:

Discount of self: "I can't do anything about this situation." (Old decision—"I'm not important or powerful.")

Discount of others: "No point in telling Maria. She will never change." (Old decision—"She is rigid.")

Discount of situation: "I see the lightning, but it won't strike here. I'll finish my golf game." (Old belief—"It will never happen to me.")

> *When a person discounts the situation or other people, he also discounts himself.*

Notice that when a person discounts the situation or other people, he also discounts himself. If John took action he might have to recognize that he *is* important. If he told Maria and she changed, he would have to update his old opinions about her. If he came off the golf course, he would be protecting himself and admitting that he is mortal. When old decisions and attitudes and the behaviors that maintain them are deeply embedded in John's past, he discounts without thinking and can be totally unaware of his denial.

How Do People Discount?

In order to discount, to distort or ignore information, problems, or options, we use grandiose thinking. We justify our denial by making something "grandly larger" or "grandly smaller" than it really is. We maximize or minimize by holding attitudes that imply "always," "never," "forever," "told you a thousand times," or "not really important."

Whenever we use grandiosity to discount, we are attempting to avoid responsibility. We are trying to shift it to others. In *Power and Innocence*[1] Rollo May defines power as the ability to keep what we want to keep and change what we want to change. When we discount, we neglect to take good care of ourselves and we prevent ourselves from taking good care of our children. We give up our power.

What Are the Four Levels of Discounting?

We can find out more about how we discount and how to stop discounting by looking at the methods people use to discount. We'll refer to these as levels of discounting. They are described in the book *Cathexis Reader,*[2] by Jacqui Lee Schiff and others.

Level 1: Discount the existence of the situation, problem, or person. "That's no problem."

Level 2: Discount the severity of the problem. "That's no biggie."

Level 3: Discount the solvability of the problem. "You can't fight City Hall."

Level 4: Discount your personal power to solve problems. "Nothing I can do about that," or "I wouldn't feel comfortable doing something about that."

You can use Discounting Chart 1[3] to help you think through the differences among the four levels and the implications of each.

> *When we discount, we neglect to take good care of ourselves and we prevent ourselves from taking good care of our children. We give up our power.*

The Effects of Discounting and Empowerment

Discounting is the process of denying, of perceiving something to be less or more than or different than it really is. We can discount our own needs or abilities, the needs or abilities of others, or the reality

LEVEL 1–NO PROBLEM	LEVEL 2–NOT SERIOUS	LEVEL 3–NO SOLUTION
Characteristics:		
A level-1 discounter responds as if the person, situation, or problem does not exist. (No problem!)	A level-2 discounter accepts that the problem exists, but ignores it because it has negligible impact. According to the discounter, this problem is not serious.	The level-3 discounter accepts that the problem exists and is serious, but believes the problem is not solvable. (There's no solution.)
Example: Family gathers before the funeral of a grandparent.		
"Hi folks. What's new?"	"You can't expect people to live forever."	"Nobody can help anyone else with their grieving. It's a lonely road."
Children May Hear the Following Messages:		
You don't know what you know; don't trust your own perceptions and needs.	You don't know what you know; don't trust your own perceptions and needs; don't take things seriously.	Nothing can be done. That's the way life is. There's nothing anyone can do.
Common Responses of Children:		
Since all four levels of discounting result in the problem not being solved, children may respond to each one with despair, anger, rage, helplessness, self-doubt, mistrust of others, mistrust of own perceptions, disdain for the discounter, and feelings of unimportance, rejection, abandonment, confusion, being unloved, shame, hopelessness, and being undermined. They may be scared about who will protect and keep them safe.	(Same as under level 1.)	(Same as under level 1.)
Decisions Often Made by Children and Often Carried into Adulthood:		
I can't trust my own perceptions. There must be something wrong with me.	I don't know if I will be taken seriously. I can't trust my thinking and evaluation.	I can't trust my world to meet my needs. I don't deserve help or assistance. There are no solutions. I am helpless.

and probabilities of a situation. There are four levels on which we may discount. Level 1 is most difficult to confront, but every level keeps a person from acting responsibly and powerfully. Discounting is done outside of awareness to defend old beliefs or because of lack of information.

LEVEL 4–NO PERSONAL POWER	EMPOWERMENT

Characteristics:

The level-4 discounter accepts that there may be solutions to the problem and accepts that it is serious, but believes he or she has no power to solve or to help solve it. (I have no power to fix the problem.)	In contrast to a discounter, an empowered person acts responsibly. The empowered person (1) evaluates the problem realistically, (2) judges its seriousness accurately, (3) knows or finds solutions to the problem, (4) assesses what is reasonable for him or her to do, and (5) takes effective action.

Example: Family gathers before the funeral of a grandparent:

"I ought to be able to help my family through this, but I just don't know how."	"I'm glad we are all here. I feel bad about Grandpa and it's hard for me to believe he's dead. How are you doing?"

Children May Hear the Following Messages:

I don't know how to help you. You or your problems are too much for me.	I respect you and myself. Your needs, problems, and feelings are important. So are mine. If we can't figure out what to do, we'll find someone who can.

Common Responses of Children:

(Same as under level 1.)	Children feel safe, cared for, listened to, relieved, loved, accepted, valued, competent, important, and powerful. They may feel joy, satisfaction, anger, or frustration, depending on the situation.

Decisions Often Made by Children and Often Carried into Adulthood

I can't count on people around me. I am abandoned. I must do this on my own. I will choose not to be aware of what I need.	It is safe for me to do the things I need to do and to grow up. I can ask for help. I am competent, capable, and effective. I can trust my senses and intuition. I know what I know.

chapter 21

Examples of the Four Levels of Discounting

While discounting at any level denies the importance of the situation, self, and others, it may help to think of each level as having a special focus. First- and second-level discounts are ways of denying the situation. Third-level discounts primarily deny the ability of others to find options. Fourth-level discounts deny the self, one's own needs, and one's own power to take effective action.

> *If you need help stopping critical voices in your head, identify the critical message and replace it with a helpful one.*

When we do not deny, when we take full account of the situation, others, and self, we respond in an empowering way for ourselves and others, a way that gives and accepts full respect and responsibility.

Look at the following events with examples of all four discounting levels. Each also includes a possible response that does not discount, but empowers, and validates respect for self and others.

If you recognize your own behavior in some of the discounting, make a note of it and go on. If you need help stopping critical voices in your head, identify the critical message and replace it with a helpful one. You can decide how much you want or need to change.

1. A child is crying. Adult responds:
Level 1: "I don't hear her." (No problem)
Level 2: "She cries a lot. It doesn't mean anything." (Not serious)
Level 3: "Look, if a kid feels like crying, there is nothing you can do." (No solution)
Level 4: "I like kids when they are smiling. Never know what to do with them when they cry." (No personal power)
Empowering: "What is the matter? Can I help you?"

2. A two-year-old child runs into a busy street. The parent:

Level 1: Does not keep track of the child, does not notice. (No problem)

Level 2: Thinks, *Well, the cars usually go slowly on this street. They'll see him.* (Not serious)

Level 3: Says, "Nobody can keep kids that age from running in the street." (No solution)

Level 4: Says to self, *I've told him and told him and he doesn't pay attention, so what can I do?* (No personal power)

Empowering: Runs and brings the child back and says seriously, "You must stay on the grass! Only cross the street with a big person." Watches child.

3. Pet dies and family member says to child:

Level 1: "Don't carry on so—it wasn't a person, you know." (No problem)

Level 2: "Look, a dog is a dog. I'll get you a new one." (Not serious)

Level 3: "There is no way to help a kid get over a dead pet." (No solution)

Level 4: "I know you feel bad, but what can I do?" (No personal power)

Empowering "I'm sorry the dog died and I'm sad. How are you feeling? Do you want me to help you plan a funeral for him?" Gives lots of comfort.

4. My child is using alcohol. Parent says:

Level 1: "No. He's not." (No problem)

Level 2: "He may take a drink on weekends, that's all." (Not serious)

Level 3: "It's those darn kids he hangs around with." (No solution)

Level 4: "I don't know what to do, but I wish he'd straighten out." (No personal power)

Empowering: "I'll remind him that using alcohol is illegal and dangerous for him and he needs to stop drinking. I know I am not in control of his decision to drink, but I can get help for him and for myself. I will make whatever supportive changes I need to make in my life and the way I respond to him."

**5. Teenager is bemoaning not having a date for a
Friday night party and family member says:**

Level 1: "I don't want to hear about it." (No problem)

Level 2: "It's not the junior prom you know." (Not serious)

Level 3: "Look, it's too late for anybody to do anything to help you." (No solution)

Level 4: "I don't know how to help you." (No personal power)

Empowering: "I love you. I'm sorry you don't have a date. Would you like to ask somebody over here Friday night?"

6. Teenager wants a date, doesn't have one, and says to self:

Level 1: "I don't care." (No problem)

Level 2: "The party probably won't be any fun anyway." (Not serious)

Level 3: "If you don't just happen to get a date, there is nothing anyone can do." (No solution)

Level 4: "I can never get a date." (No personal power)

Empowering: "I want to go to the party. I'll try three more ways to get a date. If I don't get one, I'll go with a friend or get somebody to go to a movie or watch TV with me."

How Identifying Levels Can Be Helpful

The ability to identify the four levels of discounting is a helpful tool in dealing with denial. There is more information about the four levels in Discounting Chart 2 (page 166). At this point it is enough to focus on three concepts.

1. Any level of discounting means the problem does not get solved.
2. First- and second-level discounts are harder to confront than third and fourth levels, which can often be dealt with by educational means.
3. Usually, when a person is discounting at the first or second levels, that person has to work through the third and fourth levels to reach empowerment.

Occasionally, if a crisis or a clear safety issue is involved, a person will jump from first-level passivity directly to empowered action.

Test Your Knowledge

To practice identifying empowering responses and the different levels of discounting, write the appropriate number before each statement in the following examples. When you compare your answers with the ones suggested, remember that the level of discounting can change with the ways words are delivered, the tone of voice, facial expression, and body language. Depending on their histories of broken contracts and of promises not kept, people may perceive discounts at different levels. Treat these responses as suggestions and feel free to rewrite them to make them fit for you.

Indicate the levels for each example by placing a 1, 2, 3, or 4 or an E in front of each response.

1. Discounts existence of problem.
2. Discounts seriousness of problem.
3. Discounts solvability of problem.
4. Discounts personal ability to solve problem.
E. Empowering—takes other people, the situation, and the power of self into account.

7. Teenager is driving twenty miles above speed limit.
Three of her friends and her parent are in the car. The parent:

___ Thinks, *There is never a traffic cop when you need one.*

___ Thinks, *She is driving. I have no right to embarrass her in front of her friends.*

___ Doesn't notice.

___ Says firmly, "Return to the speed limit and stay there or I will take the wheel." If teen does not slow down, parent makes her stop and parent drives. After they are home, parent sets rules and consequences for future driving.

___ Thinks, *Well, all kids speed, I suppose.*

Suggested Answers: 3, 4, E, 1, 2

8. Bonnie's daughter seems to pay much more attention to what her boyfriend wants than to what she wants. She carefully watches how she feels and frequently reassures and comforts him. He seems to like it, but doesn't return in kind. Bonnie says to herself:

___ "I get along fine with him."

___ "I will tell her about my concern for her. I will ask her to read a book about caretaking behaviors or join a support group to get another perspective. I wish my parents had taught me to expect as much care as I give so our daughter could have learned how from me."

___ "My friends say if I interfere it would make her angry and she might not listen to me anymore."

___ "What right have I to say anything? I did that myself until two years ago."

___ "Oh, they'll work it out."

Suggested Answers: 1, E, 3, 4, 2

9. Arne's son is single-minded in his devotion to the principles of his church. There is no room for discussion and he believes his church knows everything there is to know about right and wrong. He's very critical of other family members. Arne says to himself:

___ "I can't compete with the church."

___ "He's a very religious person and that's all that counts."

___ "I will listen respectfully to his beliefs and ask him to listen respectfully to mine. If he degrades my beliefs, I will insist that he stop and I will change the subject."

___ "Once that church of his hooks people, that's the end of them."

___ "He has been through these phases before."

Suggested Answers: 4, 1, E, 3, 2

Discounting in the Adult World

Denial and discounting are rampant in the adult world. Look at the following examples of ways adults discount or empower each other and themselves.

10. A friend is hoping to get a promotion. I say:

Level 1: "Look—some people don't even have a job." (No problem)

Level 2: "If you don't get it, you'll live." (Not serious)

Level 3: "Who knows how they decide on those promotions?" (No solution)

Level 4: "There is no way I can help." (No personal power)

Empowering: "I hope you get the promotion. Is there anything I can do to help you go after it?"

11. My beloved says, "I want you to spend more time having fun with me." I say:

Level 1: "We spend lots of time together and we have enough fun." (No problem)

Level 2: "Okay . . . I'll tell you a joke once a week." (Not serious)

Level 3: "Most couples have difficulty finding enough time to play." (No solution)

Level 4: "I'm really swamped for the rest of the month." (No personal power)

Empowering: "All right. Let's figure out how to do that."

12. A new mother has postpartum depression or postpartum mood disorder. She says to herself:

Level 1: "I think PPD is a myth." (No problem)

Level 2: "It will pass." (Not serious)

Level 3: "It's hormonal and you can't do anything about it." (No solution)

Level 4: "The only thing you can do is take antidepressants and they are addictive." (No personal power)

Empowering: "I didn't cause this, but I have to find ways to deal with it. I will talk to my doctor and find out about medicines that would help me. I will find some books about postpartum problems.[1] I may need a support group or some talk therapy. I'm going to keep looking until I find some answers."

13. A mother is afraid her postpartum depression is affecting her baby. Her friend responds:

Level 1: "He's too little to know the difference." (No problem)

Level 2: "If it does affect him, he'll get over it." (Not serious)

Level 3: "Well, you can't help being depressed, so why worry about the baby?" (No solution)

Level 4: "That depression runs its own course. The baby will have to cope." (No personal power)

Empowering: "In the early days of life, a baby's need for direct physical contact helps the baby establish trust and a feeling of connection with the caregiver. You might use a baby sling and sing to your baby. Is there some way I can help you so that you can stay connected with your baby while you recover from your depression?"

Test Your Knowledge

Practice identifying empowering responses and the different levels of discounting in these adult-world examples. Indicate the levels for each example by placing a 1, 2, 3, or 4 or an E in front of each response.

1. Discounts existence of problem.
2. Discounts seriousness of problem.
3. Discounts solvability of problem.
4. Discounts personal ability to solve problem.
E. Empowering—takes other people, the situation, and the power of self into account.

14. Your friend has to go back to work, but she's worried about suitable child care for her two-year-old. You say:

___ "Parents everywhere are worrying about that."

___ "Find out what's available in your area. Ask friends for referrals and call your city or state social service agency for a list of places. Visit four or five and see if the children seem to be well cared for. Find a licensed place that fits with your child-rearing values."

___ "Don't worry. You'll find something."

___ "If parents need to work, the workplace should provide child care."

___ "Find the closest, cheapest place."

Suggested Answers: 3, E, 1, 4, 2

15. My spouse has been hospitalized for a long time and I'm on the road a lot. I wonder how this is affecting our children. I say:

___ "I make sure the kids and I are together when I'm home. I'm looking for a job where I can stay home. I have the best live-in care I can find. I've asked my sister to spend more time with my kids. I'm watching their behavior carefully and encouraging them to talk about their feelings."

___ "It can't be helped."

___ "A seven-year-old and nine-year-old are old enough to take care of themselves."

Examples of the Four Levels of Discounting

___ "The kids haven't complained."
___ "Hey, I didn't plan it this way."

16. My wife has two citations for driving while under the influence of alcohol and she is having trouble at work. I say:

___ "At least she's drinking at home now and not out every night."
___ "I'll just keep on covering for her."
___ "Women are harder to treat than men."
___ "Thank goodness she is okay around me."
___ "I will stop protecting her and find out where she and I and our family can get the help we need and I will do it now."

17. My spouse looks at our child in a sexually suggestive way. They spend lots of time together without me. I say:

___ "I have an uncomfortable feeling, but I'll ignore it and not say anything."
___ "You can't control what other people do when they are alone."
___ "I am disloyal for having suspicions and I wouldn't dare say anything anyway."
___ "I will remember that the adult is always the one who is responsible. I'll talk with my spouse and I will get some professional advice now. I will call a child protection agency if I need to."
___ "Parents are supposed to spend time with their kids and look at them and touch them."

18. I have heard that my friend's spouse is sleeping with a variety of partners. I am afraid my friend will get AIDS. I say:

___ "I don't want to risk my friendship. Anyway, I wouldn't know what to say."
___ "Other people get AIDS, not my friends."
___ "However this couple live their lives is up to them. It is no one else's business."

___ "This is serious, possibly life-threatening information. I will find a way to check on it. If I believe it is true, I will talk to my friend. I hate to risk our friendship, but I would never forgive myself if my friend got AIDS because I kept still."

___ "The person who told me has been known to exaggerate. It's no big deal if my friend's spouse is seen with other partners."

Suggested Answers: 4, 1, 3, E, 2

19. My love asks, "Do you love me?" I respond:

___ "Don't embarrass me."

___ "Yes (hug, hug, kiss, kiss), I'll tell you some things I love about you. . . ."

___ "I gave you a valentine, didn't I?"

___ "Oh, by the way, did you pay the gas bill?"

___ "It's impossible to get other people to really believe that you love them."

Suggested Answers: 4, E, 2, 1, 3

20. Your friend says that people are supposed to ask for what they need. You respond:

___ "If I have to ask for what I need, it doesn't count."

___ "Other people should know what I need."

___ "I know it's a myth to believe that others know what I need, so I will ask until I find someone who will help me get my needs met."

___ "I don't have any needs."

___ "I have some needs that aren't met, but I'm surviving."

Suggested Answers: 4, 3, E, 1, 2

21. A husband and wife are grieving a miscarriage. These are comments from family, friends, and co-workers.

___ "It was God's will. You have no cause to grieve."

___ "I'm sorry it happened, but what can I do about it?"

___ "Now that you're back, I've got a new project for you to work on." (co-worker/boss)

Examples of the Four Levels of Discounting

___ "This is a really tough time for you. I'm going to do what I can to help now."

___ "You can always have another child."

Suggested Answers: 3, 4, 1, E, 2

22. A friend says, "I've been waiting to tell you about my great new ideas." I say:

___ "I usually don't understand your great ideas."

___ "I'm busy right now, but I want to hear your idea. Can you wait until this evening to tell me?"

___ "I'll listen since there is nothing else to do."

___ "There is never enough time just to talk, is there?"

___ "I want to go to a movie tonight. Do you want to come with me?"

Suggested Answers: 4, E, 2, 3, 1

Once we understand the levels of discounting, several questions arise about how to make use of that information. What happens to the problem? What results are implied for the discounted and the discounter? What kinds of confrontation are likely to be effective at each level?

LEVEL 1–NO PROBLEM	LEVEL 2–NOT SERIOUS	LEVEL 3–NO SOLUTION

Example: Person has lost a lot of weight in a short time without dieting.

"I'm fine."	"I like being thin."	"I eat a lot now and I've never had any help from doctors in the past."

Effect of the Discount on the Problem:

The problem is not solved.	The problem is not solved.	The problem is not solved.

How Adults are Affected When Discounted by Others:

Adults are apt to be most vulnerable to the level(s) of discounting they experienced most often as children.	(Same as under level 1.)	(Same as under level 1.)

Characteristics of Adults Who Discount Persistently and Frequently at This Level:

Serious detachment from reality. May be very hard to confront successfully; may need a crisis or therapeutic intervention.	Serious misrepresentation of reality. May be very hard to confront successfully. May need a crisis or therapeutic intervention.	Mistaken belief system that can often be successfully confronted with education.

Methods of Confronting Adults Who Discount:

Often requires hard confrontation related to areas of the person's life that are highly meaningful to that person. Must include information about desired change and any consequences of not changing. People who discount on level 1 usually will not move directly to empowerment, but must go through each level. Confrontation may not work. Confronting is a high-risk activity, so confronter needs to carefully assess the investment before starting and decide how to respond if the confrontation does not work.	Often requires hard confrontation with substantial, verifiable data. May need to relate to area of direct concern to the discounter. Then move to level 3, possible solutions to the problem, rather than moving directly to empowerment.	Often confronted successfully with accurate, specific, demonstrable information about how the problem can be solved. Then move to level 4, affirmation of the person's ability or suggested options within the person's power.

Methods of Confronting Children Who Discount:

Present information. Raise the child's discomfort level until he or she has to look at the problem and deal with it. Offer to help, but leave the problem with the child. Do not take on the child's discomfort.	(Same as under level 1.)	(Same as under level 1.)

LEVEL 4–NO PERSONAL POWER   EMPOWERMENT

Example: Person has lost a lot of weight in a short time without dieting.

"I wouldn't know where to go for help."	"I will call my doctor today and insist on an appointment soon to have my health evaluated."

Effect of Empowered Action on the Problem:

The problem is not solved.	The problem is solved, or a start has been made toward the solution.

How Empowered Adults are Affected When Discounted by Others:

(Same as under level 1.)	Discounts are listened to for kernels of truth, but do not stop or delay positive action.

Characteristics of Adults Who Persistently Act in Empowered Ways:

Mistaken belief that they are powerless to change themselves or the situation. May be based on lack of information or on early decisions that it is unsafe to be powerful.	Have permission to see problems clearly and to take action. Have skills for evaluating problems and choosing effective courses of action.

Methods of Supporting Adults to Become Empowered:

Often confronted successfully with information. Some persons may need support, guidance, or therapy to make new decisions that it is safe to be powerful. Then move to Empowerment.	Offer support and encouragement. Confront discounts.

Methods of Supporting Children to Become Empowered:

(Same as under level 1.)	Balance nurture (stimulation and recognition) and structure. Confront discounts.

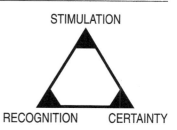

STIMULATION

RECOGNITION   CERTAINTY

chapter 22

Stop the Many Ways of Discounting

There are many ways of belittling people. Who among us has not cringed from derisive laughter, cruel teasing, sarcasm, or ridicule? Abuse and abandonment are profound ways of discounting. Let us sharpen our sensitivity to each of these practices and replace them all with love. Let us look at the underlying decisions that support discounting, and find ways to get off the merry-go-round and on with healthy lives.

Laughter

Laughter can either block healing or be healing. In *Anatomy of an Illness,*[1] Norman Cousins describes how he used laughter to recover from a serious illness. Joyous laughter at a joke that disparages no one, or laughing in an empathetic way, builds esteem and offers intimacy. It invites people to feel special and signals that they are "insiders." For example, Charlie brought flowers to his wife for her birthday, not realizing he was one week early. Ginny and the children genuinely enjoyed the surprise of his "mistake" and he joined in the laughter.

> *Laughter can either block healing or be healing.*

But laughter can also discount, alienate, and disconnect when it puts people "on the outside." Look at the following situation and think how laughter would sound at each of the four levels of discounting.

You fall and break your tailbone. The pain is intense.

Level 1: "Ha, ha, ha." (No problem)

Level 2: "Chuckle, chuckle. Some fancy spill you took there." (Not serious)

Level 3: "Ha, ha, people fall on those steps every time it drops below freezing." (No solution)

Level 4: "I'm glad it wasn't me who fell. Ha, ha, ha." (No personal power)

Compare these with the empowering, responsible response: "Are you hurt? Can I help you?"

When someone is hurt, laughter is never appropriate—not even nervous laughter. Laughing at pain is sometimes defended as "having a sense of humor." Any laughter that happens at the expense of someone's safety or self-esteem is destructive, not humorous. That includes laughing or smiling at our own distress. We may sometimes laugh ruefully at the human condition as we reflect on our past ineptness, but this kind of forgiving laughter comes only after anger, sadness, grieving, and acceptance of the situation and of one's humanity are completed.

Parental Laughter

Being laughed at is one of the cruelest ways of being discounted because it ridicules the person at the same time it discounts the problem. Derisive laughter is a form of abuse. Hurtful parental laughter can ring in the ears of a child for days, and that same long-forgotten laughter, years later, triggers the old messages, *You are not important. Don't dare to get close.* This laughter engenders timidity, withdrawal, rebellion, and other habits of thought and behavior harmful to self and others. The message of such laughter is that familial love and support are scarce or unreliable. Before you laugh at a child's mishap that seems amusing to you, stop to think: *Will the child find this as funny as I do, or is it painful to the child?* Wait to see if the child laughs. If the mishap is truly not serious or painful, you can laugh together.

> *Derisive laughter is a form of abuse.*

Children Who Laugh at Their Own Pain

Disparaging laughter is especially harmful to children. When they are laughed at disrespectfully, they learn to laugh at their pain in an attempt to be one of the "in group" or "in" the family.

If Davy smiles or laughs at his own pain, either physical or emotional, before he acts hurt or confused or embarrassed, his parents need to stop and take stock. Has he already learned that he is supposed to laugh at his pain? If so, Davy's parents can expect him to neglect to take care of himself because he has learned to discount the information that pain sends: that he needs to do something to protect or care for or heal himself.

What can a parent do to discourage children from laughing or smiling at themselves in discounting, self-destructive ways?

- Stop laughing at pain or mishaps, or at dangerous, mean, or destructive behavior yourself.
- Say, in a loving way, "That does not seem funny to me," or "Let's talk about what we can do to help you instead of laughing at your problem (pain, embarrassment, or mistake)," or "I feel uncomfortable when you laugh at pain," or "Please don't do that."

If your young child is in a play group that expects him to laugh at his own pain, do something. Tell the other kids to stop. Enlist the aid of other adults. Find a new play group for the child. Change day care or nursery schools. Move if that is the only way you can stop the laughing at pain.

If your junior high school child is engaging in the frequent ridicule practiced by her group, teach her that this is common behavior among kids her age, that it is destructive, that you expect her to outgrow it shortly, and not to use it at home.

If, in spite of your parental love and structure, your child continues to smile about her own misfortune or misbehavior, that is a signal that the child has internalized being discounted and is now internally discounting herself. Get whatever help you need, including therapy, to get this discounting stopped before you are faced with even more serious behaviors.

Gallows Smiles: The Unconscious Signals

At one time it was the practice for a condemned person on the gallows to tell a joke just before hanging so the onlooking crowd would be laughing as the prisoner died. Eric Berne, the father of transactional analysis,[2] called an unconscious smile at our own pain a "gallows smile" because we are, in effect, smiling at our own destruction.

As awful as it sounds, many of us do smile automatically at our pain and misfortune. Such smiles signal that we have touched some early area of our lives where our needs were not met, nor could we get them met, so we learned to discount them. Our smiles signal that we are still discounting those needs and ourselves. As children, we had to accept the situation. It is understandable that we decided whatever we did in order to stay alive and grow. But, if years later, we are still smiling about our pain and about not getting what we need, this discounting keeps us from being responsible to ourselves and others. It is a poor decision to hold on to. We need to stop smiling at pain and take action to alleviate it.

> *As awful as it sounds, many of us do smile automatically at our pain and misfortune.*

To find out if you are using gallows smiles and laughter and modeling them for your child, ask a friend to tell you if you are smiling or laughing at something painful or disturbing. Choose a friend who will report honestly, with love, and who will not use this opportunity to "get" you. If you aren't sure about a friend, ask a counselor or therapist to help you with this.

Talk about what concerns you most about your life or your family, and your friend or counselor can soon tell you if you are smiling inappropriately. If you are, welcome this as a physical signal that you are doing internal discounting. At first you may want to deny the smile, or you may feel angry or embarrassed about it. Remember that a gallows smile or laugh is usually done outside of your awareness. Now that you are aware of it, you can change it!

If you have ever denied having a gallows smile, check your discounting response with these examples of the four discounting levels.

Your friend or counselor says, "You asked me to tell you if you smiled when you described pain, embarrassment, or failure. Did you know that you smiled when you told me you failed your test?"

Level 1: "I didn't smile." (No problem)

Level 2: "Well, one little smile isn't such a big deal." (Not serious)

Level 3: "Everybody laughs at that sort of thing—nobody wants to see a grown person cry." (No solution)

Level 4: "I can't help it. Sometimes my mouth just smiles." (No personal power)

Watching your own gallows smile on videotape is a compelling way to face the truth. If you have no video, check your physical response by placing your fingers firmly on either side of your mouth to feel your smile. Repeat what you said when you smiled. If you feel your cheek muscles push for the smile, press firmly with your fingers to prevent the smile and repeat what you said before. Notice that as soon as you prevent your smile, you stop discounting your sadness, fear, anger, or whatever you were denying. Now you are ready to get on with the healing of that particular pain.

Remember, as you learn to stop using discounting types of laughter, you create lots of opportunities in your life for delightful, healing, joyous laughter.

Teasing

Teasing, like laughter, can build esteem and encourage intimacy, or it can cruelly discount. Teasing used to irritate, provoke, annoy, disturb, deceive, or ridicule is sometimes an attempt to make ourselves look better at someone else's expense. Anytime we are tempted to tease in a hurtful way, it is important to stop and do something healthy instead. Teasing can be damaging if offered to children instead of needed information, rules, or love.

Harmless teasing between people who feel secure with themselves and each other is often called banter, pleasantry, or joking. The message it sends is, "I like you; I want to laugh with you (not at you); here's a funny way of telling you that I care about you or that I notice you." This kind of banter is friendly, even loving. Nevertheless, be very cautious about its use. People who grew up with hurtful teasing often misunderstand and are offended by it, even if they pretend to be jolly about it. Also, since children under six are working at the developmental task of separating reality from fantasy, they may miss the friendly intent unless very broad hints such as winks, big smiles, or little rituals assure that this is joking and not ridicule.

> *Anytime we are tempted to tease in a hurtful way, it is important to stop and do something healthy instead.*

Benjamin's daddy knows how to do this. Four-year-old Benjamin came racing into the house, interrupted his father who was watching television, placed himself squarely in front of his dad, and announced, "I had an ice-cream cone."

His dad asked quizzically, "You did?"

Benjy replied seriously, "Yes."

His dad said, "Did you bring me one?"

Benjy shouted, "No!"

Benjy's father jumped to his feet and shouted, in a singsong voice, "How could you do that? You turkey! You know I love ice-cream cones! What shall I do to you because you didn't bring me ice cream?"

Benjy shouted delightedly, "Restel me!"

Dad and son rolled on the floor, wrestling, hugging, and laughing. Here are aspects that made the teasing positive:

- The child initiated it.
- Dad was willing to be interrupted.
- Dad paid attention to Benjamin's invitation to play.
- Dad exaggerated his actions by jumping up and shouting in a special, ritualized way.
- Dad and Benjy ended the interlude with positive touch and laughter.

Sarcasm and Ridicule

Sarcasm and ridicule are forms of discounting that strike at a person's being. They issue a bitter and mocking invitation for contemptuous laughter that says, "You are not important and your needs are not serious." Because sarcasm and ridicule are difficult to counter and leave people feeling ashamed, exposed, stupid, or diminished, these forms of discounting should not be excused as friendly teasing.

Sarcasm and ridicule command an instant response from children and thus may seem momentarily attractive to parents. But parents may not realize that criticism, sarcasm, and ridicule not only stop unwanted behaviors, they also wither important aspects of a child's growth. Think about Katlin's response: She was in the backseat of the car, chatting merrily with her mother about the

> *Sarcasm and ridicule are forms of discounting that strike at a person's being.*

school day. Grandpa, riding in front, said scornfully, "She's some talker, isn't she?" Katlin didn't speak for the rest of the drive and would not respond to her mother's request to finish the story. It is healthier for everyone when adults replace ridicule and sarcasm with appreciation or instruction. Tell children what you want them to do and how to do it. And remember, such instruction works better with adults too.

Using Sarcasm to Toughen?

Some people believe sarcasm toughens children. The theory is that if children can learn to survive sarcasm at home and in the play group, they will be able to let it roll off when they encounter it in the outside world. On the surface, this seems to work. But people trained this way pay a price. They often use ridicule in their relationships and against themselves.

Girls who are ridiculed for not being as good at math as boys often believe it and do not extend themselves to become proficient at math. These girls may even mistrust other women who are good at math. When boys are ridiculed for being sensitive, they learn to hide their sensitivity or they sometimes decide to discard it. Members of minority groups sometimes trash themselves—they do to themselves and each other what their oppressors have done to them. In "Playing the Dozens," a game used by street kids to prove their toughness, players hurl scathing insults at each other until one player breaks down and loses face.

Think about people who learn to use put-downs skillfully; they continue to put down themselves and their peers. Wouldn't it be better to change the culture so people don't learn to expect and honor ridicule, sarcasm, and other discounts?

Double Binds—Messages That Create Dilemmas

Double binds are especially confusing and immobilizing discounts. They discount by saying two things that, when considered individually, are understandable, but, when offered as a pair, are impossible to reconcile. They are mutually exclusive experiences and both true. (See the discussion of double binds in chapter 17, page 134)

Double binds discount the other person by creating a box, a corner, or a Catch-22, where that person can do no right. They discount the self by creating life situations that yield confusion and pain rather than support and joy. In *Adult Children of Alcoholics*,[3] Janet Woititz identifies double-bind messages common in families where alcohol is abused.

- "I love you." / "Go away."
- "Always tell the truth." / "I don't want to know."
- "Being drunk isn't okay." / "Anything a drunk does is okay."

Examples of double binds created by overindulgence are listed on page 136.

You can use the suggestions in Getting Free of Double Binds in appendix A to help you recognize, counter, and avoid double binds. You can also explore the following Double-Bind Chart[4] to get ideas about how double binds may be put on children of different ages. If you recognize that you may have been putting a child in a double bind, endeavor to send only one message.

A *double bind* is a set of two or more messages, each of which seems to be true when given separately, but when given in combination are contradictory. Double binds create a Catch-22

STAGE 1: BIRTH TO 6 MONTHS	STAGE 2: 6 MONTHS TO 18 MONTHS	STAGE 3: 18 MONTHS TO 3 YEARS
Characteristics:		
Conflicting verbal and nonverbal messages are sent about child's being; getting needs met; unconditional love; trust; being close, safe, and connected in healthy ways.	Conflicting messages are sent about child's doing; initiating; exploring; trusting self, others, and the environment; ability to be creative, to be active, and to get support while doing and exploring.	Conflicting messages are sent about child's thinking, being separate, expressing and acting upon feelings.
Examples:		
Your needs are important. / Your needs conflict with mine. Your needs are important. / Your needs are too much for me. I love you. / Go away. I'm here for you. / Don't bother me.	Explore. / Don't touch, get dirty, put things in your mouth, etc. Perform in order to get love and approval. / What you do is never enough. I will keep you safe. / Ignore harmful situations. Explore. / Don't embarrass me.	Your feelings are okay. / You must feel the way I feel. Don't hit. / Parent hits. It's okay to think for yourself. / Don't say NO to me. Hurry and grow up. / Here, I'll do that for you.
Children May Hear the Following Messages:		
You don't know what you need. The needs of others are more important than your needs. You are a bother.	You are not enough and whatever you do is not enough. It's not safe to explore. What you do is wrong. Be perfect. You are a bother. What you do gets in others' way.	Don't be separate. Don't be different. Don't think of yourself. Take care of others by thinking for them or letting them think for you. You are lovable and accepted when you are like me. Please others.
Common Responses of Children:		
Fears for emotional safety and connectedness. Holds onto life through physical tension, holding breath, anger, and fighting to stay alive. Engages in behaviors to "prove" or justify being and life. In later life, may eat or drink excessively, or engage in other addictions to cope with "pain" of being alive.	Does tricks to get approval. Later engages in lots of DOING—tasks, projects, etc.—in order to justify and validate self. Doesn't know what enough is. Has difficulty making decisions. Focuses on what is wrong. May be judgmental and critical of self and others.	Shows difficulty in making decisions and thinking for self. Later, exhibits inappropriate rebelliousness, "chip on shoulder," or overcompliance. Needs to be "right" or corrects behaviors of others. Has difficulty with boundaries and setting limits for self. Has difficulty or fear of saying no. Is overly responsible or second-guesses others. Feels tired or overwhelmed at pleasing so many people.
Decisions Often Made by Children and Often Carried into Adulthood:		
I'm not important or valuable. My needs are not important but are bothersome. I'm just in the way. The needs of others are more important than mine. My needs are too much for me or anyone else. I don't trust love from others.	I'm not enough. It's not safe to reach out. Decides to Do within the given parameters in order to Be.	Others ideas are more important than mine. I have to take care of others by thinking for them. I have to do whatever I'm asked to do or am told to do. Whatever anyone says about me must be true.

where the person can do no right. Messages may be verbal or nonverbal and may be given simultaneously or at different times.

STAGE 4: 3 YEARS TO 6 YEARS	STAGE 5: 6 YEARS TO 12 YEARS	STAGE 6: 12 YEARS TO 19 YEARS
Characteristics:		*Characteristics:*
Conflicting messages are sent about child's identity, learning skills, and role and power relationship with others.	Conflicting messages are sent to child about rules: establishing them, following them, and the relevancy of rules and values.	Conflicting messages are sent about youth's identity, sexuality, separation, and competence.
Examples:		*Example:*
Grow up. / Stay little. Be smart. / Don't be smarter than I am. Don't tattle. / Tell me everything. Think for yourself. / I'll tell you what to do.	Get good grades. / Parent fills child's homework time with chores, errands, activities. Don't fight. / When someone hits you, hit them back. It's just a mistake. / Don't let that happen again. Be successful or skillful. / Don't be more successful than I am. Tell the truth. / Lie to protect me. Figure out how to do things. / Do it my way.	I'm glad you are growing up. / Don't leave me. Be popular like your friends. / Don't do what your friends are doing. Grow and mature. / Don't be sexy. Make your own decisions. / I make decisions for you. Be independent. / Stay dependent.
Children May Hear the Following Messages:		*Youth May Hear the Following Messages:*
Others are more important than you.	Rules aren't important. You can't trust rules. Rules aren't fair. Rules are for kids and not grown-ups. Rules are to be circumvented.	I don't trust you. Don't leave home because I need you.
Common Responses of Children:		*Common Responses of Youth:*
May seek power over others or look to others to define who they are. Needs approval from others. Later, engages in either/or thinking. Gives up personal power. Has difficulty setting priorities. Shows confusion about safety of growing up.	Exhibits helplessness, confusion about what is valuable. Later, has difficulty making decisions and setting boundaries.	Feels trapped and confused about growing up, being separate, leaving home, being independent. Expresses sexuality inappropriately.
Decisions Often Made by Children and Often Carried into Adulthood:		*Decisions Often Made by Youth:*
If people really knew me, they wouldn't like me. I can't trust feedback from others. There is something wrong with me. It's not safe for me to be powerful. I am a powerless victim.	I don't have to follow rules or I don't trust rules. Children have consequences for not following rules; grown-ups do not. The powerful people have the rules. I am powerless. I don't need internal rules. I don't know what I know.	I can't trust my own decision making. It isn't safe to grow up.

Abandonment

Abandonment of any kind is a first-level discount of the other person. It is probably the most serious way that parents can discount children. Abandonment implies, *Caring for you is not important, you do not exist, or I wish you didn't exist.* The child interprets the behavior of a parent who walks out, is drunk, or is preoccupied as abandonment.

> *Abandonment is probably the most serious way that parents can discount children.*

Sometimes a parent abandons a child by refusing to accept her as she is. "We wanted a boy, but Ashley does very well. She is quite a tomboy." In such a sad circumstance, the child often attempts to make sense of a no-sense situation by taking the blame on herself for not being a boy. As mentioned in chapter 14, this is called *victim blame* because the child is the victim, but she blames herself. This kind of self-blame during childhood perpetuates itself in adult life. As an adult, Ashley needs to stop blaming herself, stop pretending what her parents did was okay, deliberately sort out what really happened, and find the support and healing she needs and deserves.

Underlying Decisions That Lead to Denial and Discounting

Denial and discounting protect previously made decisions. You can practice understanding how discounting springs from old decisions or beliefs by looking at the following examples and guessing what the underlying decision for each might be. There is also an empowering response for which you can guess an underlying decision or attitude.

Pat's friend Jamal asks: "Will you help me with the decorations for my club party?" Pat responds:

Level 1: "You are always doing something for that club. You should spend as much time with me." (No problem)
Level 2: "They don't need decorations to have a party." (Not serious)
Level 3: "Decorating is a lot of work. There isn't time to get it done." (No solution)
Level 4: "I'm no good at artsy-craftsy things." (No personal power)
Empowering: "Sure. What do you want me to do?" or "No, I can't commit to do that, but I hope you find someone to help you."

Guess what the underlying decision for each response might be.

1.

2.

3.

4.

E.

Compare your guesses with this possible list.
1. My needs are more desperate than yours.
2. I need to do things perfectly and I feel ashamed if I don't.
3. I am not artistic.
4. I can't decorate well enough and someone would criticize me.
E. I am competent.

Every level of discounting protects old decisions. Other decisions that could be behind any of the above levels of discounting might be:

- I am an artistic klutz.
- I don't dare to get close. If I help people once, they bug me forever.
- It is not okay for me to say no directly.
- Jamal might get to know me better if we do this together and that's a risk I can't take.
- I am not important, so I am jealous of people who belong to clubs.
- Jamal might want to be intimate and I don't know how to be intimate as a friend. I only know about sexual intimacy.

Remember, when other people discount you, it makes no difference what their reason is. It is your responsibility to deal with the discount without discounting them in return and without internalizing the discount yourself.

We can identify our own underlying decisions and beliefs. Some of the ways we can do that are by exploring the dynamics of our families of origin, by noticing what bothers us so much in others, by journaling, by attending to our feelings and letting them guide us to thoughts and memories of old experiences and decisions, and by therapy.

New Decisions

If you uncover old destructive decisions and the situations that led to them and expose them to the light of day, you will discover yourself as a child whose needs were not met, a child who made lifesaving decisions anyway. Applaud those decisions. Grieve the situation and make new decisions that will help you take better care of yourself and others now.

Robert Subby in *Lost in the Shuffle*[5] calls children who had to make unfortunate decisions "victims," but adults who continue to base their current actions upon them "volunteers." Perhaps you are tired of being a volunteer discounter but find it hard to maintain new, empowering behaviors because the old decisions keep playing in your head, tugging you back to old behaviors. Here are ways people have helped themselves find new attitudes and behaviors and make new decisions:

- Laura read and used self-help books.
- Ron took parenting classes.
- Stephanie told her story in her support groups and got suggestions for making new decisions.
- Marty got the help of a therapist.
- Fred participated in grief workshops.
- Alice used her Twelve Step support group.
- Connie did all of the above and more.

We all have different life-affirming tasks to accomplish and will choose different ways to do them. This book, the class, the program, the therapist are there to help. It is up to us to take the risk and experience the discomfort, to do the grieving and make the changes. Since it is damaging to stay stuck and not change, let yourself be worth the discomfort, the determination, the discipline, and the effort to grow. The rewards are inner peace, health, happiness, and joy. Another great reward for changing is the satisfaction that we are improving the parenting legacy we pass on to our kids.

> *Remember, we do change. We can't stay the same.*

Remember, we do change. We can't stay the same—either we are growing and expanding or we are tightening our defensive denials every day.

Getting Off the Merry-Go-Round

Here are questions people often ask about discounting. You may have been wondering about them yourself.

What if I realize that other people are discounting me?

Stop to think if you are discounting yourself or your needs in some way. Then decide what you want to change in this situation. Usually, if we are clear about our needs, desires, skills, and goals, we can think of several options for managing the discounts of others without discounting ourselves or them.

My world is filled with discounts. How can I remember to recognize them?

As you use the thinking techniques in this section to identify discounts, be aware of your feelings. You may have a clutch in your stomach or tightening of your throat when you receive a discount. Or you may have a sneaky feeling of relief when you seem to get by with a discount. Acknowledge and learn from these feelings or any other sensation you have. You can learn to trust your feelings to help you know when you are discounting or being discounted. You can use feelings to remind you to take responsibility for yourself.

So many people discount. Isn't it normal and can't we just ignore it?

No and no. With people, "frequent" doesn't necessarily mean normal. It is normal for members of families to help each other survive and to treat each other with love, support, and respect. If we have lost that birthright, we need to reclaim our right to be treated and to treat people this way and stop our discounting. True, there are many discounts in the world around us. In some situations there are too many for us to deal with and we may have to change jobs or friends or withdraw from our families of origin for a while.

> *It is normal for members of families to help each other survive and to treat each other with love, support, and respect.*

What can I do to help my family?

Improve your ability to nurture and structure others and yourself. Teach family members to give warm nurture and clear structure to you. Replace your discounting behavior with responsible parenting.

It is important for us to remember that although it is easier to overcome third-level (no solution) and fourth-level (no personal power) discounts, from the child's point of view, all levels are the same because the child's problem remains unsolved; the child's need remains unmet.

There is a big problem in our family and we don't talk about it. Is this discounting?

Yes. You may not feel like facing up to it either. You may feel too scared or mortified to even mention it, so your family treats it as a secret. Often, big family problems stem from some unfinished business. That is the time to get some outside help.

Sometimes two or more people have made outside-of-our-awareness secret contracts, such as, "I won't mention what you are doing if you don't notice what I am doing," or "I'll ignore your drinking problem if you don't confront my martyrdom," or "I won't mention your cocaine use if you don't notice my sexual addiction," or "I'll ignore your overeating if you accommodate my workaholism," or "I won't mention your frequent absences if you don't get mad at my gambling." These are examples of mutual discounting agreements.

The first partner to become aware of a double-destruct contract should run, not walk, for competent outside help and do everything possible to resolve the problem. Even with goodwill and determination to get well, the people in this kind of relationship usually need strong outside support over time to help develop more satisfying and loving relationships. (See Where to Go for Additional Help in appendix B.)

> *Often, big family problems stem from some unfinished business.*

Can People Stop Discounting?

If our habits of denial are long-standing, can we change our discounting behavior? Yes, we can change a bit at a time by deliberately becoming aware of our behaviors. We can think about them. We can gather information by asking other people for their feelings and thoughts about situations. We can deliberately contract with ourselves to pay thoughtful, loving attention to evaluating and making changes in one piece of discounting behavior at a time. It is helpful to put aside any tendencies of self-blame and look upon discounts with an attitude of *Oh shucks—well, here is something I can change and I will.*

You can use the following seven steps to become aware of discounting behaviors and to replace discounting with empowering, responsible thinking and behavior.

1. Choose a recent situation that disturbed you, but that you did nothing about.
2. Ask yourself what you discounted. What information or feeling did you ignore? What did you not attend to or value? Yourself, others, the situation? Remember that doing nothing is, in fact, an action or a decision. When we do nothing, we cast a powerful, apathetic vote that says, "I take the action of ignoring or denying."
3. Brainstorm four or five things you could have done instead. Remember, ideas collected by brainstorming don't have to be sensible. Generate lots of ideas; don't evaluate them until later.
4. Predict the probable outcome of each of these actions and decide for each if it would likely have made the situation better.
5. Select the action you plan to use the next time you are in the same situation.
6. Think about how often you discount. How often do you ignore things or fail to think things through because you feel powerless or not responsible? Compare that to how often you choose to ignore or remain silent because that option is the most powerful way you could help the situation.
7. Think about whether you allow others to discount you, and instead of addressing the discounting, you stay in denial and keep yourself in a powerless position.
8. Choose a new decision that will support your new plan of action, such as, "I am powerful and responsible. I will decide upon appropriate action and take it."

Here is how Virginia went through the seven steps.

1. Choose a situation.

I was in the grocery store when I observed a mother spanking her two-year-old and then glaring at her baby and threatening, "You keep your mouth shut or you will both go to the car!" Later, as I left the store, I noticed the two children alone in a closed car, screaming. It was a hot day. I did nothing.

2. Ask yourself what you discounted.

Self: I discounted myself by thinking, *They are not my kids so I'm not responsible and I wouldn't know what to do.*

Other: I discounted the mother by assuming she would verbally attack me if I spoke to her, and I discounted the needs of the children by telling myself that babies are tough.

Situation: I discounted the situation by ignoring the fact that closed cars can be heat traps and that I know of instances where children have died in closed automobiles on a hot day. I did nothing when I could have done something.

3. Brainstorm.

What could I have done?

   a. I could have told the store manager.

   b. I could have offered to take care of the children for a half hour.

   c. I could have asked the mother if there was some way I could help. "Excuse me, but I remember when my children were little and I needed to get my shopping done. I have some extra time right now. Is there some way I can help you?"

   d. I could have given the mother the name and address of a nearby drop-in center that provides child care for shoppers.

   e. I could have called the Child Protection Agency.

   f. I could have told the police officer who was having lunch across the street.

   g. I could have told the mother, "You stop this—you are abusing your children. You are not a good mother."

   h. I could have told the mother, "When you leave the children, they could be harmed. Better to take them with you."

4. Predict the probable outcome.

Working backward through my list, I decided: Forget h., it would probably be heard as blaming; forget g., blaming seldom helps; F. probably would have been successful and it would have been easy to do; E. was a good bet, but it might have taken them awhile to get there; D. might have worked; C. could have worked, but I was too scared to try that; B. wouldn't have worked because I didn't have the extra half hour; A. was possible.

5. Select action to use in future.
If this happens again, I'll try telling the police. If they won't come and help the children, I'll call the Child Protection Agency.

6. How often do I discount in similar situations?
I often ignore how adults treat children. Yet I believe that adults should protect children. Next time I'll brainstorm options. I'll ignore only if I have decided that is the most effective thing to do, not because I am acting powerless.

7. Am I used to being discounted?
I will examine how the discounting I have done has been done to me. Am I accepting another's discounting of me and if so, how will I address this?

8. Choose a new decision.
Adults should protect children and that's what I'll do.

If you recognized yourself in Virginia's story, accept that information without blame or shame. We all learned to discount because we needed to. Don't be hard on yourself; that only keeps you stuck. Remember that sometime in the past, when we felt confused or were in pain, we learned to deny and discount by pretending things didn't matter. But, in the long run, they do matter and we pay a price for ignoring what is really going on.

How Can I Confront My Own Discounts?

How can I stop discounting and start empowering? Read through the following list of actions. Select two or three to start doing, and do them. When you are ready, add others.

- Start by accepting yourself as human. All people discount sometimes.
- Honor yourself for having decided to block, deny, or accept victim blame when that was the only choice you could make to survive.
- Accept the fact that old, once-helpful decisions often get us in trouble now.
- Set some long-term goals to stop discounting and to start empowering yourself in several areas important to you and your family. Set a short-term goal to change one of those areas.

- Use empowering responses or initiate responsible action at least once every day for a week. Do not be deterred if you feel awkward. Remember, if you do not stumble as you learn this new skill, you will probably be the first person in the history of the world to achieve instant competence without practice.
- Encourage yourself and your children to be responsible by using responsible language that avoids discounting and indicates clearly who is to do what. (See Encouraging Responsibility through Language in appendix A.)
- Get outside support. Join a therapy group, a support group, or a Twelve Step group. Get a friend who won't discount the area you are working on to cheer for you and plan celebrations for you.
- Plan celebrations to mark your successes.
- Use a journal to record your progress.
- Think about how discounting creates scarcities in your life. Decide to go for abundance.
- Ask a friend to point out ways you discount. Choose someone who will do so with love and who will never, never use your request as an opportunity to "get" you, get even, embarrass you, or hurt you.
- Likewise, do not use your knowledge of discounting to blame or shame others. Find solutions to problems without using accusations, name-calling, or put-downs.
- Be in charge of updating your beliefs to form the life base most helpful for you and your family now.
- If you have great difficulty replacing a particular discount with empowerment, get therapeutic help in identifying and remaking the underlying decision.
- Love yourself, discounting and all.

Shall I Confront Discounts from Others?

You can ask yourself if the discount is a minor one or a major one that makes a difference. Then ask yourself:

- Shall I confront this discount?
- If no, can I let it go? and if I can't, where will I store it in my body?
- If yes, how shall I confront it?
- If no, do I contribute to the discounting?
- If yes, do I have the energy to deal with any escalation?
- If no, will someone get hurt?

Will Doing Less Discounting Help My Parenting?

Greatly. The less you discount, the better you parent. The unspoken contract between parents and children is that parents will nurture and structure, and children will learn and grow.

> *The less you discount, the better you parent.*

chapter 23

Problem Solving

Putting It All Together

Now that we have examined structure, nurture, and discounting separately, we can combine them into a powerful problem-solving tool.

At the end of this chapter you will find a blank Problem-Solving Worksheet (page 193)[1] and two examples already filled out. Using the worksheet can help you clarify a problem. The solution to the problem will show on the right side of the sheet. The left side will provide clues to how and why you may be avoiding or sabotaging the solution. Feel free to photocopy the worksheet for use time and time again.

Follow the step-by-step instructions for using the Problem-Solving Worksheet.

Fill in the Problem-Solving Sheet

1. Identify the problem and write it in The Problem box. If the problem has two or more parts, use separate sheets for each one. Be clear about the problem. Is this your internal problem or does it involve other people? Do you want to change a behavior or an attitude or deal with a feeling?
2. Fill in all of the boxes on the left, answering the question, "What would I do or say if I were going to be rigid, criticize, marshmallow, etc." Notice that every position on the left, every shoulder and ditch of the parenting highway, involves some kind of discount.
3. Fill in the boxes on the right answering the question, "What is needed here?" Remember that support or negotiable rules

are not appropriate in some situations. Notice that the solution to the problem appears in the boxes on the right—the driving lanes of the parenting highway and the empowered response.

Look for the Solution

4. Read all of the information on the right side and decide if those actions would probably get the desired result. If they would not, add whatever is needed.

Deal with the Hindrances

5. Examine the responses on the left side. Circle each one that you often do or are likely to do or would like to do. "I know what I should do, but I really want to blast them (criticize) or hit them (abuse) or give in (overindulge); what I usually do is try to save them the pain (marshmallow) or forget the whole thing (discount) and hope it goes away (neglect or abandon)."

6. For each response circled, ask yourself, "What do I need so that I could get past wanting to _____ and get on with solving the problem?" For example:

   - I want to criticize. I will get the criticism out of my system by writing a blasting, no-holds-barred letter and then tearing it up. Then I will think clearly about the problem.
   - I am in the habit of marshmallowing. I will look at my old rules about protecting children from pain and see if I am giving in to them because of a wish that the children would always be happy, or because I don't have clear boundaries between them and me, or because I don't know how to enforce discipline. Then I will update my rules or get help firming up my structure or do both.
   - I want to abandon. I will get other people who care about me to support me and encourage me and hold me accountable when I want to run away.

7. Get whatever you need to help you move off the left side to the problem-solving right side. Sometimes, when we become aware of what we have been doing or have been wanting to

do, we can simply say, "I'll stop that," and stop it. But if we can't let go of it completely, if we push it down, it is apt to pop up later and tug us back to ineffective behaviors. We can choose and use the affirmations that will support us (see chapter 25). It is worth the time and effort to get the help we need. This is part of growing up again.

Take Action

8. Return to the right side of the sheet and **put the solution into action.** Use your power for a positive resolution of the problem.
9. When you do the things you identified on the right-hand side of the chart and the problem remains, reexamine the definition of the problem. You may have lumped several problems into one. If so, divide the problem into its separate pieces and do a Problem-Solving Worksheet for each one. Or you may have been working on a symptom so the underlying problem resurfaced. If so, look for the underlying problem and attend to that.

Expect the process of filling in the sheet to take awhile the first few times you use it. After people become experienced with the process, they can usually work through a problem very quickly. If a problem is hard to get onto the sheet, it may be a big problem that requires outside help to solve or an old problem that has been hanging around for a long time. Now is a good time to resolve it. Give yourself all the permission you need to use your power for a positive resolution of the problem.

PROBLEM-SOLVING WORKSHEET

THE PROBLEM: My child doesn't listen to me.

STRUCTURE CONTINUUM

RIGIDITY:
"I only say things once, no matter what."

SOLVING THE PROBLEM

CRITICISM:
"You never listen to me! Are you deaf?"

NONNEGOTIABLE RULES
"You will sit here until I'm sure you heard me because this is important."

MARSHMALLOW:
Remind child again and again and again and again . . .

NEGOTIABLE RULES
"Since you must listen to me, how shall we arrange that? Sit where? Should we have a hand signal that each of us can use when we need the other person to listen?"

ABANDONMENT:
Don't expect child to listen.

NURTURE CONTINUUM

ABUSE:
Grab child by shoulders and shake him, hard.

CONDITIONAL CARE:
"I can't love you if you don't listen."

ASSERTIVE CARE
Touch child on shoulder and say, "Hear me and repeat what I say."

OVERINDULGENCE:
Ask once and then take care of situation for child.

SUPPORTIVE CARE
"Can you listen to me now or shall I ask you when you finish. . . ?"

NEGLECT:
Ignore the child's ignoring.

LEVELS OF DISCOUNTING

LEVEL 1–NO PROBLEM
It doesn't matter if kids don't listen.

LEVEL 2–NOT SERIOUS
That's just kids. Don't get so upset about it.

LEVEL 3–NO SOLUTION
There is no way to get kids to listen. They just don't.

LEVEL 4–NO PERSONAL POWER
I don't know how to get kids to listen.

EMPOWERMENT
I will stop reminding and try out as many ways as I need to in order to get my child to listen.

E

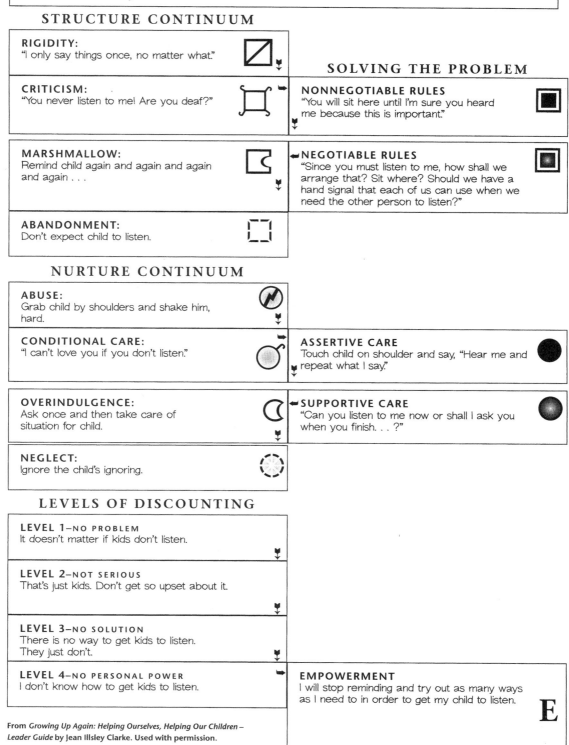

From *Growing Up Again: Helping Ourselves, Helping Our Children – Leader Guide* by Jean Illsley Clarke. Used with permission.

PROBLEM-SOLVING WORKSHEET

THE PROBLEM: My seven- and ten-year-olds are hitting each other.

STRUCTURE CONTINUUM

RIGIDITY:
Send children to separate rooms for the rest of the day.

SOLVING THE PROBLEM

CRITICISM:
"You are bad kids! You are always fighting. Can't you ever be quiet?"

NONNEGOTIABLE RULES
"If you start to hit, you must sit at opposite sides of the room and use words to decide how to solve your problem."

MARSHMALLOW:
"I wish you children wouldn't hit each other. Are you bored?"

NEGOTIABLE RULES
"Do we need new rules about what to do instead of hitting?"

ABANDONMENT:
Walk away.

NURTURE CONTINUUM

ABUSE:
Hit them harder than they were hitting each other.

CONDITIONAL CARE:
Remind them that you like children who get along.

ASSERTIVE CARE
Stop the hitting and provide protection if either child is getting hurt.

OVERINDULGENCE:
Dish up two bowls of ice cream to distract them.

SUPPORTIVE CARE
"Do you want ideas from me about how to solve your problems peacefully?"

NEGLECT:
Don't notice they are hitting or automatically yell at older child.

LEVELS OF DISCOUNTING

LEVEL 1–NO PROBLEM
So?

LEVEL 2–NOT SERIOUS
Fighting makes kids tough.

LEVEL 3–NO SOLUTION
Kids hit!

LEVEL 4–NO PERSONAL POWER
I can't control their every move!

EMPOWERMENT
I will remind them of the no-hitting rule. I will notice what happens just before they hit and see if I can interrupt at that time. I will notice when they solve problems without hitting, congratulate them, and ask how they did that and how they can do that in the future.

E

From *Growing Up Again: Helping Ourselves, Helping Our Children – Leader Guide* by **Jean Illsley Clarke.** Used with permission.

PROBLEM-SOLVING WORKSHEET

THE PROBLEM:

STRUCTURE CONTINUUM

RIGIDITY:

CRITICISM:

SOLVING THE PROBLEM

NONNEGOTIABLE RULES

MARSHMALLOW:

← **NEGOTIABLE RULES**

ABANDONMENT:

NURTURE CONTINUUM

ABUSE:

CONDITIONAL CARE:

ASSERTIVE CARE

OVERINDULGENCE:

← **SUPPORTIVE CARE**

NEGLECT:

LEVELS OF DESCOUNTING

LEVEL 1–NO PROBLEM

LEVEL 2–NOT SERIOUS

LEVEL 3–NO SOLUTION

LEVEL 4–NO PERSONAL POWER   → **EMPOWERMENT**

E

From *Growing Up Again: Helping Ourselves, Helping Our Children –
Leader Guide* by Jean Illsley Clarke. Used with permission.
Reproduction for educational purposes is permissible.

The Prenatal and Birth Experience

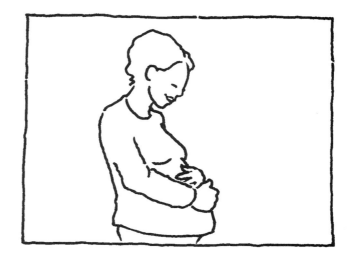

Human infants, we can safely conclude, like infants of other species, are preprogrammed to develop in a socially cooperative way; whether they do so or not turns in high degree on how they are treated.

JOHN BOWLBY

chapter 24

Becoming

The Prenatal and Birth Experience

Does the Prenatal and Birth Experience Really Matter?

Does the prenatal experience or the birth experience really matter to a child? Can a child remember what happened in the womb? Conflicting assumptions abound about the significance of the prenatal and birth experience on the life of a human person. In the past, no one was able to observe the experiences of the fetus and relate those experiences to later attitudes and behaviors. Technological advances now allow researchers to observe the growth, behaviors, and reactions of a fetus; consequently some of the questions people have asked about conception, pregnancy, and birth finally have answers.

Using ultrasound and other data-gathering methods, researchers have recorded specific prebirth and birth experiences and then observed children's behaviors to see if there were connections. Their research findings offer some clear directions not only about managing pregnancy and birth but also about understanding and supporting an infant's growth and our own growing up again.

We shouldn't be surprised. It is common knowledge that alcohol, nicotine, and other drug use by a pregnant woman can create serious problems for her child during pregnancy and after birth. New research indicates that the mind and the body are not separate, that we all have a mindbody. Therefore it shouldn't surprise us that the mother's emotions also affect her unborn child. It shouldn't amaze us to learn that a child in the womb has a negative emotional response if the mother is beaten, that a forming baby receives pleasure-giving endorphins when the mother is happy, or that a child will be calmed

> *It shouldn't surprise us that the mother's emotions affect her unborn child.*

after birth by hearing voices or music that gave the mother pleasure during pregnancy. Many parents know this is true from experiences with their own infants.

The Abundance of Research

Popular interest is growing in the abundance of research on prenatal, birth, and perinatal topics. Research reports are appearing everywhere from scholarly journals to the mainstream press. The *Newsweek* Special Edition "Your Child from Birth to Three" and the *Time* article "Fertile Minds" are good examples.[1] These articles highlight the astounding effect the environment has on the development of the brain, not just on attitudes but on the very structure of the brain itself.

Craig Ramey, a leading pediatrics professor and researcher at the University of Alabama,[2] asserts that the research reported in the popular press is "the tip of the iceberg." According to Dr. Ramey, it reflects only a thousandth of what is now known about brain development, learning, memory, emotions, and ways in which experience shapes genetics.

In the Spring 1996 *Journal of Psychohistory* Lloyd deMause reported on more than forty controlled studies.[3] He included research from many disciplines on the impact of *in utero* and birth experiences and how these experiences are later reflected in child and adult behaviors. Several themes emerge that challenge common myths about prenatal memory.

- Do Babies Remember?
- Is it Nurture v. Nature or Nurture/Nature?
- How Can the Genetic Map Be Enhanced?
- What are the Hazards of Being Unwanted?
- Is There Hope after a Rough and Bumpy Start?
- What Are Some Ways the Results of Rough Starts Show Up?
    Fear of Progress in Life—Isaac, the Kid Who Held Back
    Resurfacing Early Emotions—Greta's Old Pain
    Growing Up Again—Connie's Story
- Nurture/Nature Revisited

Babies Do Remember

To many people, the idea that fetal memory exists is absurd. They believe that babies cannot think before they are born or cannot feel real pain or emotions for some time afterward. Such assumptions led to the belief that we could say derogatory things to the baby because he or she wouldn't remember, and we could (and still sometimes do) perform circumcisions and other surgery on infants without anesthesia. Now we know that was a mistake.

Research shows that some children remember their births and can actually describe birth experiences until the age of three.[4] Many adults have reexperienced early traumas through spontaneous or guided regressions. Many more adults, upon getting specific information about their fetal, birth, or early childhood experiences, say, "Finally! That makes sense of some things in my adult life that I could not explain."

> *Research shows that the fetus both feels and builds memories throughout its development.*

Think of it in another way, and the idea that fetal memory does *not* exist is absurd. Why would we accept that the fetus develops from two cells into a complex human system, complete *except for* feelings and memory? Research shows that the fetus both feels and builds memories throughout its development.

Since the brain takes a long time to mature, a child's early memories are stored in the *early emotional memory system* (in the amygdala). Our usual recall is from the *declarative memory system* (in the hippocampus), which develops in later childhood. Therefore, in later life, early memories are often identified only through body work (such as massages, chiropractic, cranial sacral therapy, Traeger, Feldenkrais, Alexander Technique) or by relating otherwise unexplained attitudes, feelings, and behaviors to early traumas. Sometimes an infant's memory of prenatal experiences can be easily identified by observing the baby's behavior. Listen to the story of baby David.

The "Jeopardy" Story

David, just a few days old, was being rocked in the crook of Grandma's arm while his mother took a few peaceful minutes for herself. Television droned in the background and the 5:30 news was drawing to a close. David's eyes were busy studying his grandmother's face when he turned his head suddenly and quite deliberately toward the television. The look on his face was one of recognition and relieved satisfaction, just as an adult might look deeply pleased at the sight of a dear friend approaching. His mother walked into the room just in time to see all this. She smiled. David had turned his head toward the theme song for the television quiz show *Jeopardy*. His mother, a *Jeopardy* fan, had watched the program nearly every night of her pregnancy. It was apparent that David had not only heard the theme song before, but also it clearly had a calming effect on him. Discovering this effect was a boon. By singing the theme song, David's mother was able to calm him while he was waiting to be fed. This strategy worked well for the first three or four months of David's life.

Not only do babies benefit from the pleasure a mother gets watching a favorite television program, but also they benefit from intentional prenatal stimulation. Chairat Panthuraamphorn, who has researched the effects of prenatal stimulation, reports:

> While positive maternal emotions have been experimentally shown to increase later growth, alertness, calmness and intelligence—the fetus even benefits from the mother singing to it in the womb—and prenatal infant stimulation, particularly being bathed in pleasant music, improves fetal development compared to control groups.[5]

Nurture v. Nature or Nurture/Nature?

The amazing and powerful information that we can positively influence our child even before birth can energize us to improve the way we care for pregnant women and young children, but what of children who have had a less-than-desirable fetal experience? Is it too late for them? No. Can anything be done? Yes! Does the environment make a difference? YES!

For years people have argued over the relative importance of environment versus genetics in raising children. The question could start a lively debate in any gathering from the coffee shop to the academic conference. New parents could hear their infant pronounced lucky because "It's all in the genes; it's all there; look at this baby; she has everything she needs!" Then the next visiting adult pronounced with equal conviction, "She is so lucky to have you as parents because she will have the environment she needs and that's what counts."

As it turns out, both observations are correct. The explosion of information from research about the brain includes descriptions of how nature and nurture intertwine to build the brain. Driven by genetics, the brain creates nerve cells and lays out circuits to prepare for vision, language, and other functions. Then the flood of sensory experiences that the environment provides during gestation and following birth triggers a biochemical cascade that reaches not only the nucleus of the cells but also the coils of DNA in the genes.

Enhancing the Genetic Map

Instead of merely wondering if our child will be bright, we now know that we can enhance a child's genetic intelligence by providing the fetal experience of acceptance, love, and stimulation. But if it is possible to increase intelligence, can the prenatal and neonatal environment also decrease it? Yes, it is now commonly accepted that maternal distress and chemical toxins have been shown to produce not only low birth weights, increased infant mortality, respiratory infections, and asthma but also reduced cognitive development. For more information, read Thomas Verny's *The Secret Life of the Unborn Child*.[6]

Despite the good intentions of any parents, life can go awry during a pregnancy. Some difficulties can be eased—a woman who is depressed can find a listening friend, clergy person, or counselor to help her. Medical help can be sought for any illness, including depression. Other events are beyond the parents' control. The illness or death of a family member, the loss of a job, a betrayal in a relationship—these are just a few of the external events that can have a profound negative impact on the growing fetus.

> *A pregnant woman can deliberately comfort her fetus.*

There are strategies parents can use, however, when a negative stressor occurs. A pregnant woman can deliberately comfort her fetus by thinking reassuring thoughts, singing, and telling the aware being inside her body that she, the mother, will be in charge and that the fetus will be all right. *Baby dear, my sister is very ill and I am worried about her. You go ahead and grow. You don't need to worry about her or me. The grown-ups will take care of this. I'll let you know what we do, but this is our job, not yours. I'm glad you are safe and well.* Perhaps the words will not comfort the little being; but, since the mother's emotions produce hormones that are transmitted to the blood of the fetus, the confidence and calming will have a positive effect.

The most crucial period in a baby's development is the nine months prior to birth. Many parents find it helpful to have information about fetal development so they can track their child's progress.

> *The most crucial period in a baby's development is the nine months prior to birth.*

The little stand-up calendar *Affirmations for Your Healthy Pregnancy: Daily Affirmations with Fetal Developmental Stages*[7] is especially easy to use. Placed on a counter or a table, it offers one fact about fetal development and an affirmation for each day. For example, Week Five: Tuesday, your baby begins to form its heart, which at this stage is a single tube. "Dear little one, your mommy sends you lots of love from her heart to yours." or Week Seven: Sunday, your baby's lungs are in the process of forming. "Breathe in life, sweet baby! Life is our most precious gift." Laurie Kanyer's book *The Journey of Becoming a Mother*[8] looks at the needs of both the fetus and the parents.

The Hazards of Being Unwanted

Since the emotional state of the mother can have such a profound positive effect upon the fetus, could it not have a negative effect as well? Unfortunately, the answer is yes. Statistical studies have correlated negative maternal attitudes with negative effects on children, including premature births, more physical illness, and greater school failure. One of the most alarming findings is the correlation between maternal rejection during pregnancy and violent criminal behavior during the child's teen years. One Danish study showed that boys who were unwanted and who had difficult births were four times as likely as those in the control group to participate in violent crimes.[9]

This points to the importance of taking care of all infants in a society by supporting pregnant women and their children.

Hope after a Rough and Bumpy Start

Fortunately, not all birth traumas lead to violence. And, of course, not all problems in life are the result of prenatal, birth, or early childhood experiences. But, if early negative experiences are reinforced by a series of later happenings that echo the earlier trauma, the child can lay a foundation of mistrust that will have a profound influence in later life. However, positive early experiences can mitigate the effects of the earlier trauma. This is why early interventions are so vitally important. According to Dr. Craig Ramey, programs that have a high degree of success with infants to three-year-olds share the following six qualities:

- Encouragement of exploration
- Mentoring in basic skills
- Celebration of developmental advances
- Guided rehearsal and extension of new skills
- Protection from inappropriate disapproval, teasing, and punishment
- A rich and responsive language environment

All of us can replicate these qualities. A rich and responsive language environment is especially important for cognitive development. This includes both the worldwide singsong way parents and caretakers talk to babies and exposure to the extended vocabularies adults use with each other. It is the basis for all of the other learning subsystems. When you talk to your infant, you are creating patterns not only for later speech development, but also for math, music, and other forms of expression.

Fear of Progress in Life

Sometimes the early traumas do not get rewritten during childhood years, even in a thoughtful and supportive family. Then understanding the *potency* of early experiences and the propensity of the infant to use them as a basis for long-lasting decisions can help us look for clues to difficult behaviors in adolescents and adults. For example, therapists and researchers have documented the inclination of people who experienced prenatal trauma or problematic births to fear progress, growth, and individuation—perhaps to find all transitions difficult. Researcher Lynda Share suggests it is as if the fetus decided, "that going forward in life led to disaster; and that to hold back will avoid a repetition of the horrible start."[10]

Some people need therapeutic help to overcome this hesitance. With other people, the information and understanding are freeing and help them overcome their reticence. This knowledge can also help parents be more understanding of behavior that up until that point had been only perplexing. Consider the story of Isaac, a kid who held back.

Isaac, the Kid Who Held Back

As a preschooler, Isaac held back and watched a long time before he entered the play group. He started grade school without the excitement of the other kids who had been on the corner practicing waiting for the bus. He gradually became an excellent student. But in high school he was still slow to try new things. When the school attempted to motivate seniors to apply for colleges, he remained inactive.

Isaac's parents pondered the whys of this behavior pattern. They couldn't make sense of it because once Isaac finally decided to do something, he did it well. It was the *moving-on* part that could put the whole family in turmoil.

When Isaac's parents, during his senior year in high school, learned that *fear of going forward* often results from early trauma, they connected it with the fact that Isaac had almost died at birth. So, on the chance that this information would be helpful, they talked with Isaac about his birth. This discussion helped him make sense of his fears. Starting something new had always meant knots in his stomach for weeks and terrible dreams of trying to escape from life-threatening situations. Isaac's parents stopped being irritated with his procrastination, gave up commanding him to "get on with it," and turned to gentle nudges, reassurances, and support to help him apply for college entrance. Isaac moved somewhat less reluctantly and the family turmoil around his transitions ceased.

His parents decided how long they would give Isaac financial support for college and then left his decisions to him. Once in college, still a good student, he stayed a long time, always seeming to need one more quarter before leaving school and looking for a job. He was able to earn his own way and his family was able to say, "You can move on when you are ready."

Often, when we as parents understand the real cause or possible cause of children's behavior, we are able to switch from exasperation and irritation to some form of help and support that the child can accept. When we understand the real cause or possible causes of *our own* behavior we are able to switch from self-blame and shame to self-understanding and acceptance. We overcome our blocks or get the help we need to heal old wounds.

Early Emotions That Resurface

Since early experiences are encoded in the primitive part of the brain, not the conscious part of the brain, the pain from early trauma sometimes surfaces in later life in ways that can be very perplexing. When a grown-up says, "I can't think why I feel this way," that person may be speaking the truth. The person is not thinking with the part of the brain that holds the old memory. But the old pain can still come up in a demanding way as if it were saying, "Heal me now!"

Healing these old wounds often involves body work, emotional support, therapeutic support, spiritual support, or all four and more. Other times these pains can be handled in everyday life through a combination of nurture, willingness to grow, and perhaps luck and intuition. This was the case with Greta.

Greta's Old Pain

Greta was conceived during her parents' honeymoon and developed during a difficult pregnancy. Her mother had Asian flu twice, worried a great deal about the fetus, and regretted getting pregnant so soon. The birth was difficult. Greta was born before the family's new home was finished and before the newlyweds had successfully sorted out their husband and wife relationship, let alone their mother and father role expectations.

After a fussy infancy and a childhood fraught with illness, Greta entered adolescence with improved physical health and a generally sunny attitude. However, during her sixteenth year, she became moody and despondent, couldn't sleep or slept a lot, and acted more and more withdrawn.

Her parents did not know what was wrong, and neither did Greta. She could offer no reasons why she felt so lousy. Fearing that she might be seriously depressed, her parents were planning to get therapeutic help for her. Her father summed up their decision this way: "Your teenager has a toothache, you take her to the dentist. You don't try to fill a molar yourself. Besides, I don't have a clue how to help her with this." Her mother agreed but decided to try talking one more time, this time affirming, not asking, as questions about what was going on only brought irritable, "Nothing, go away" responses.

After Greta was in bed, her mother knelt by the side of the bed to deliberately give her daughter affirmations for being. The affirmations that support adolescent development (page 235) had been spurned by Greta so her mom decided to try the Being affirmations (see page 221), the messages at the base of decisions about identity. Greta buried her head in her pillow.

"Greta, listen to me." No response. "I'm glad you were born to this family." No response. "I'm glad you were born just who you are, a girl, who looks the way you look and thinks the way you think." Mumble. "I'm glad you were born when you were born."

Greta's voice lashed out, "No, you aren't! I've heard all my life about how I was born too soon and the house wasn't finished and there weren't any doorknobs and the neighbor's dog ran through the house! You're NOT glad I was born!"

> *I'm so glad you were born!*

Greta's mom drew in her breath, thought fast, and decided the whole truth would be the safest way to go. "Greta, what you say *is* true! I had so many dreams about how our nest would be ready for you and how I would take care of you and how you would be a healthy, smiling baby. It *was* too soon at that time and you were miserable and I was too. But Greta, I got past that. That was sixteen years ago and now it's fine with me. I had almost forgotten it. I didn't realize how important that was for you. But, if you *hadn't* been born, then I wouldn't have this very you here at this very time! I'm so glad you were born! Can you hear that? Can you let it be okay *now*? I truly am glad and I love you dearly!"

Greta opened one eye and peered suspiciously at her mother. "Are you sure?"

"Yes, I'm sure. Really, truly, I don't mind now. You are my darling daughter and I wouldn't have it any other way."

Greta sat up, hugged her mom, and announced that she was ready to sleep. And sleep she did. In the morning she was her cheerful, teasing self again. Awesome? Yes. Unusual? Maybe. Maybe many times we heal old wounds without knowing that is what we are doing.

Greta's mother hadn't known what the problem was. She told her husband, "I just went fishing and I happened to hit on it. Poor child. When we told those stories about the house not being done, it never occurred to us that they might be hurtful to Greta."

Greta's family was lucky. Greta was lucky because she had parents who were willing to notice what was going on and to take action. The parents were lucky because Greta's mother happened to find the key that unlocked the depression. They were also lucky that Greta was willing to accept the cause of her despair and to believe and incorporate the new health-giving messages. If the depression recurs, the family can call on the therapist. If Greta's mother had understood the impact of her experience during pregnancy, she could not have changed the Asian flu, but she could have deliberately offered the fetus comfort and reassurance instead of worry. And the parents could have been willing to accept Greta's birth time and encouraged everyone else to do that.

Sometimes problems stemming from a rough and bumpy start are solved this directly, but often the early wounds cannot be resolved by nurturing support alone. Then good therapeutic help is in order. Consider Connie's story.

Growing Up Again—Connie's Story

Connie had done therapy on all the issues about everyone important in her life. But something still didn't feel quite right. Then she happened to read *The Secret Life of the Unborn Child*,[11] in which Verny describes information gathered from researchers all over the world about how babies, before they are born, are so very aware of what's going on around them, inside the womb and out.

To Connie, this was miraculous information. *Well,* she thought, *no wonder I felt there was a piece missing! My birth mother was ashamed of being pregnant out of wedlock and knew immediately, for many reasons, she couldn't keep me. How could she have given me messages of wantedness when she was scared and secretive about sending me away?"*

Finding out about the many influences on a fetus led Connie to breakthroughs in her journey to heal the past. She grieved the loss of her birth mother and was able to surmise what her mother's messages to her must have been, "I'm so ashamed of being pregnant." "This is really hard. It's too painful for me to love you so go away." Somewhere, deep in her heart, Connie had known those messages all the time.

Corrective parenting therapy helped Connie put new messages of being wanted in place. She now experiences a fullness and joy not possible before.

Remember, experience is the chief architect of the brain. Not only do sensory experiences *in utero* become part of the wiring of the brain, but repeated experiences after birth can rewrite or override early physical traumas. This provides a profound basis of hope, for our children and for our own *growing up again*. Creating a firm attachment (see pages 43–45) with the child is a crucial factor in helping children recover from prenatal and birth trauma.

Now the nurture/nature formula reads like this:

1. During the prenatal period the *genetic map* (nature) is laid down and is influenced by positive and negative experiences (nurture). The *nurturing climate* includes nutrition, the mother's attitude, sounds, light, and touch from the world outside the womb.
2. Following birth the positive or negative treatment of the baby supports or alters the genetic material.
3. The child makes early coping decisions that can be affected both by further experiences (nurture) and by a genetic predisposition to some temperament style (nature).

As the research on the brain continues and becomes known, parents and society will find more and better ways of supporting positive growth of fetuses, infants, and children.

Remember, parents are responsible for the process, for providing the best environment they can. Children build their own thinking systems and make their own life decisions. Section 7 offers guidelines for doing the nurturing the first time around and for growing up again.

SECTION VII

Growing Up
Again and Again

Not many years ago I began to play the cello. Most people would say that what I am doing is "learning to play" the cello. But these words carry into our minds the strange idea that there exists two very different processes: 1) learning to play the cello; and 2) playing the cello. They imply that I will do the first until I have completed it, at which point I will stop the first process and begin the second; in short, that I will go on "learning to play" until I have "learned to play" and that then I will begin to play. Of course, this is nonsense. There are not two processes, but one. We learn to do something by doing it. There is no other way.

JOHN HOLT
author of *How Children Fail*

chapter 25

Ages and Stages

"It's just a stage she is going through. It's not important. Just ignore her and she'll forget it soon." That is what Mother said when Lois was eight and stubbornly pursued some interest that inconvenienced another family member. Was Mother right? Partly. Mother was right about stages, but wrong about their importance. We all go through stages as we grow and *each stage is important.* Children and adults need to be supported, not ignored, in their mastery of the developmental growth tasks for each stage. Lois may have forgotten the discounts she received, but the skills Lois learned and the decisions she makes at each stage remain with her unless overshadowed by later, bigger events or unless Lois deliberately decides to change them. Understanding the tasks of the various developmental stages can help her do this.

> We all go through stages as we grow and each stage is important.

In this section we will address

- What is a developmental stage?
- What are some developmental tasks of each stage?
- What is Growing Up Again?
- Charts for each stage
- Activities that support Growing Up Again—recycling and others

What Is a Stage?

A developmental stage is a describable segment of growing up. During each segment of time, the person is busy with age-appropriate tasks that help answer the all-important questions Who am I? Who am I in relation to others? and How do I acquire the skills that I need? Some tasks flow through each stage, for example, the path of spiritual growth as described by Mary Kaye Ashley. (See Supporting Spiritual Growth through the Early Developmental Stages in appendix A.) Other tasks seem more focused to specific stages.

We will use nine stages to describe development; but, since each person has his or her own timetable for growth, the ages listed are approximations. Here are the main questions to be addressed in each stage:

Prenatal Stage (Becoming)–conception to birth
Is it safe for me to develop fully and be born?

Stage 1 (Being)–birth to six months
Is it okay for me to be here, to make my needs known, and to be cared for?

Stage 2 (Doing)–six months to eighteen months
Is it safe for me to explore and try new things and to trust what I learn?

Stage 3 (Thinking)–eighteen months to three years
Is it okay for me to learn to think for myself?

Stage 4 (Identity and Power)–three years to six years
Is it okay for me to be who I am, with my unique abilities? Is it okay for me to find out who others are and learn the consequences of my behavior?

Stage 5 (Structure)–six years to twelve years
How do I build an internal structure that supports me and others? How do I develop the competence to master the technical and social skills I need to live in my culture?

Stage 6 (Identity, Sexuality, and Separation)–twelve years to nineteen years
How can I become a separate person with my own values and still belong? Is it okay for me to be independent, to honor my sexuality, and to be responsible?

Stage 7 (Interdependence)–adult
How will I balance my needs for competence, intimacy, connectedness, and separateness with the demands of caring for others, and how will I move from independence to interdependence?

Stage 8 (Integration)–adult
How do I complete the meaning of my life and prepare for leaving?

The experiences and decisions made at each developmental stage shape an adult's ability to offer and receive nurture and structure.

The Nurture/Structure Shield

How would you describe your ability to care for yourself and others if you were to think of it as having a concrete shape? Would it be an umbrella? A cloak? A bubble of white light? A shield?

We will use a shield as a symbol for the skills we use to nurture and structure ourselves and others. If you think of your ability as something other than a shield, as a cloak for example, each time you read "shield" change it to "cloak" so it will fit for you.

Our shields are built from the accumulation of our experiences in each developmental stage. By examining our experiences and decisions from each stage, we can see the many skills we have developed that are working well for us, and we can also see the holes, the gaps, we need to repair or fill in. If you would like to try a visualization exercise to picture your shield, cloak, or whatever symbol you choose, use the guided imagery exercise at the end of the book. (See Seeing Our Own Shields in appendix B.)

When children experience consistent, loving parenting, they have the opportunity to build strong shields. But such consistent loving comes only from mature, dedicated, healthy parents whose parenting efforts are continuous. Many of us grew up with adults whose energy was diverted from us by alcohol or other drugs or by compulsive relationships with food, people, work, or religion. They may have neglected or abused us physically, sexually, or psychologically because of their own pain or inhibited development. For these and many other reasons such as war, poverty, or illness, our parents weren't able to meet our needs adequately.

It is interesting that although such families suffer from very different problems, the effects of uneven parenting are much the same. From the outside, for example, a family with a member addicted to alcohol may look very different from a family that adheres to rigid religious practices or one struggling to care for a chronic invalid. In the end, the dynamics of neglect are often the same: Children in those situations lack the opportunity to develop the nurture and structure that builds strong shields.

Although such families suffer from very different problems, the effects of uneven parenting are much the same.

Also, our shields, like trees, are strongest if they have a healthy center. The center is the part we acquired during childhood. If our shields have holes in the center part, we have probably learned to deny and discount our needs and to defend our early decisions. Such decisions, which were necessary at one time, can be damaging to us now. We need to begin repairing those holes or weak spots.

What Is Growing Up Again?

Growing up again and again is getting what we missed earlier so we don't have to go on living without what we need now. We grow up again so we can parent better, so we can feel more alive. Growing up again is the process of choosing *one* small hole at a time in our shields and filling it in, or repairing one small corner of a large hole.

> *Growing up again and again is getting what we missed earlier so we don't have to go on living without what we need now.*

"But, I don't want to grow up again," you might say. "Isn't it enough that I got through childhood the first time? Who wants to go back and relive old pain?" Claudia Black points out in her book *It Will Never Happen to Me*[1] that we must go back or the pain does happen again. The pain, the old behavior, the old patterns never really get resolved unless we go back and recognize the parts of our experiences that were painful. Then we can truly grow up again. Fortunately, growing up again is about going forward. It is the process of being active in ways that help us make new decisions and use new behaviors.

How Do We Know When We Need to Grow Up Again?

Several signals let adults know it is time to do some growing up again. You may suspect a hole in your shield if an uncomfortable number of the discounting examples sounded all too familiar, or if structure still sounds like criticism, or if you continue to reject nurture. You can use the Ages and Stages charts in this chapter to help you assess, by developmental stage, the strengths and holes in your shield.

How Do We Grow Up Again?

There are several ways to grow up again. Sometimes we teach ourselves how to grow up again as we learn to parent our children well.

Living with children working on specific developmental tasks seems to stimulate parents to rework those same tasks. For example, when a two-year-old is saying no and being resistant, the parents often find themselves feeling resistant and refurbishing their ability to say no and to think independently.

We also strengthen our shields as we experience the rhythms of our own growth, moving through the developmental tasks of our adult years (page 238) at the same time we recycle or learn to do earlier tasks in more sophisticated ways. For example, the identity tasks, the job of defining who we are, are recycled every time we experience a major change such as marriage, divorce, giving birth, losing family members, losing a mental or physical capacity, or attaining a new level of competency. Pamela Levin describes her helpful theory of recycling in her book *Becoming the Way We Are*.[2]

The Ages and Stages charts on pages 218–242 include examples of tasks adults can recycle for each developmental level, to support the process of Growing Up Again. When we missed a great deal the first time we grew up, however, when the holes in our shields are large, the activities suggested in *Growing Up Again* will not be enough to repair them. Then we need the help of competent support groups, therapists, or therapy groups to help us with our healing. (See Where to Go For Additional Help in appendix B.)

Stay Underwhelmed

Many of us, when we glimpse what we can do to improve our lives, want to do it all at once. We want to be finished last week. Some of us may even have gone to a therapist and said, "Fix me. NOW."

We want to grow up fast.

It doesn't work that way. It works more like this: a sharp upward growth swing, and then a plateau while we consolidate new skills, attitudes, and beliefs. Often there is a little backsliding or turmoil before we start the next growth swing. If you feel discouraged, remember that as you grow up again, each plateau is higher than the last. Growing up again is a process, not a one-time accomplishment. When you feel impatient, repeat to yourself:

> *Growing up again is a process, not a one-time accomplishment.*

- One hole at a time
- One task at a time
- One experience at a time
- One new decision at a time
- One new behavior at a time
- One day at a time

Each hole you repair will strengthen your entire shield and make future growing up again easier. Visualize yourself with your eyes filled with wonder and appreciation. Remember, you can be scared and still think and go ahead. Healing involves grieving for what you had or did not have. Part of the grief work will include facing your anger[3] and frustration. Eventually you will reach the place where you can notice another bit of repair work and say, "Okay. What is it I am to learn now? I may as well get on with it."

Meanwhile, you can grow at your own pace. Stay underwhelmed.

Using the Ages and Stages Charts

You can use the charts on the next pages to remind yourself of what your children need and what you need. Each chart includes the following:

- A brief list of important *developmental tasks* for that particular stage
- *Behaviors common* to children of that stage
- *Affirmations* focusing on the tasks of that stage
- Parent *behaviors that are helpful* and ones that are *unhelpful* for children of that age
- *Tasks adults may revisit* while they are recycling each stage
- *Clues to growing up again* (a sample of attitudes and behaviors that can indicate the need for adults to rework developmental tasks from that stage)
- *Activities that support growing up again* (examples of small and big things that adults can do to support healing and growing)

A developmental chart specifically for adopted children appears on pages 269–270.

The Power of Affirmations

The specific affirming messages we need to hear and learn to give at each stage of growth are included in each stage chart. Developmental Affirmations: How to Use Them in appendix B suggests ways you can incorporate the developmental affirmations into your life.

Affirmations can be delivered by look, word, or deed. They can be offered as gifts, said, sung, or acted upon. There is more information about affirmations in the book *Self-Esteem: A Family Affair*[4] by Jean Illsley Clarke.

If you are familiar with the power of affirmations, you already know that the developmental affirmations can help you identify the exact messages that you and your children need. If affirmations are new to you, a few words about them are in order.
An *affirmation* is anything we say or do for others to let them know that we believe they are lovable and capable. Affirming encourages self-esteem. But the affirmations we deliver to others must be sincere or they become crazy-making double-bind messages.

Self-affirmations are all the things we say, do, think, and feel, externally and internally, that indicate we are lovable and capable. Self-affirming builds our self-esteem and self-love and can be especially important when we are tempted to discount our needs and not believe that the affirmations are important or true for us. We can start using the developmental affirmations by saying the messages to ourselves as "you" messages, speaking from our own nurturing parent to the child within us—"I'm glad *you're* alive."

> It is important to use "I" messages to ourselves only when we have chosen them and not because someone else told us to say them.

Later, we can affirm ourselves with an "I" message, when the child within is willing to make that statement as a celebration or to claim that statement as a conviction that the inner child does believe or wants to believe—"I'm glad *I'm* alive."

It is important to use "I" messages to ourselves only when *we* have chosen them and not because someone else told us to say them. Self-esteem cannot be built around the desire to please someone else; it is an internal process about an internal set of beliefs. Affirming ourselves and visualizing ourselves as if the affirmations we have chosen are already true help us make them so.

Prenatal Stage, Becoming
From Conception to Birth

The prenatal stage lays the groundwork for all the stages to follow. During these nine months, if all goes well, the baby's body is developing from the genetic gift of the egg and the sperm to a full-term infant with all life-support systems intact or ready to grow to full potential. Simultaneously, the new being is making life-shaping decisions in response to the environment of the womb and the relationship experiences of the mother with other people and with the baby.

1. Job of the prenatal child (developmental tasks)

- To grow; to develop all body systems.
- To experience the ultimate in being separate and connected at the same time.
- To accept nourishment, acceptance, reassurance, and love.
- To move—starting early, probably by week ten when still under two inches long. (By week twenty the mother can feel the movement.)
- To gain a familiarity with the mother.
- To recognize voices (father and others) and begin to learn language (at least by six months).
- To form some deep decisions about trust.
- To initiate and move through the birth process.

2. Typical behaviors of the prenatal child

- Develops a sleeping and waking rhythm.
- Turns away from, or gives other physical responses to, a bright light or a loud sound, an amniocentesis needle, or other intrusion.
- Stops drinking when amniotic fluid is toxic (e.g., alcohol).
- Learns to recognize the voice of the mother and father or other close people.
- May learn to respond. For example, baby kicks. If parent taps that spot three times and says, "kick again," baby may kick again.

3. Affirmations for becoming[5]

BECOMING
I celebrate that you are alive.

BECOMING
Your needs and safety are important to me.

BECOMING
We are connected and you are whole.

BECOMING
You can make healthy decisions about your experiences.

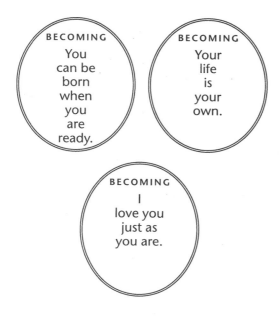

BECOMING
You can be born when you are ready.

BECOMING
Your life is your own.

BECOMING
I love you just as you are.

4. Helpful parent behaviors

- Mother gets proper nutrition, exercise, and rest.
- Mother gets helpful prenatal medical care.
- Father provides for and protects mother.
- Both mother and father review their own prenatal experiences and resolve any leftover traumas from that period of their growth.
- Both parents resolve their grief from any prior miscarriage losses.
- Both parents examine their expectations for this child and put those aside so they can welcome this child for who he or she is.
- Both parents talk and sing lovingly to the child.
- Both parents experience joy about this child and other parts of their lives.

- Both parents prepare the extended families to welcome this child in his or her uniqueness.
- Both parents prepare for the birth, by setting up a crib, gathering clothing, and so on.
- Mother arranges for a trusted female support person, a labor doula, to be present at the birth.
- Both parents determine how to spend the most time possible with the child after birth. If needed, they find the best surrogate parent possible.
- Parents identify ways they will take care of each other and help each other get their needs met after the baby is born when the majority of their caring energy and time will be directed toward the baby.
- Parents anticipate balancing their new roles as parents with their partnership contracts.
- Parents line up ongoing support for their "new family."
- If child is to be adopted or relinquished to adoption, see chapter 27.

5. Unhelpful parent behaviors

- Mother's use of alcohol, nicotine, or other harmful substances.
- Father's lack of support for mother's abstinence.
- Either parent ignoring the pregnancy, for example, neglecting sleep, nutrition, and exercise needs.
- Either parent thinking/talking about the fetus as a burden instead of taking responsibility for the pregnancy and doing necessary problem solving.
- Speaking roughly to the fetus.

- Either parent being proud of the mother's "not showing."
- Physical or verbal abuse.
- Mother failing to get proper monitoring or medical care.
- Either parent failing to find a way out of emotional distress.

6. Becoming tasks adults may recycle
- To take excellent care of own physical health.
- To reexperience needs for dependency and support.
- To update old decisions about trust.
- To celebrate the joy of being alive.
- To grieve any mishaps during own prenatal stage or birth.

7. Clues to a need for adults to grow up again
- Feeling an unaccounted for incompleteness in self.
- Lack of joyfulness not otherwise accounted for.
- Stuck, not able to get started and no words to describe that feeling.
- Any addiction, compulsive behavior.
- Water—strong desire to be in water or reaction against being in water.
- Eating—struggle to get food or wanting to be waited on or served.
- Boundaries—need to sleep all curled up and tucked in or reaction against someone who gets too close.
- Believing you have to do everything by yourself, trying to start things and not finishing.
- Feelings of grandiosity or abject worthlessness.

- Self-destructive behaviors, recklessness, extreme risk taking.
- Strong and intense reactions to minor disappointments.
- Irrational fears or chronic anxiety not otherwise accounted for.
- Chronic depression.
- Thoughts of suicide.

8. Activities that support growing up again
- Suspend disbelief that pre- and perinatal experiences matter. (See chapter 24).
- Treat yourself to a therapeutic massage or body wrap.
- Listen to lullabies while wrapped up closely in blankets.
- Perform rhythmic movements (e.g., swing in a hammock, sit in a rocking chair, row a boat).
- Take naps with a sheet over your face.
- Eat comfort foods like bananas.
- Do therapy with a skillful, corrective parenting practitioner; try kinesthetic, body-memory, affective therapies.
- Eat twenty minutes before a warm bath so you feel satisfied in your tummy. Listen to soothing music or affirmations during your bath. (Use of hot tubs and Jacuzzis needs to be checked with medical advisor, especially during pregnancy.)
- Ask someone to hold you heart to heart in a nonsexual way and hum with no talking.
- Listening to fetal heart sounds or mother's heartbeat tapes and meditate.

Stage 1, Being
From Birth to Six Months

Stage 1 is about deciding to be, to live, to thrive, to trust, to call out to have needs met, to expect to have needs met, to be joyful. These decisions are important to nourish and amplify throughout our whole lives.

1. Job of the child (developmental tasks)

- To call for care.
- To cry or otherwise signal to get needs met.
- To accept touch.
- To accept nurture.
- To bond emotionally, to learn to trust caring adults and self.
- To decide to live, to be.

2. Typical behaviors of the child

- Cries or fusses to make needs known.
- Cuddles.
- Makes lots of sounds.
- Looks at and responds to faces, especially eyes.
- Imitates.

3. Affirmations for being

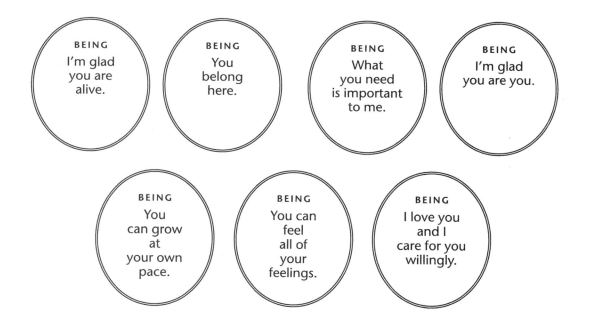

BEING
I'm glad you are alive.

BEING
You belong here.

BEING
What you need is important to me.

BEING
I'm glad you are you.

BEING
You can grow at your own pace.

BEING
You can feel all of your feelings.

BEING
I love you and I care for you willingly.

4. Helpful parent behaviors

- Affirm child for doing developmental tasks.
- Provide loving, consistent care.
- Respond to infant's needs.
- Think for baby.
- Hold and look at baby while feeding.
- Talk to child and echo child's sounds.
- Nurture by touching, looking, talking, and singing.
- Get help when unsure of how to care for baby.
- Be reliable and trustworthy.
- Get others to nurture you.

5. Unhelpful parent behaviors

- Not responding to baby's signals.
- Not touching or holding enough.
- Rigid, angry, agitated responses.
- Feeding before baby signals.
- Punishment.
- Lack of healthy physical environment.
- Lack of protection, including from older siblings.
- Criticizing child for anything.
- Discounting.

6. Being tasks adults may recycle

- To ask for care.
- To find ways to get own needs met.
- To accept touch that you want.
- To accept nurture.
- To bond emotionally, to learn to trust caring adults and self.
- To decide to be and live more fully.

7. Clues to a need for adults to grow up again

- Not trusting others.
- Wanting others to know what you need without your asking.
- Not knowing what you need.
- Not needing anything. Feeling numb.
- Believing others' needs are more important than yours.
- Not trusting others to come through for you.
- Not wanting to be touched, or compulsive touching or joyless sexual touching.
- Unwillingness to disclose information about self, especially negative information.

8. Activities that support growing up again

- Use and adapt this stage's "Helpful parent behaviors" to care for your inner child.
- Take a warm bath and get a therapeutic massage.
- Sing lullabies to the little child in you.
- Get more hugs.
- Close your eyes. Visualize yourself as a child. If the all-perfect mother or father could see this child right now, what would she or he do? What would she or he say? Do those things and say those things to yourself or ask someone who loves you to do or say those things for you.
- Do something to make your house more comfortable.
- If you have not done so, grieve any untimely infant separation from parents (hospitalization, divorce, adoption).
- Get therapy if you need it.

> ## Stage 2, Doing
> ### *From Six Months to Eighteen Months*
> Stage 2—the "doing" stage—is a powerful time when it is important for the child to decide to trust others, to trust that it is safe and wonderful to explore, to trust his or her senses, to know what he or she knows, to be creative and active, and to get support while doing all these things.

1. Job of the child (developmental tasks)

- To explore and experience the environment.
- To develop sensory awareness by using all senses.
- To signal needs; to trust others and self.
- To continue forming secure attachments with parents.
- To get help in times of distress.
- To start to learn that there are options and not all problems are easily solved.
- To develop initiative.
- To continue tasks from stage 1.

2. Typical behaviors of the child

- Tests all senses by exploring the environment.
- Is curious.
- Is easily distracted.
- Wants to explore on own but be able to retrieve caregiver at will.
- Starts patty-cake and peek-a-boo.
- Starts using words during middle or latter part of stage.

3. Affirmations for doing

DOING
You can explore and experiment and I will support and protect you.

DOING
You can use all of your senses when you explore.

DOING
You can do things as many times as you need to.

DOING
You can know what you know.

DOING
You can be interested in everything.

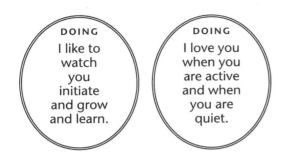

DOING
I like to watch you initiate and grow and learn.

DOING
I love you when you are active and when you are quiet.

4. *Helpful parent behaviors*

- Affirm child for doing developmental tasks.
- Continue to offer love.
- Provide a safe environment.
- Protect child from harm.
- Continue to provide food, nurturing touch, and encouragement.
- Say two yesses for every no.
- Provide a variety of sensory experiences (massages, music, peek-a-boo and patty-cake, pots and pans, blocks, soft toys, toys that make noise, etc.) for child.
- Refrain from interrupting child when possible.
- Refrain from interpreting child's behavior. "You like looking at yourself in the mirror."
- Instead, report child's behavior. "Emma is looking in the mirror."
- Echo sounds child makes.
- Talk to child a lot.
- Respond when child initiates play.
- Take care of own needs.

5. *Unhelpful parent behaviors*

- Fails to provide protection.
- Restricts mobility.
- Criticizes or shames child for exploring or for anything.
- Punishment.
- Expects child not to touch "precious" objects.
- Expects toilet training.
- Discounts.

6. *Doing tasks adults may recycle*

- To explore and experience the environment in new and safe ways.
- To enhance sensory awareness by using all senses.
- To signal needs; to trust others who are trustworthy; to trust self.
- To continue forming secure attachments with loving, caring people.
- To get help in times of distress.
- To find options and accept that not all problems are easily solved.
- To expand initiative.
- To continue tasks from stage 1.

7. *Clues to a need for adults to grow up again*

- Boredom.
- Reluctance to initiate.
- Being overactive or overquiet.
- Avoiding doing things unless you are able to do them perfectly.
- Being compulsively neat.
- Not knowing what you know.
- Thinking it is okay not to be safe, supported, protected.

8. *Activities that support growing up again*

- Use and adapt this stage's "Helpful parent behaviors" to care for your inner child.
- Explore your house on your hands and knees. Notice how different things look.
- Ask a friend to take you some place you have never been before.

- Explore some safe objects. Shake, smell, taste, look at, listen to, stack the objects. Pay close attention to the objects. Think how you feel when you devote yourself to learning about familiar things in a new way.
- Explore new talents, foods, activities, and cultures.
- Drive to work a different way.
- Get therapy if you need it.

Stage 3, Thinking
From Eighteen Months to Three Years

In order to separate from parents, children must learn to think and solve problems. Learning to express and handle feelings is also important. These lessons are the focus of stage 3—the "thinking" stage.

---

1. *Job of the child (developmental tasks)*

- To establish ability to think for self.
- To test reality, to push against boundaries and other people.
- To learn to think and solve problems with cause-and-effect thinking.
- To start to follow simple safety commands: stop, come here, stay here, go there.
- To express anger and other feelings.
- To separate from parents without losing their love.

- To start to give up beliefs about being the center of the universe.
- To continue tasks from earlier stages.

2. *Typical behaviors of the child*

- Begins cause-and-effect thinking.
- Starts parallel play.
- Starts to be orderly, even compulsive.
- Sometimes follows simple commands, sometimes resists.
- Tests behaviors: "No, I won't, and you can't make me."
- May try out the use of tantrums.

3. Affirmations for thinking

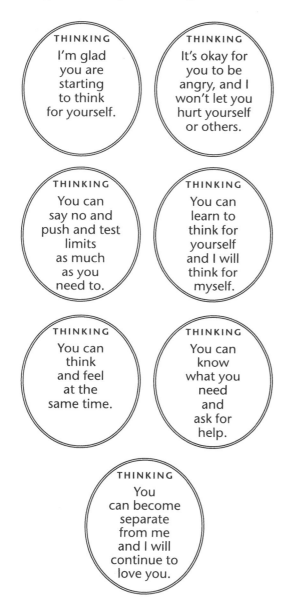

THINKING
I'm glad you are starting to think for yourself.

THINKING
It's okay for you to be angry, and I won't let you hurt yourself or others.

THINKING
You can say no and push and test limits as much as you need to.

THINKING
You can learn to think for yourself and I will think for myself.

THINKING
You can think and feel at the same time.

THINKING
You can know what you need and ask for help.

THINKING
You can become separate from me and I will continue to love you.

4. Helpful parent behaviors

- Affirm child for doing developmental tasks.
- Continue to offer cuddling, love, safety, and protection.
- Help child transition from one activity to another.
- Give simple, clear directions child can follow; encourage and praise achievement.
- Teach child basic safety commands, (e.g., come, no, go, sit, stay).[6]
- Set reasonable limits and enforce them.
- Celebrate child's new thinking ability.
- Provide time and space for child to organize thinking.
- Accept positive and negative expression of feelings.
- Teach options for expressing feelings instead of hitting or biting.
- Encourage cause-and-effect thinking.
- Expect child to think about own feelings and start to think about others' feelings.
- Provide reasons, explain "how-to's," and give other information.
- Teach names of things.
- Refrain from getting into win/lose battles.
- Remain constant in face of child's tantrums or outbursts; neither give in nor overpower.
- Think of and refer to child as a "terrific two."
- Take care of own needs.

5. *Unhelpful parent behaviors*

- Use too many don'ts and not enough dos.
- Get caught in power struggles.
- Try to appear to be a good parent by having a compliant child.
- Refer to child as a "terrible two."
- Refuse to set limits or expectations.
- Set expectations too high.
- Expect child to play "with" other children before learning to play "near" others.
- Refuse to use discipline for not thinking.
- Shame child.
- Discount.

6. *Thinking tasks adults may recycle*

- To reaffirm ability to think for self.
- To test reality, to reexamine boundaries and push against other people in safe ways when needed.
- To expand ability to solve problems using cause-and-effect thinking.
- To be able to follow simple or complex commands with adult evaluation, without being overly adaptive or rebellious.
- To express anger and other feelings appropriately.
- To separate from relationships or change parts of relationships when needed.
- To replace codependent attitudes and behaviors with self-reliance.
- To give up any remnants of an old belief about being the center of the universe and to encourage high esteem for self and others.
- To continue recycling tasks from earlier stages.

7. *Clues to a need for adults to grow up again*

- Inappropriate rebelliousness (chip on shoulder).
- Rather be right than successful.
- Bullying and use of anger to cover fear or sadness.
- Think the world revolves around self.
- Fear of anger in self or others.
- Saying no or yes without thinking.
- Scared to say no; allow others to dominate.
- Indirect expressions of anger through behaviors.

8. *Activities that support growing up again*

- Use and adapt this stage's "Helpful parent behaviors" to care for your inner child.
- Make a "No List" of things it is important for you to say no to and say no to them.
- Get a new recipe or something to assemble. Follow directions exactly. Get three people to tell you how well you did.
- Do something to improve your memory. Learn about memory: Read a book, take a workshop, practice. Pick seven things it is important for you to remember and remember them.
- Get therapy if you need it.

Stage 4, Identity and Power
From Three Years to Six Years

The tasks of this stage focus on learning and activities that help the child establish an individual identity, learn skills, and figure out role and power relationships with others.

1. Job of the child (developmental tasks)

- To assert an identity separate from others.
- To acquire information about the world, self, body, and sex role.
- To learn that behaviors have consequences.
- To discover effect on others and place in groups.
- To learn to exert power to affect relationships.
- To practice socially appropriate behavior.
- To separate fantasy from reality.
- To learn extent of personal power.
- To continue learning earlier developmental tasks.

2. Typical behaviors of the child

- Engages in fantasy play, possibly with imaginary companions.
- Gathers information: how, why, when, how long, and so on.
- Tries on different identity roles by role playing.
- Starts learning about power relationships by watching and setting up power struggles.
- Practices behaviors for sex-role identification.
- Starts cooperative play.
- Practices socially appropriate behavior.
- Begins interest in games and rules.

3. Affirmations for identity and power

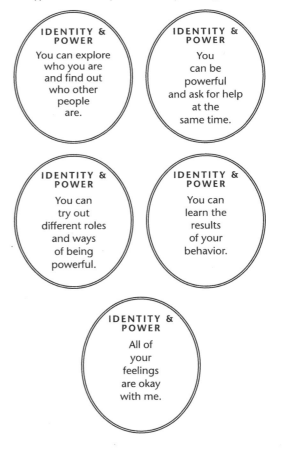

IDENTITY & POWER
You can explore who you are and find out who other people are.

IDENTITY & POWER
You can be powerful and ask for help at the same time.

IDENTITY & POWER
You can try out different roles and ways of being powerful.

IDENTITY & POWER
You can learn the results of your behavior.

IDENTITY & POWER
All of your feelings are okay with me.

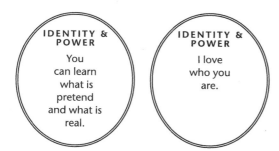

IDENTITY & POWER
You can learn what is pretend and what is real.

IDENTITY & POWER
I love who you are.

4. Helpful parent behaviors
- Affirm child for doing developmental tasks.
- Continue to offer love, safety, and protection.
- Be supportive as child continues to explore the world of things, people, ideas, and feelings.
- Encourage child to enjoy being a boy or a girl; teach that both sexes are okay.
- Expect child to express feelings and to connect feelings and thinking.
- Provide information about child's environment and correct misinformation.
- Give answers to questions.
- Provide appropriate positive or negative consequences for actions.
- Use language that is clear about who is responsible for what. (See Encouraging Responsibility through Language in appendix A.)
- Encourage child's fantasies and separation of fantasy and reality.
- Compliment appropriate behavior.
- Respond matter-of-factly and accurately to child's curiosity about the human body and the differences between boys and girls.

- Maintain contact with supportive people who help nurture self.
- Resolve own identity problems that surface.

5. Unhelpful parent behaviors
- Teases.
- Is inconsistent.
- Not expecting child to think for self.
- Unwilling to answer questions.
- Ridicule of role play or fantasies.
- Responds to child's fantasies as if real.
- Uses fantasy to frighten or confuse child.
- Engages in judgments or arguments over who is right or wrong or who/what is better or worse.
- Discounts.

6. Identity and power tasks adults may recycle
- To maintain an identity separate from others.
- To update information about the world, self, body, and sex role.
- To choose behaviors based on the consideration that all behaviors have consequences, positive or negative or both.
- To learn socially appropriate behavior for new roles and situations.
- To expand ability to separate fantasy from reality.
- To examine own personal and cultural frame of reference for archaic prejudices.
- To access accurately what you have power over and what you do not have power over and to exercise your power to enhance self and others.

- To continue recycling earlier developmental tasks.

7. Clues to a need for adults to grow up again

- Having to be in a position of power.
- Afraid of, or reluctant to use, power.
- Unsure of personal adequacy.
- Identity confusion—needing to define self by a job or relationship.
- Feeling driven to achieve.
- Overuse of outlandish dress or behavior.
- Frequently comparing self to others and needing to come off better.
- Wanting or expecting magical solutions or effects.

8. Activities that support growing up again

- Use and adapt this stage's "Helpful parent behaviors" to care for your inner child.
- Make a list of ten things you would like to do.
- Give or go to a costume party.
- Join a men's group if you are a man or a women's group if you are a woman. Talk and think about your idea of sex roles.
- Find out about a different job or career.
- Write a story starting with "In my next life I will . . ."
- Learn about appropriate manners to use in another culture.
- Get therapy if you need it.

Stage 5, Structure
From Six Years to Twelve Years

During stage 5, children learn more about structure and install their own internal structure. This includes understanding the need for rules, the freedom that comes from having appropriate rules, and the relevancy of rules. Examining the values on which rules are based is important. Another major task of this stage is acquiring many kinds of skills.

---

1. Job of the child (developmental tasks)

- To learn skills, learn from mistakes, and decide to be adequate.
- To learn to listen in order to collect information and think.
- To practice thinking and doing.
- To reason about wants and needs.
- To check out family rules and learn about structures outside the family.
- To learn the relevancy of rules.
- To experience the consequences of breaking rules.
- To disagree with others and still be loved.

- To test ideas and values and learn value options beyond the family.
- To develop internal controls.
- To learn what is one's own responsibility and what is the responsibility of others.
- To learn when to flee, when to flow, and when to stand firm.
- To develop the capacity to cooperate.
- To test abilities against others.
- To identify with one's own sex.
- To continue to learn earlier tasks.

2. Typical behaviors of the child

- Asks questions and gathers information.
- Practices and learns skills.
- Belongs to same-sex groups or clubs.
- Compares, tests, disagrees with, sets, breaks, and experiences consequences of rules.
- Challenges parental values, argues, and hassles.
- May be open and affectionate, cantankerous, or self-contained, or may alternate among these.

3. Affirmations for structure

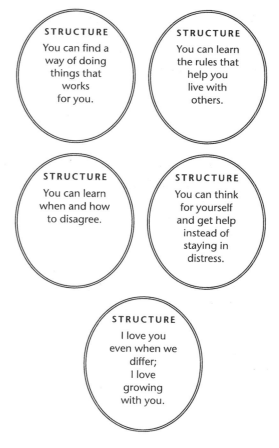

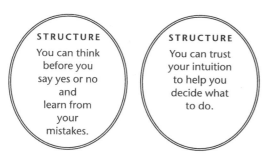

4. Helpful parent behaviors

- Affirm child for doing developmental tasks.
- Continue to offer love, safety, and protection.
- Make an accurate assessment of the safety of child's world and teach conflict-resolution skills.[7]
- Affirm child's efforts to learn to do things in own way.
- Give lots of love and lots of positive strokes for learning skills.

- Be a reliable source of information about people, the world, and sex.
- Challenge negative behavior and decisions; encourage cause-and-effect thinking.
- Confront discounting.
- Be clear about who is responsible for what.
- Affirm child's ability to think logically and creatively.
- Offer problem-solving tools.
- Discuss with child how and when to flee, flow, or fight.
- Set and enforce needed nonnegotiable and negotiable rules.
- Allow child to experience nonhazardous natural consequences for actions and ways of doing things.
- Point out that you continue to care for child even when child disagrees with you.
- Promote the separation of reality from fantasy by encouraging child to report accurately.
- Be alert to teenage-type behaviors and discourage child from growing up too fast.
- Be responsible yourself and encourage child to be responsible for own decisions, thinking, and feeling. (See Encouraging Responsibility through Language in appendix A.)
- Encourage child's skills development by finding teachers and mentors in the area of child's interest: first, a teacher who is encouraging and enthusiastic, then one who teaches skills and insists on quality performance; still later, probably not until adolescence, one who acts as model and mentor.[8]

5. *Unhelpful parent behaviors*
- Uneven enforcement of rules.
- Insisting on perfection.
- Expecting child to learn needed skills without instructions, help, or standards.
- Filling all of child's time with lessons, teams, and activities so child lacks the unstructured time to explore interests and learn the relevancy of rules.
- Overindulging child by not insisting on completion of household chores and other ways of being a contributing family member.
- Unwillingness to allow child to feel miserable for brief times.
- Rules and values too rigid or lacking.
- Unwillingness or lack of ability to discuss beliefs and values, to reevaluate rules, and to expect child to develop skills for personal responsibility.
- Discounting.

6. *Structure tasks adults may recycle*
- To become adequate at new skills and to continue to learn from mistakes.
- To expand ability to listen, look, and experiment in order to collect information and think.
- To expand your intuitive abilities.
- To become more clear about the difference between wants and needs.
- To evaluate family rules and learn about structures inside and outside the family.
- To examine the relevancy of old personal and family rules.
- To be willing to accept the consequences of breaking rules without blaming or whining.

- To improve skills for disagreeing with others and still being able to stay connected with them.
- To test ideas and values and learn value options beyond the family and beyond your own culture.
- To examine your internal controls and be sure they are helping you accomplish what you want for your life.
- To reassess what is your own responsibility and what is others' responsibility and set appropriate boundaries.
- To increase your capacity to cooperate.
- To choose when to test abilities against others, when against standards, and when against self.
- To identify with your own sex in supportive ways.
- To continue to learn earlier tasks.

7. Clues to a need for adults to grow up again

- Having to be part of a "gang" or only functioning well as a loner.
- Not understanding the relevance of rules.
- Not understanding the freedom that rules can give.
- Unwillingness to examine own values or morals.

- Needing to be king or queen of the hill.
- Trusting the thinking of the group more than your own thinking and intuition.
- Expecting to have to do things without knowing how, finding out, or being taught how.
- Being reluctant to learn new things or be productive.

8. Activities that support growing up again

- Use and adapt this stage's "Helpful parent behaviors" to care for the child in you.
- Join a club and figure out what the rules are.
- Watch television for one evening and list the morals and values presented. Compare the number of alcoholic drinks versus cups of coffee or tea, soft drinks versus water, incidents of violence versus incidents of nurturing, and so on.
- Clean and organize something—closet, drawers, sewing kit, tool kit, garage.
- Learn a new system of organization.
- Learn a new skill.
- Get therapy if you need it.

Stage 6, Identity, Sexuality, and Separation
From Twelve Years to Nineteen Years

The tasks of this stage focus on identity, separation, sexuality, and increased competence.

---

1. Job of the adolescent (developmental tasks)

- To take more steps toward independence.
- To achieve a clearer emotional separation from family.
- To emerge gradually, as a separate, independent person with own identity and values.
- To be competent and responsible for own needs, feelings, and behaviors.
- To integrate sexuality into the earlier developmental tasks.

2. Typical behaviors of the adolescent

Adolescents make some of their identity and separation choices by revisiting or recycling the tasks of earlier stages—being, doing, thinking, identity and power, and structure—with new information and with the sometimes confusing pressures of their emerging sexuality. Therefore, adolescents may act very grown up one moment and immature the next. The ages at which they usually recycle and incorporate these earlier tasks are as follows:

Onset of puberty or about age thirteen, recycling the being and the doing or exploratory stages of infancy:

- Sometimes independent and sometimes wanting to be fed and cared for.
- Exploring new areas without necessarily being concerned with standards or finishing.

Age fourteen, recycling age two and independent thinking:

- Sometimes reasonable and competent with intermittent rebellious outbursts.

Ages fifteen, sixteen, and seventeen, recycling ages three to five years, and identity and power:

- Asking questions, "Why?" and "How come?" Working out new role identity with same sex and opposite sex with both peers and adults. Learning to solve complex problems.

Ages sixteen through nineteen, recycling ages six to twelve years, and structure.

- Being adult and responsible with sudden short journeys back to earlier rule-testing behaviors.
- May also break rules as part of separation from parent.

3. *Affirmations for identity, sexuality, and separation*

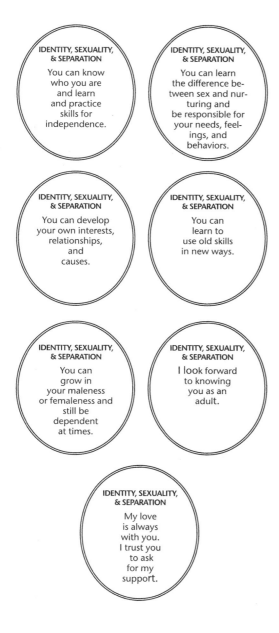

IDENTITY, SEXUALITY, & SEPARATION

You can know who you are and learn and practice skills for independence.

IDENTITY, SEXUALITY, & SEPARATION

You can learn the difference between sex and nurturing and be responsible for your needs, feelings, and behaviors.

IDENTITY, SEXUALITY, & SEPARATION

You can develop your own interests, relationships, and causes.

IDENTITY, SEXUALITY, & SEPARATION

You can learn to use old skills in new ways.

IDENTITY, SEXUALITY, & SEPARATION

You can grow in your maleness or femaleness and still be dependent at times.

IDENTITY, SEXUALITY, & SEPARATION

I look forward to knowing you as an adult.

IDENTITY, SEXUALITY, & SEPARATION

My love is always with you. I trust you to ask for my support.

4. *Helpful parent behaviors*

- Affirm adolescent for doing developmental tasks.
- Continue to offer love, safety, and protection.
- Accept all of the adolescent's feelings and talk about what it was like when you had emerging sexual feelings.
- Confront unacceptable behavior.
- Be clear about position on drug use and on sexual behaviors.
- Confront discounting.
- Identify the ways adolescent is becoming separate and affirm the ones that are supportive of independence.
- Understand and affirm reworking of tasks from earlier developmental stages.
- Celebrate adolescent's growing up and welcome to adulthood.
- Encourage growing independence and accept the identity that adolescent is forging, urging adolescent to be true to self and to find accommodations with socially acceptable behaviors. This may be different from the parent's expectations or dreams for child.
- Take community action to make schools and streets safe.

5. *Unhelpful parent behaviors*

- Unresponsive, uncaring behavior.
- Withholds loving touch.
- Responds sexually to adolescent's developing sexual maturity.
- Uses rigid rules or no rules or unevenly enforced rules or refuses to negotiate rules.
- Neglects to expect thinking and problem-solving behavior.

- Cruelly teases about sexuality, interests, fantasies, dreams, appearance, or friends.
- Fails to confront destructive or self-defeating behaviors—anything from drug abuse to limited friends and interests.
- Attempts to keep child from separating.
- Unwilling to allow child to feel miserable for brief times.
- Discounting.

6. Identity, sexuality, and separation tasks adults may recycle

- To achieve a cleaner separation from and connection with family of origin.
- To practice independence in a way that leads to interdependence.
- To emerge gradually, as a separate person, independent of teenager, with own identity and values while accepting teen's values or challenging them when appropriate.
- To be responsible for own needs, feelings, and behaviors.
- To integrate sexuality appropriately into current adult situation.

7. Clues to a need for adults to grow up again

- Preoccupation with sex, body, clothes, appearance, friends, or sex role.

- Unsure of own values; vulnerable to peer pressure.
- Problems with starting and ending jobs, roles, and relationships.
- Overdependence on or alienation from family and others.
- Irresponsibility.
- Trouble making and keeping commitments.
- Looks to others for definition of self.
- Confuses sex with nurturing.
- Unsure of maleness or femaleness or lovableness.

8. Activities that support growing up again

- Use and adapt this stage's "Helpful parent behaviors" to care for the child in you.
- Write an essay starting with "What I want most to accomplish in my life is . . ."
- Do something for a cause you believe in.
- Have a long talk with a mentor about what is important to you.
- Get a new hairstyle, some new clothes, a new look.
- Go to a romantic movie or play or read a sexy novel.
- Separate from a person who hurts you.
- Join a support group.
- Get therapy if you need it.

Young Adults Living at Home

Parenting does not stop when the child reaches nineteen or twenty-one or ever. A parent is always a parent. The way that parents offer and accept support changes through the decades, but the love and caring do not end.

For many young adults there is a transition stage of both dependence and independence, when they are not yet financially or perhaps fully emotionally independent adults, so they need to live at home. This stage is made more difficult for the young adults if their parents treat them as children, cook, clean and do laundry for them, or support them financially with no expectation that they provide for part of their expenses. It is also made more difficult if parents demand that the young adults rigidly adhere to rules established during their teen years.

It is helpful for parents and young people who live together to remember some things about each other:

- The young people are starting to move into the adult steps, interdependence (page 238)
- Parents are still expected to set nonnegotiable rules about any area of lifestyle crucial to their values and beliefs, and young people must comply as long as they remain at home.
- Most other rules can and should be negotiated.
- It is usually better to anticipate needs, to set or negotiate rules, and to plan divisions of labor before the young adult and parents begin their joint living arrangement.
- It is usually better not to make any assumptions about who will do what, but to ask about and negotiate all tasks.
- It is okay for parents to help their grown children as long as the help does not marshmallow or overindulge the young adult and as long as the parents do not resent it.

- It is all right for young adults to live with parents, if the young adults pay room and board, share fully in household tasks, and participate with the same consideration and courtesy they would if they were living with some other family.

It is helpful for parents to be aware that young people separate from parents in four ways:
1. Some leave home and return grown up.
2. Some stay home and grow up.
3. Some leave and come back several times.
4. Some break family rules so their parents will force them to leave.

The way a young person chooses to leave may be different from the way the parents separated. The important issue is not how young people leave, but that they do become separate adults, capable of making their own decisions, and willing to interact with their parents as supportive adults.

- It is important for parents to encourage their children to become adults and to treat them as such no matter where they are living.
- It is important for young adults to let their parents grow up, to see, experience, and treat their parents as growing people, and not to cling to the images they had when they were four or nine or seventeen years old.
- It is all right for young adults to parent their parents in areas where the young adults have information helpful to their parents.
- It is wonderful for both young adults and their parents to realize that these years can be a source of satisfaction and enjoyment while they discover each other as caring adults.
- It can be an ideal time for both young adults and parents to do some important growing up again.

Stage 7, Interdependence
Adults

The developmental tasks of adulthood focus on the journey from independence to inter-dependence, and they include regular recycling of earlier tasks in ways that support the specific adult tasks.

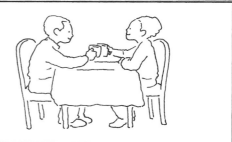

1. Job of the adult (developmental tasks)

- To master skills for work and recreation.
- To find mentors and to mentor.
- To grow in love and humor.
- To offer and accept intimacy.
- To expand creativity and honor uniqueness.
- To accept responsibility for self and to care for the next generation and the last.
- To find support for own growth and to support the growth of others.
- To expand commitments beyond self and family to the community, the world, and possibly beyond.
- To balance dependence, independence, and interdependence.
- To deepen integrity and spirituality.
- To refine the arts of greeting, leaving, and grieving.

2. Behaviors of the adult

Many behaviors are typical of the long years of the adult stage. The important ones for you right now are the ones you are doing; so list behaviors typical for you now in the space above.

3. Affirmations for adults

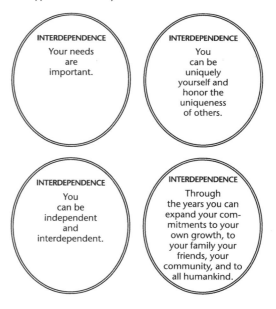

INTERDEPENDENCE
Your needs are important.

INTERDEPENDENCE
You can be uniquely yourself and honor the uniqueness of others.

INTERDEPENDENCE
You can be independent and interdependent.

INTERDEPENDENCE
Through the years you can expand your commitments to your own growth, to your family your friends, your community, and to all humankind.

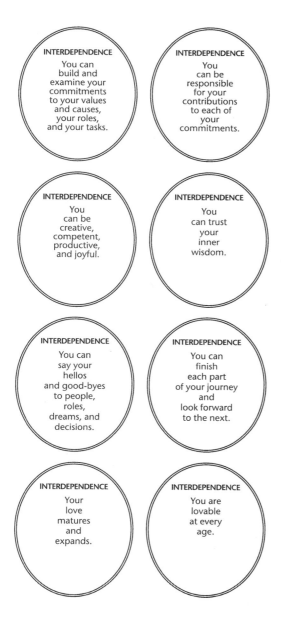

INTERDEPENDENCE
You can build and examine your commitments to your values and causes, your roles, and your tasks.

INTERDEPENDENCE
You can be responsible for your contributions to each of your commitments.

INTERDEPENDENCE
You can be creative, competent, productive, and joyful.

INTERDEPENDENCE
You can trust your inner wisdom.

INTERDEPENDENCE
You can say your hellos and good-byes to people, roles, dreams, and decisions.

INTERDEPENDENCE
You can finish each part of your journey and look forward to the next.

INTERDEPENDENCE
Your love matures and expands.

INTERDEPENDENCE
You are lovable at every age.

4. Helpful adult behaviors toward self

- Affirm developmental tasks.
- Be willing to look at self with love, objectivity, and forgiveness.
- Be willing to celebrate successes, however large or small.
- Be willing to grow and change.
- Make and meet your commitments toward family and community.
- Participate in behaviors that support the fulfillment of the affirmations.

5. Unhelpful adult behaviors toward self

- Resistance to age changes.
- Unwillingness to learn, grow, and change.
- Competition with others for emotional needs.
- Imposing own definition of the world on others.
- Accepting the definition of the world imposed by others.
- Passivity, addiction, and codependency.
- Discounting.

6. Interdependence tasks adults may recycle

- Any adult task may be recycled any time circumstances call for it. See chapter 26, General Activities for Deliberately Growing Up Again.

7. Clues to a need for adults to do growing-up-again tasks from the adult stage

- Overdependency.
- Afraid to be dependent.
- Independence to the exclusion of interdependence.

- Difficulty making and keeping commitments.
- Role inflexibility.
- Afraid to grow old.
- Unwilling to say hello and good-bye.
- Unwilling to grieve and then move on with life.
- Living in the past.
- Living in the future.
- Living through others.

- Not knowing or getting what you need.
- Denial and discounting.
- Codependency.

8. Activities that support growing up again
See chapter 26, General Activities for Deliberately Growing Up Again.

Stage 8, Integration
Toward Death

During the last part of our lives, or whenever we face death, we are called to finish putting all the pieces together. Some of us don't wait for the imminence of death to do this. We do and redo this "wrapping-up," celebrating and grieving, process throughout our lives.

If we have lived our lives through all the stages and reached the last part of adulthood—past the hustle and bustle of growing up, rearing families, and acquiring things; past the building of our work lives and caring for the aged; past the stage of devoting great effort to changing the world—then we shall reach the stage of elder and crone. Some call this the time when old ones pass on wisdom to those who seek it.

Dying is a part of living and this stage of life could properly be called "Living Until You Die." No matter what our circumstances, this can be a time of being in charge in a new way. We can be in charge of how we see ourselves and the world. We can be in charge of what we make of every day we live to the greatest degree we are able.

We sum up what we have learned from life's experiences. We begin to sharpen our observations and come to accept life as it is without thinking it must be changed to suit us. We prepare to relinquish certain responsibilities to those we have mentored. We understand that just about everything has both a light and a dark side. There are no simple answers. We recognize the demons we may have created and devise ways to lay them to rest.

If we haven't yet asked, "What has this life been all about?" and "What was my job here?" and "What of that job have I accomplished?" we're likely to ask those questions now.

We take inventories. We look back and ask, "What is my unfinished business? If I died today, what would I regret not having said, not having repaired, not having done, not having been? And what will I, or what can I, do about it now?"

We are called upon to revisit not only our beliefs about life and death, but also our concepts of an afterlife. What happens after our bodies give out? This exploration usually involves becoming clear about our beliefs, about how a power within ourselves connects with a power beyond ourselves.

A wise older woman who looks back, looks forward, and lives for each day's revelations said, "My life has had its epochs: Twenty years with my family of origin, twenty years of marriage and child rearing, twenty years of improving my various communities, and twenty years of preparing for death. I have lovingly let go of my wish to direct the lives of my children. I have had to let go of old friends and family who have died before me. I have let go of old dreams, decisions, outworn ideas and judgments of myself and others. I have reassessed my attachment to many of my belongings. I keep the things with me that enrich my life."[9]

We meet each day as it comes. Development continues until we die. The tasks of this part of life call for the integration of the past with the present and preparation for the future.

1. Job of the older adult (developmental tasks in addition to the adult developmental tasks)

- To prepare for death; to make conscious, ethical preparation for leaving.
- To explore connections with humankind and connections with a higher power.
- To reassess artificial barriers—the judgments that keep distance between self and others.
- To continue to learn and to grow each day.
- To experience every situation with all the senses, mind, and heart.
- To adjust to and grieve the loss of any physical and mental capabilities.
- To integrate life experience with personal beliefs and values.
- To be willing to share your wisdom; to be clear about what you have wisdom about and what you do not.
- To refine the arts of greeting, leaving, and grieving.

2. Signs of avoiding the developmental tasks

- Failing to put your affairs in order.
- Meeting life with rigidity and flatness.

- Maintaining one's attitudes, beliefs, and behaviors in spite of knowing they have harmful impact on self or others.
- Being unwilling to thoughtfully pursue an understanding of one's self.
- Failing to make mindful transitions from one role, career, or relationship to another.
- Looking back upon life with regret, and doing nothing about it.
- Being in denial of the aging process and mortality.

3. Signs of doing the developmental tasks

- Having the courage to "see with one's own eyes"[10] and speak one's own truth.
- Telling the truth and doing no cruelty.[11]
- Feeling the fullness of life on a daily basis.
- Making the connection between the past and the present.
- Tolerating ambiguity and the tension of opposites.
- Facing the uncertainties without becoming immobilized by them.
- Planning for dying and death.
- Approaching death as a natural part of living.
- Experiencing and accommodating a range of declining physical, and perhaps mental, faculties.
- Asking appropriate people for help and accepting help graciously.

4. Affirmations
(in addition to adult affirmations)

You can grow your whole life through.

You can look upon the process of dying as a natural transition.

You can make your preparations for leaving and die when you are ready.

You can celebrate the gifts you have received and the gifts you have given.

You deserve the support that you need.

You can share your wisdom in your way.

You are lovable just the way you are.

chapter 26

General Activities for Deliberately Growing Up Again

Two types of activities support growing up again. One is to identify episodes from adult life and redo them, making new decisions and claiming new attitudes about who we are. The other is to recycle tasks for each earlier developmental stage as many times as necessary.

Recycling Earlier Tasks

Recycling is doing earlier developmental tasks in ever more sophisticated ways to meet current adult needs.

Notice Clues

One way to recycle is to respond to the anxieties, needs, or clues that we identify in our daily lives, to notice the developmental stage they may spring from, and to use the affirmations and activities that support growing up again in that stage.

> *Recycling is doing earlier developmental tasks in ever more sophisticated ways to meet current adult needs.*

Pick a Theme

Another way to grow up again is to pick a theme and choose activities to help recycle that theme at each developmental stage. The following are examples of themes:

- Knowing what I know
- Knowing that I need nurturing and accepting it
- Being willing to be seen and valued
- Being responsible for myself and to others
- Building strong, not rigid, boundaries

Here are ways Eric explored the "Knowing that I need nurturing and accepting it" part of stage 1 (being) development. A couple of times each week he chose three or four activities he thought would support just "being."

- He gave himself the affirmations for that stage and arranged for other people to take care of him for a specified length of time (twenty minutes or one hour) and to give him the affirmations in the way that he wanted them.
- He focused on just being and on knowing what he knew about his body.
- He thought about how his body felt during and after each activity.
- He got a therapeutic massage.
- He soaked in a hot tub; he wandered around aimlessly; he listened to soft music.
- He got lots of hugs and back rubs from his family.
- He drank cocoa and hot cider; he looked at his baby pictures; he visualized himself as a wonderful infant; he exercised when he felt like it and took naps or rested when he was tired.
- Then he made it a point to notice if he was more aware of needing nurturing and was more willing to accept it.

Get Outside Help

Sometimes we can use our intelligence and ingenuity to create these experiences for ourselves in our daily living. Sometimes we get the help we need in a book such as Muriel James's *Breaking Free: Self-Reparenting for a New Life*.[1] Sometimes we need the help of a respectful, caring support group. Sometimes we need the help of a therapist and a therapy group.

> *The ability to intellectualize is the strength and hazard of the adult stage.*

The ability to intellectualize is the strength and hazard of the adult stage. The temptation to avoid healing work, feeling work, and body work is a signal that we need loving help in order to deal with our old defenses, to stop intellectualizing away the importance of our needs.

We also can benefit from finding new parent figures to mentor and nurture us. Muriel James suggests that we need many good fathers and many good mothers, many smart people to think with, and many people to play with, and they don't all have to be the same people.

We may choose a "new-parent" therapist as described in Jonathan and Laurie Weiss's book *Recovery from Codependency: It Is Never Too Late to Have a Happy Childhood*[2]—or we may contract with other people to play limited, new-parent roles with us.

Revising Specific Episodes from Adult Life

The other type of activity that supports growing up again is to identify specific events in adult life, do them over again, let go of old negative feelings and decisions, and keep the new, positive, good ones. For example:

- Several unfortunate happenings surrounded Mary and Jerry's wedding, so they are going to do their wedding over again and have it be the way they want it this time.
- Barbara regrets events on her fortieth birthday, so she is going to give herself a fortieth birthday party on an unbirthday date.
- Betty harbors bad feelings about the way she was fired from her job, so her support group is going to role-play a job termination that is respectful. Betty will indicate what she wants to have happen.
- Sometimes it's not possible to do things over, so we have to use other methods. Ted wants to resolve his feelings about his experiences in the Vietnam War. He found a therapy group created specifically to help veterans grieve and heal from their war and postwar experiences.

When you create an adult growing-up-again experience, it is important to let the new feelings and lessons in, to make new and healthy decisions about yourself and your life. Often, doing this about an episode in adult life is healing and satisfying. Other times, it seems to be not enough. That usually means we need to go to an earlier developmental stage to do additional healing there.

> *When you create an adult growing-up-again experience, it is important to let the new feelings and lessons in.*

Affirmations for Starting to Grow Up Again

Anytime we make changes in what we believe or how we behave, we must keep several things in mind. First, people around us may not be enthusiastic about our changes. They may be more comfortable with us the way we are now. They may try hard to get us not to change or to thwart our efforts to change. Nonetheless, we must get the support we need and persist.

Second, we may not always be enthusiastic about the changes ourselves. This is especially true if we jump into them and don't take time to honor and grieve our old decisions as we replace them with new ones.

Here are affirmations for starting to grow up again:

- It's okay to start today.
- It took a long time to build the defenses. It can take time to heal. Healing any weak spot strengthens other weak spots.
- It's okay to welcome feeling stuck as a signal that the next healing is especially important and has a wonderful new freedom waiting.
- You have all the courage you need; the more you use, the more you will have.
- You are worth the effort.

Rest assured that as you make necessary changes, when you realize you have said or done something you regret, you can apologize and do it again in a healthier way. As the old carpenter said, "I like to work with wood. I can shave it and shim it and get it to work for me." Shim and shave your words and behaviors. Make them work for you. An "I'm sorry I said what I said yesterday. I'm going to try again" can help. Solving problems or resolving differences means making the effort and making some mistakes, acknowledging them, learning from them, and repairing them now.

Rest assured that you will run into a few surprises in the journey ahead. You may celebrate some, grieve some, honor some. Looking at both the past and the present for useful information is necessary in order to create a better present and future. Avoiding, denying, and blaming keep you in a painful present and ensure a painful future.

Rest assured that the notion of living a life free of discord, conflict, and difficulty is a myth. Those who subscribe to this myth inflict pain on themselves and others. Take the path of courage. Be tenacious and be willing to give and receive love.

Rest assured that growing up again is worth it. Remember the popular saying, "The woods would be very silent if only those birds sang who sang the best." So sing! One day at a time.

SECTION VIII

Adoption

Here, root yourselves beside me.
MAYA ANGELOU

chapter 27

Adoption

Parenting Someone Else's Children as Your Own

Growing up again is an important job for any parents who wish to improve what they pass on to their children. It is an absolutely critical job for adoptive parents. This chapter is meant for them. It is also for adult adoptees, who may read it with an eye toward seeking to identify repair work for themselves. It will help them think about their separation and adoption experiences and how these experiences may be affecting what they pass on to their children.

There is not room in this chapter to include everything about adoptive parenting or the experience of being adopted. Many other good books and resources are available to help. A starter list appears at the end of the chapter. For the family formed by adoption, this chapter elaborates upon and adds to the material found in other chapters of *Growing Up Again*. Many suggestions will also apply to parenting foster children. An Ages and Stages Chart for the adopted child appears on page 269.

This chapter includes sections on:

- The adoptive family's uniqueness
- The adoptee's uniqueness
- The importance of paying greater attention to the infant's experience
- Advice to parents adopting
- The attachment process and how to facilitate it

- Challenging possible early decisions of adoptees
- Honoring grief
- When to get help
- Adoptions that occur after failed parenting
- The importance of having information about the child and his prior experiences
- Search and reunion
- Adoptees as parents
- Nurture, Structure, and Discounting examples of adoption situations, and
- Growing up adopted, hope for all involved

All Adoptive Parenting Isn't the Same

The definition of *adoptive family* includes not only couples or committed partners who adopt but also single men and women who form a family through adoption. Each adoptive family is unique, and each member's experience is also unique. Nevertheless, there are similarities between families created by adoption and other families. All families have day-to-day problems. Although adopting parents are scrutinized in ways that birth families are not, they range in their abilities to nurture and structure just as birth families range in their abilities to do so.

> *Although adopting parents are scrutinized in ways that birth families are not, they range in their abilities to nurture and structure just as birth families range in their abilities to do so.*

There are also general similarities among adoptive families. They all have to figure out how to bring their children into the family circle, how to overcome attachment problems, and how to deal with the ramifications of the child's connections to two other parents. Issues common to all parents—such as feelings of inadequacy and low self-esteem, need for ownership and excessive control of the child, or competitiveness—may have an additional urgency or twist in adoptive families.

Despite these similarities, all adoptive parenting is not the same due to the wide variety of genetic features and prior experiences adopted children bring to the relationship.

David Kirk, an adoptive father and respected researcher, reported the results of a study indicating that adoptive families who paid attention to the differences between them and other families were generally more successful than those who denied that adoptive families were different.[1] There are also many dimensions to adoptive parenting that go beyond "usual" parenting which make it different.

For instance, the behaviors of a child who has had a rough and bumpy first three years of life can baffle parents. This can be true of infant adoptees too. Parents are not automatically equipped to parent a child whose idiosyncrasies call for understanding and skills outside the realm of the parents' own experience: the outgoing and energetic girl in the home of a quiet and reserved couple or the well-coordinated and athletically inclined boy in a family of studious scientists, for instance.

All Adoptees Are Not the Same

Rather than referring to "adoptees" as one monolithic group, this chapter distinguishes among three subsets of adoptees who share certain common circumstances of their adoption.

- *Infant adoption:* Children adopted at or shortly after birth or after three months spent with birth mothers who took good care of them. The adoption may be open or closed.
- *Adoption after failed parenting:* Children adopted after termination of parental rights, often after sustaining abuse and/or neglect, including children with difficulties related to the birth mother's poor self-care during pregnancy. Adoptees kept for a long time in orphanages and foster homes, internationally or domestically, are part of this group.
- *Adoption by a stepparent:* Children living with one biological parent and the parent's new spouse who adopts the child. These adoptees usually have full access to genetic, medical, cultural, and family information. Their circumstances differ from families parenting from a greater void of information. For that reason, this chapter focuses on infant adoptions and adoptions, internationally or domestically, because of failed parenting.

Children who have lost a known parent may manifest the same coping behaviors as adoptees. Even though they remain with kin, children orphaned by the death of one or both parents, kidnapped by an alienated parent, or abandoned by a parent who leaves home permanently may feel uncertain, confused, or insecure. The loss of a parent at any age has a powerful impact on a child's decisions about safety and entitlement.

Infant Adoption

We used to believe that moving an infant from one parent to another didn't have much effect on the child. We told ourselves that it didn't make a difference or that the child would not *know* the difference. The child would put the names "Mom" and "Dad" on two new faces and would have family to love and care for him or her and that was all that mattered.

> *Babies who suddenly lose all that is familiar have an inborn survival system that overwhelms them with fear.*

Now we know that adoption is much more complex. Babies who suddenly lose all that is familiar have an inborn survival system that overwhelms them with fear. The feelings of fear tell them that they are in danger. But they are powerless to get themselves into a safer place or position. They must rely on the new mother and father to understand their losses and their fear and to help them adjust.

Wendy McCord of the Association for Pre- and Perinatal Psychology and Health asserts that adoptive parents who understand separation trauma are able to have true empathy for infants' reactions to their losses. They may come with colic, or heightened startle responses, and be unwilling to allow the new parents to comfort them. Parents should not interpret these behaviors as rejection. Dr. McCord suggests that parents begin to say things to reassure the baby. "You must feel really sad; you must feel really lost. You miss your mother. You've lost something very important, and I understand. I'm not the mom you expected. I don't smell like her. I don't sound like her. I'm a different mom and I love you, and I'm not going to leave you."[2]

Babies are a lot "smarter" than we once thought, even before they are born. Indeed, babies may sense or know they will not be staying with the birth mother before they physically part, as suggested in the following anecdote: During a college class about adoption for professionals working with children, the instructor talked about the awareness and abilities of the newborn. "We know that birth mothers experience separation from their babies as a traumatic event. How could it not also be a traumatic event for the infant?"

Two middle-aged women sitting together looked at one another before one of them raised her hand. "I am a nurse in the labor and delivery unit of a large hospital. They know they will be separated from their mothers."

The instructor asked, "How do you know they know?"

"They are different from the others. Their cries are forlorn and kitten-like. I just know they know they're leaving." Her colleague nodded agreement. Both had tears in their eyes.

> *The baby is already Someone.*

Having read chapter 24 on the extraordinary capabilities and adaptations of the human fetus and infant, you know that newborn children are not blank slates. The baby is already Someone. The adoptive parents' job is to support the infant in grieving losses and be ready to marvel at the infant's unfolding, all the time falling in love with the person he or she is.

An adoptee's identity work will eventually need to be done with four parents. The legacies of other genetic lines, of other cultures, of other socioeconomic levels, of other personalities, of other experiences are an undeniable part of the child, and it is too dangerous to pretend they aren't there. Or said another way: One of the purposes of adoptive parents should be to parent without discounting themselves, the adoptee, or the birth parents. (See the chapters on Discounting, page 149.)

Advice to Parents Adopting

Several axioms can guide the process of adopting. First, truth is your strongest ally. Second, attachment and trust are learned behaviors. Love alone is not enough. Third, all behavior is either an expression of love or a call for it. And now, the advice to parents:

If you chose adoption because of your infertility, consider grieving your infertility by attending Resolve groups or other groups for people dealing with failure to conceive or the death of a child pre- or perinatally or seeing a therapist before you enter into the process of adopting. The adopted infant should never be put in the position of having to replace the child you would have had.

You might revisit your own babyhood and make any needed repairs in order to buoy your confidence and self-assurance in caring for an infant. (See Ages and Stages, Birth to Six Months, page 221.) Strengthen the relationship between you and your spouse or partner. It's important not only that you are singing from the same hymnal but also that you are on the same page.

Spend time getting to know the birth mother and father if you can. This will allow the baby to hear your voices before being born. Some experts suggest that adoptive mothers also adopt such things as the diet and favorite scents of the birth mother. All this is an intentional effort to create a smoother transition for the baby from one environment to another.

Hope that the birth mother will be strong enough to give her baby messages of wantedness and to tell her baby she's found a family to love him and teach him how to be capable. Think about involving the birth parents in a ritual for moving the child from one family to another. Include the presence of support persons for them and for you.

Take lots of time with your baby. He will be grieving, which doesn't mean you should be sad *for* him. It does mean that in your understanding, you provide a quiet environment for the baby to grieve and to adjust to you and his new home with greater ease. Remember, the separation he has just sustained gives rise to a primitive fear. Helpless to meet his own needs, he is being transferred from the person who is naturally intended to care for him to someone else. He will need your sureness, your quiet confidence, and your time.

Talk to him. Tell him the affirmations for being (see Ages and Stages, page 221) in your own words. Your behaviors and your demeanor speak these affirmations most powerfully and in a way your baby surely understands.

Wear the baby—in a pack on your front and then in a pack on your back. This gives him a chance to hear your heart and become familiar with the way you smell and the way you sound. Rock him, sing to him, gaze at him, look into his eyes, be quiet. Study him. You may wish to consult your doctor and/or a lactation specialist and prepare for breast feeding the baby.

If you can arrange to have one parent with the baby for at least his first three years, so much the better. An adopted infant needs to have "enough" of his primary caregivers to decide on their reliability. Since his beginnings were in being separated, he needs time and many interactions with you to decide if he can trust you and himself.

Keep an album of pictures of his birth folks in plain view. He needs to know he is not a secret, and he doesn't have to keep secrets in order to protect you. Be easy with this, not reminding him daily that he's adopted and not refraining from mentioning it at all. Hold all the best attributes of his birth parents in your mind. If he thinks your regard for his origins is negative, he may believe that he is lacking or "less than" or scripted to be "bad" because his parents were. Any self-defeating behaviors of birth parents can be treated as a case of their having made poor decisions or as a matter of their not having learned how to conduct their lives more positively.

Empathize with the feelings he expresses to you and reassure him of your love and commitment. "You can count on me," expressed in your words, and "You can count on me" expressed in your behaviors will reassure him of the permanence of your relationship.

Parenting the Adoptee: The Attachment Process

Children born to other parents, because of the profound trauma of their separation experience and their primitive survival decisions about that experience, may not be wholeheartedly ready to trust or accept the new Mom and Dad. They may be suspicious and resistant because they have already lost everything familiar. This is why caring for a child who has been separated from all known sounds, smells, rhythms, and persons calls for more confidence, more thoughtfulness, more skillfulness, and firmer love than does parenting infants who have not been separated. They will test the adoptive parents, maybe lightly and subtly or maybe tryingly and for a long time. They must satisfy themselves that the new parents can do the job.

Children may be "parent-defensive" if they have decided it is foolish to trust *any* adults to meet their needs. They may be protecting themselves from the possibility of being abandoned or separated once again. These children assume an "I'll-do-it-myself" posture in order to keep safe distance from those who would connect with them. Sometimes this behavior is all too noticeable and sometimes it's very hidden.

> *Children may be "parent-defensive" if they have decided it is foolish to trust* any *adults to meet their needs.*

As an adoptive parent, you will probably not be immediately trusted by your child. One way to become more trustworthy is to identify any unfinished business from *your* time in your mother's womb, your babyhood, your childhood. Look for markers such as bouts of depression in your parents, especially your mother, and

- hospitalizations, yours or those of a primary caregiver
- neglect
- multiple caregiving breaks
- any emotional unavailability of your caregivers

These situations may signal some fragile or raw places it would be wise to shore up, perhaps with professional help.

Why is this important? Adopted children can hook a parent's anger by pushing on raw or empty places. Reluctant to expose themselves to more hurt, they may be extraordinarily good at getting a parent to act out their anger. In doing so, the parent relieves the children's fear of not being in control. They test the parent this way, not out of meanness, but out of a perceived need to assure their own safety. Adoptive parents need to become well acquainted with their own growing up. Repair whatever holes you might have so you don't fall into them. Strengthen your ability to separate your child's wounds from your own so you are free to use structure with consequences and nurture with clarity.

Another way to be tried and true is to strengthen your couple, family, and support relationships. Your adopted child may decide to focus more on taking care of you and your needs than on his or her own growing-up tasks. If there are weaknesses in your relationships or in what you know about your own needs and how to meet them, your child may decide that, in order to keep from being abandoned again, he or she has to take care of you. Bad idea! The child doesn't know how but will do it anyway, arresting his or her development to buttress yours. (See pages 43 and 44 for more on attachment.)

Parenting the Adoptee: Challenging Early Decisions

A thoughtful eighteen-year-old woman who is *not* adopted was asked, "What do you think when you hear the word 'adoption'?"

She responded, "My worst fears as a child were that my parents would get divorced and that I would find out I was adopted."

"What would be so bad about finding out you were adopted?"

"That I wouldn't have an identity. That I wasn't wanted. 'Loved' is more an emotional thing. 'Wanted' is more a physical thing. I would think I was too much to take care of."

The young woman's words are amazingly close to what many adoptees feel, often at a deep level and often outside of their conscious awareness. Words meant to be reassuring—such as "Your birth mother made a loving plan for you" and "How lucky for you your parents wanted a child and you didn't just happen"—don't match the adoptees' experience of how it feels not to have been kept by their birth mothers.

Because they may have deep questions about their (1) entitlement to live, (2) lovability, and (3) belonging, adoptees may oil their feathers enough to let good nurture and structure slip off. Or they may keep as much as they can tolerate, as much as is congruent with what they believe they deserve, and discount the rest. Some will convert good structure into criticism and discount good nurture because it conflicts with what they decided early on to believe about being unwanted and unimportant.

Parents must watch carefully, first to observe and then to understand what adopted children do with good structure and nurture from the Nurture/Structure Highway. Do they take just a little bit of it? Do they throw most of it away? Do they keep nearly all of it? If you observe your child discounting or converting structure and nurture, challenge the child to change whatever belief keeps him or her from accepting it. Reach out to connect with touch that's okay with the child, saying something like, "I think you didn't hear what I meant to say. Let me try again. This time, just listen and think about it." Then give the child the time and space to think about it. (See discussion on accepting love from others in chapter 7.) Remember, all children benefit from being nurtured from the care and support positions and structured from the nonnegotiable and negotiable positions.

> *Parents must watch carefully, first to observe and then to understand what adopted children do with good structure and nurture.*

Honor Your Own Grief

Normal grief about infertility will resurface again and again. Be prepared to acknowledge and deal with it just as adoptees face recurring grief about their losses. How? First, be observant. Pay attention to your feelings. Second, let your feelings help you identify your loss. Honor and experience your feelings. Let them teach you. Third, when you have been sad and mad for as long as you need to, ask yourself what will help you to move to acceptance and forgiveness. Grief about losses is something that will visit you in a variety of costumes and in a number of ways. It is something you and your adopted child have in common, something that connects you, if you both learn to recognize grief when it knocks at the door. *Loss of Dreams* by Ted Bowman and *Good Grief Rituals* by Elaine Childs-Gowell offer help for the grieving process.[3]

Remember that this child is not a replacement child for the one you might have had. Adopted children need to be seen for themselves. Their job is to master the knowledge and skills to become successful human beings and the parent's job is to help them to do that. The child's job is not to stay within the bounds of the parent's comfort zone. The child does not exist simply to make the parent proud. If you ask your adopted child to be and do as you dreamed your birth child would be and do, the child may do the opposite to get your attention. Mourning will make room for acceptance.

When to Get Help

> *It's better to go for help early rather than wait until the problem is firmly entrenched and more resistant to change.*

A number of books with excellent information and help for parenting adoptees is available. To find out which are the most helpful, ask other adoptive parents. They are the ones who know.

If your child persists in behaving in self-defeating ways, seek out a support group or a therapist who understands adoption and knows how to teach you skills beyond the repertoire of usual parenting skills. Don't wait too long and don't overreact. Pay attention to your intuition. When you first detect a problem, observe both your behavior and your child's behavior. If the problem persists, assume it's not going to get better or change without help. It's better to go for help early rather than wait until the problem is firmly entrenched and more resistant to change.

Adoption after Failed Parenting

When we hear "adoptive parents," a picture of parents who adopted infants usually springs into mind. Yet, many older children are adopted and come with a conflicted history of time spent with other parents who were unable or incapable of caring for them well.

The experience of parents who adopt an older child can be dramatically different from the experience of parents who adopt an infant. It's safe to say that parenting infant adoptees calls for more skill and strength than parenting a birth child. It's also safe to say that parenting a child adopted after he or she has experienced questionable parenting and inadequate care calls for even more parent strength and skill.

Children who come to their families after experiences of abuse, abandonment, or neglect tend to have all the issues of infant adoptees plus a few more. They are more likely to have greater difficulties making attachments to new parents, and the parents will more likely need to seek help from professionals. The children's defensiveness may be too great, their protective walls too formidable, to let the love that is offered to them into their hearts.

When these children have severe behavior problems, the parents can automatically become the focus of blame from well-meaning friends and professionals. They often hear questions such as: "What's wrong with your marriage?" and "What's wrong with your parenting?" Those things may need strengthening; but, without looking at the child's early experiences and assumptions about life, the would-be helpers miss the point. In cases where older adopted children have behavior problems, we must believe that at least *some* of the reasons for the problems lie in the children's lack of trust, their loyalty to their first families, and their refusal to accept more competent parents.

> *When these children have severe behavior problems, the parents can automatically become the focus of blame from well-meaning friends and professionals.*

These youngsters have learned to relieve themselves of responsibility and to place it on someone else. If they succeed in giving you their problem, they can usually see to it that you fail to solve it. The books *Parenting with Love & Logic* and *Parenting Teens with Love & Logic* by Foster Cline and Jim Fay can help you deal with this dilemma.[4]

Adoptive parents can be vulnerable to overindulging because they are so sensitive to the emotional pain of these youngsters. Parents would like to be loving and protect children from further distress, but in their concern, may fail to hold the children accountable. Such parental overprotection can be seen by a child as vulnerability and can invite a control game of "gotcha," which makes the children look like winners and the parents look like losers. In reality, both parents and children are losers.

The children of failed parenting can be expert in engaging all authority figures in control battles they believe are winnable on their terms. If you have an ongoing, powerless feeling because you're failing to reach your child, or you have used all your parenting skills and they still aren't enough, find help. And don't delay. Find the professionals that understand and do good work with youngsters with attachment difficulties. (See Where to Go for Additional Help in appendix B.)

The Importance of Information in Adoption

As an adoptive parent, you need information. Information is your friend. It is imperative to know all you can about the various histories of your child and to know as much as possible about the child's experiences and heritage, whatever they are. You can deal better with the knowns than with the unknowns.

Thorough medical histories going back at least two generations are of enormous importance. Many adult adoptees are unable to provide medical histories when asked by their physicians. This deprives the doctor of some of the most helpful information used in making diagnoses and makes life more dangerous for adoptees and any children and grandchildren they might have. But that's not all.

Information helps you know what gifts the child brings so you are better able to support them. It helps you provide your child with the truth about his or her origins, even the difficult truths about addictions, antisocial behavior, and poor decision making.

> *Knowing about their origins reduces confusion and increases feelings of security in adoptees.*

Certainly, the child's developmental capacity to understand the information must be considered when you sensitively share it. However, knowing about their origins reduces confusion and increases feelings of security in adoptees. It is better for them to deal with reality, with the help of parents, than to fantasize as they struggle to work out their identities.

Be careful to work through your feelings about the birth parents. If adoptees sense that adoptive parents are judging the first parents as faulty, immoral, or evil, they may take that picture of their origins into themselves and make it so. They will benefit from empathy and support for their ability to challenge and overcome their first parents' harmful behaviors. If you feel unable to share information about your child's origins in a healthy manner, ask a knowledgeable therapist to help you prepare for this process.

Because of sealed adoption records, many adults adopted as infants do not have ready access to birth families who could provide them with what they need. They make us aware of the importance of having this information during the growing-up time. This information will also help you understand and parent your child. If you are about to adopt or have a way to get this information for your child, here is a list of things to look for. This list is not meant to be exhaustive, so trust yourself to know what you need to know.

Histories

Prenatal/Pregnancy

- Circumstances of becoming pregnant; planned, unplanned
- Mother's attitude toward pregnancy and toward life in general during pregnancy
- Involvement of father
- Medical care/medical difficulties
- Use of alcohol and other drugs (mother and father)
- Nutrition, exercise before and during pregnancy
- Any significant repetitive sensory stimulus (music, languages spoken, dance, etc.)
- Quality of emotional support during pregnancy
- Physical or emotional abuse during pregnancy
- Other significant stressors

Birth Experience

- Onset of labor: spontaneous or induced?
- Length of labor
- Circumstances/difficulties/interventions
- Father present?
- Support person(s)
- Nature of contact with birth mother postdelivery

Birth Mother and Birth Father

- Ages, physical description
- Medical histories for at least two generations
- Mental health history
- Ethnic backgrounds
- Career, work, and school
- Interests, talents, and strengths
- Challenges, weaknesses
- Names of persons who will know whereabouts of relinquishing parents
- Description of child's experiences in birth family, if applicable

Orphanage/Foster Care

- Number of placements and duration of each
- Description of each placement setting, circumstances
- Child's behaviors in response to separations
- Child's experience in each setting, including features of care (e.g., held often; given eye contact; rocked, bounced, moved gently; caregiving reliable, attentive, sensitive to child)
- Possible access by child abusers
- Reasons for moving child from one placement to another
- What did or didn't go well in each placement
- "Life Book" containing pictures of important people, places, and events and names of favorite books, toys, and comforting objects
- Ongoing contact with birth family? foster families?

Search and Reunion

Many current infant adoptions are "open" or semiopen, which means the adoptive parents and birth parent or parents or birth family have made certain agreements regarding contact. Most adoptions before the late 1970s, however, are "closed." Agencies or attorneys ordinarily arrange these adoptions with the goal of keeping the identities of the people involved a secret. When the adoption was finalized, the baby's original birth certificate was sealed and a new one was issued with the adopters' names replacing the birth parents' names. At this writing, whether an adoption is "open" or "closed," in all but three states, laws require that the original birth certificate be sealed. It is available only through petitioning the courts, which rarely grant these petitions, or through, for a fee, court-appointed intermediaries.

Regardless of what it says on paper, the birth families continue to exist in fact and most adoptees continue to have questions about the parents they don't know. They seek information about themselves that can only be answered by relatives who have the missing pieces of the puzzle. Some adoptees fare better being raised by parents other than their birth parents. And some don't fare as well. Nevertheless, adoptees are not ordinarily seeking a replacement for their adoptive parents and family. They just want the whole picture.

Adoptive parents who support the adoptee's search ordinarily find that their relationship is strengthened as a result. And those who thwart this need, choosing to pay attention to their own fears, risk severe impairment to the relationship with their (now-adult) child. As one adoptee said; "When adoptive parents give their adult children permission to search, they are saying, 'Your needs are important and I support your growing up. I love you.'"

Adoptees as Parents

If it is true that we grow up treating ourselves and others the way we were treated, adoptees would do well to look not only to the care they received from their adoptive parents but also to the legacies from their birth families. Doing so will help them locate the spots in which they might grow up again and aid their own parenting. Pre- and perinatal information, if it can be found, can be very helpful. The story of an adopted middle-aged woman named Laurie is an illustration.

Laurie's Story

I'm over sixty now, but I remember how much I looked forward to nursing my firstborn. My milk was slow to come in. The doctors could find no reason that my body would not respond to the usual ways of helping, so I was sent home with hot packs and, "Good luck."

My baby nearly starved before I, with the help of a friend, decided to weigh him before and after breast feeding. He lost an ounce! I felt an overwhelming helplessness and didn't know what to do. Thank goodness my friend said, "Call the doctor and ask him what he recommends you feed this baby."

I felt like a failure. I had so looked forward to breast feeding. Mothers have been doing that for centuries. It is supposed to be instinct. Why couldn't I do it?

Shortly before she died, Mother told me the story of my birth. I had been born to a twenty-year-old unmarried woman who left immediately after my birth. I was left in the care of a midwife. I remember meeting her when I was in college. She was small in stature, frail, with bony hands. These were the hands I knew during my first week of life. It was she who fed me, diapered me, bathed me. Mother said the midwife told her I cried all of the time and she had put whiskey in my formula so she could get some sleep.

So, I had never been breast fed; I had been moved from one

woman to another to another. My formula had been "medicated." No wonder I had no bone knowledge of how to nurse my firstborn. By the time my daughter was born, I had learned about breast feeding and I got that turned around. My daughter seemed to "instinctively" know how to nurse her own firstborn and my first grandchild.

The Importance of Personal Research

Lack of "bone knowledge" is not the only problem adoptees can experience while parenting. As parents, some adoptees are hypervigilant, unconsciously or consciously trying to prevent their children's experiences from echoing their own. Or they may employ an opposite parenting style to prevent what they experienced. For instance, if they grew up feeling criticized, they may parent by marshmallowing, instead of by using nonnegotiable and negotiable rules.

Some parents spent part of their growing-up time in orphanages or in foster care. Or they were moved back and forth between foster homes and birth families. Being separated from what gave them meaning, from their natural place of belonging, without their say, is perhaps one of life's most rage-producing experiences. Each and all of these experiences make a difference in how they build an attitude toward themselves and their lives. The decisions about these childhood experiences also affect the parenting they do—of themselves and of others.

For instance, between 1890 and World War II, in an attempt to assimilate Indians into white culture, the U.S. government took many Native American children from their homes and placed them in boarding schools where all that was theirs by tradition, heritage, and family had to be left behind. Separated from loved ones, they learned that their Indianness, *who they were*, was unacceptable. They were whipped if they used their language. They were regimented and never touched or nurtured. They learned to be ashamed to be Indian. When those children became parents, they had a unique and not always completely serviceable model of how to parent children.

The daughter of a mother reared in an Indian boarding school from the age of four reports having no memories of being touched or held by her mother. As a forty-five-year-old mother herself, she asked permission to touch her mother's arm "for the first time." She's also had to learn about and reclaim her heritage. She grew up learning it was desirable to pass for non-Indian. Now she holds her own children and teaches them how many ways they have to be proud of who they are. With her intention to change the negative effects of her mother's separation, she and her children are correcting the mistakes of the past.

For parents who were themselves adopted, healing from the wounds of separation is one part of growing up again. The other part is putting the pieces in place that will help them pass on better parenting than the parenting they may have received.

Examples of Nurture, Structure, and Discounting

The experiences of adoptive parents, adoptees, and birth parents are too often the stuff of myths and generalizations. When adoptive parents talk about adoption with sensitivity and honesty, they search for the "right" words. The same is true for adoptees and birth parents.

Because they are too often on the receiving end of misplaced judgments, all people involved in the adoption may have learned to tread lightly, not saying anything for fear of saying the wrong thing. Or, even from a good heart, they may have said something hurtful, because they either lacked information or failed to consider the other's experience.

Going back and redoing what was said or went unsaid or what was done or left undone is a hopeful option. Repairing old hurts, thoughtlessly inflicted, is largely a matter of identifying them, taking personal responsibility for one's part in the wounding, saying "I'm sorry," and then making amends.

Some examples of adoption-related situations are presented here to help you identify what you want to keep and what you want to change. As you read, remember that neglect can be passive abuse.

NURTURE EXAMPLES
Situation: Adult adoptee says to a friend, "Sometimes I feel I don't belong in my family—that I don't belong anywhere."
The friend says:
   Abuse: "Oh, get real!" (Hits on arm)
   Conditional Care: "How can you say that after all they've done for you?"
   Assertive Care: "Of course you belong, but I understand your feeling the way you do." Connects in way appropriate to relationship.
   Supportive Care: "I'm sorry. Do you want to tell me how it feels to you?"
   Overindulgence: "That must be just awful. I feel so sorry for you."
   Neglect: "That's nothing. Neither do I and I was born there!"

Situation: Adopted daughter, age ten, says to her mother, "My birth mother didn't want me."

The mother says:

Abuse: "I don't want to hear about it." Takes to bed for two days with migraine headache.

Conditional Care: "But *I'm* your mother and I don't like to hear you say that."

Assertive Care: "Your birth mother had you at the wrong time for her to take care of you. I'm sorry. I want you and love you and care for you."

Supportive Care: "I think I understand that's how it feels sometimes. Would you like some cuddle time with me?"

Overindulgence: "You don't need her. I'll take care of you forever. You're mine."

Neglect: "Don't think about it."

Situation: Birth parent says to a friend, "I can't forget about the child I relinquished."

The friend says:

Abuse: "Why do you hang on to that? Get on with your life."

Conditional Care: "I'm uncomfortable when you talk about that."

Assertive Care: "Relinquishing your child must have been a very hard thing to do." Touches friend's hand gently.

Supportive Care: "I know someone who is a specialist in counseling for these issues. Would you like to have her name?"

Overindulgence: "You poor thing."

Neglect: No response. Changes the subject.

STRUCTURE EXAMPLES

Situation: Adoptive parents talk with the placing agency. The social worker says the parents will be provided with information about the child.

The parents respond:

Rigidity: "We're adopting from a foreign country. We don't think having information matters. We don't need to know that. She's going to be *our* child."

Criticism: "We don't know why you want us to have all this. We just want our baby. What difference does it make anyway?"

Nonnegotiable Rules: "We want every piece of information we can possibly get because we know it will be important at some point."

Negotiable Rules: (In addition to the above) "What are some ways we can get more information as time goes on?"

Marshmallowing: "Whatever you have will be okay for us."

Abandonment: Parents don't ask.

Situation: Birth mother who relinquished a son for adoption says to her mother, "I'm anxious to find my birth son now that he's twenty-one." *The mother responds:*

Rigidity: "Oh, for heaven's sake! You don't need to do that. You gave him up and that's that."

Criticism: "Why do you want him to know *you*?"

Nonnegotiable Rules: "Take care of any unfinished business left over from the relinquishment before you make the effort to contact him."

Negotiable Rules: "When you are ready to find him, if you want me to, I'll go to a search-and-support group meeting with you."

Marshmallowing: "It's best if you don't stir up old stuff, but if you must, I'll make the search for you."

Abandonment: Changes the subject. Pretends not to hear.

DISCOUNTING EXAMPLES

Situation: One adoptive parent says to another adoptive parent, "I've read that adoptive families are different from other families, but I don't want it to be that way."

Level 1: "A family is a family!" (No problem)

Level 2: "If they are different, they aren't much different, so don't worry about it." (Not serious)

Level 3: "I believe it! But what can you do about it?" (No solution)

Level 4: "I can't think of anything to do about it." (No personal power)

Empowerment: "I've got my head out of the sand about that! We're not better or worse, but we have some dynamics in our families that other families don't have."

Situation: Adult child of adoption tells adoptive parent about wanting to search.

Level 1: Ignores. (No problem)

Level 2: "But we're your family. You already have a family." (Not serious)

Level 3: "The records are sealed." (No solution)

Level 4: "I can't help you. Anyway, I don't know what to do." (No personal power)

Empowerment: "I understand. How do you want me to help you? I'm a little nervous about it and I will be responsible for my feelings."

Growing Up Adopted

Going back and redoing what was said or what went unsaid and what was done or left undone is a hopeful option. Repairing old hurts, thoughtlessly inflicted, is largely a matter of identifying them, taking personal responsibility for one's part in the wounding, saying "I'm sorry," and then making amends.

If you find something here that triggers a need for more understanding, you can start with the brief reading list at the end of this chapter. If you want more help than reading provides, check through the list of resources, also at the end of the chapter.

Adoptive parents, build your half of the bridge to the child by being the sort of human being and parent that a reluctant-to-attach child will be inclined to trust. Decide whether you support the changing of sealed records laws. If you do, take some action. Do not discount yourself, the adoptee, and the situation.

Adoptees, accept responsibility for improving not only the quality of your lives, but also the legacy you pass on to your children.

Parents and adoptees, if you have regrets about what's happened in the past, it is never too late to say so, apologize if you need to, and move forward with your new understandings. Remember, we have all done the best we could at any given time.

Many mental health professionals are becoming more knowledgeable about how to help adoptive parents and adoptees. However, many still do not understand the dynamics of adoptive parenting or the experience of growing up adopted. Research carefully to find the help you deserve.

Adoption isn't right or wrong, good or bad. It just IS. Whatever happened in the past can't be changed, but the *decisions* made about past experiences *can* be changed and replaced with joyful, life-supporting beliefs.

Adoption Developmental Chart
This information for adoptees and adopters is in addition to the developmental information in the Ages and Stages chapter.

---

1. Job of the adoptee
(across developmental stages)

- To develop an attachment with adoptive family.
- To grieve losses.
- To accept affection, care, and love.
- To test trustworthiness of caregivers.
- To develop own understanding of adoptive status.
- To do identity work with all four parents in mind.
- To ask questions about adoptive status.

2. A range of behaviors that may be true of an adoptee

- Assumes defensive, protective postures in intimate relationships.
- Attempts to have control by manipulating people and situations.
- Shows signs of recycling grief on anniversaries of separation.
- Sabotages success.
- Shows signs of depression.
- Acts out perceived experiences (stealing, lying, being sneaky, losing things chronically, throwing away valuable items, drug and alcohol abuse, and a host of others).
- Exhibits behaviors outside those explained by history in adoptive family.
- Exhibits behaviors or emotional states related to neurological/ organic causes.
- Is "too good" or "too bad."
- Resists receiving affection or demands an inordinate amount of affection on his terms.

3. Affirmations for the adoptee
(in combination with the affirmations in the stage that applies to the child's age, plus the ones for the prenatal and birth-to-six-months stages. These affirmations are also useful with foster children and stepchildren.)

I will do my part to make a connection with you.

You can count on me.

You can push, but I will not let you push me away.

I will care for you and for myself.

We can both tell the truth and be responsible for our behaviors.

I support you in learning what you may want to know about your history and heritage.

You are lovable just the way you are.

4. Helpful Parent Behaviors

- Give even, confident care.
- "Wear" the baby; practices strong attachment behaviors.
- Comfort grieving child.
- Have albums of child's birth relatives and prior foster care settings available.
- Talk to child about being adopted.
- Listen nondefensively; answer questions truthfully.
- Expect responsible behavior.
- Know that child may be recycling earlier developmental stages more than most non-adopted children.
- Remember child has four parents.
- Deal with own pain; do not project it onto child.
- Grieve infertility.
- Be willing to support adoptee's search for birth family.

5. Unhelpful parent behaviors

- Acting as if own the child.
- Withholding information or giving at inappropriate time.
- Failure to answer adoptee's questions truthfully.
- Too much or too little emphasis on child's adoptive status.
- Believes rearing an adoptee is no different from rearing a birth child.
- Failure to grieve infertility.
- Failure to be honest about personal motives for adopting.
- Failure to get help to solve problems.
- Demanding exclusive loyalty to adoptive family.

6. Clues to adult adoptee's need to grow up again

- Engaging in self-defeating or self-destructive behaviors.
- Failure to follow through on commitments.
- Presence of any addiction.
- Failure to eat properly.
- Failure to get enough sleep or getting too much sleep.
- Failure to pay attention to own needs.
- Being overly dependent, or chronically giving way to others.
- Being rigidly self-reliant, oppositional.
- Being a perfectionist.
- Being stuck in a younger than adult developmental stage.
- Having chronic difficulty in intimate relationships.

Selected References

Arms, Suzanne. *Adoption: A Handful of Hope*. Berkeley, Calif.: Celestial Arts, 1990.

Bascom, Barbara, and Carole McKelvey. *The Complete Guide to Foreign Adoption*. New York: Simon and Schuster Pocket Books, 1997.

Brodzinsky, David M., Marshall D. Schechter, and Robin Marantz Henig. *Being Adopted: The Lifelong Search for Self*. New York: Doubleday, 1992.

Childs-Gowell, Elaine. *Good Grief Rituals*. Barrytown, N.Y.: Station Hill Press, 1992.

Cline, Foster, and Jim Fay. *Parenting with Love & Logic*. Colorado Springs, Colo.: Pinon Press, 1990.

———. *Parenting Teens with Love & Logic*. Colorado Springs, Colo.: Pinon Press, 1992.

Jewett, Claudia L. *Helping Children Cope with Separation and Loss*. Cambridge, Mass.: Harvard Common Press, 1982.

Kirk, H. David. *Adoptive Kinship*. Port Angeles, Wash.: Ben-Simon Publications, 1981.

Levy, T., and Michael Orlans. "Intensive Short-Term Therapy with Attachment Disordered Children." In Vol. 14, *Innovations in Clinical Practice: A Source Book*, L. Vande Creek, S. Knapp, and T. L. Jackson, Sarasota, Fla.: Professional Resource Press, 1995. P.O. Box 15560, Sarasota, FL 34277-1560.

Lifton, Betty Jean. *Lost and Found*. New York: Harper and Row, 1988.

———. *Journey of the Adopted Self*. New York: Basic Books, 1994.

Magid, Ken, and Carole McKelvey. *High Risk: Children without a Conscience*. New York: Bantam Books, 1990.

McKelvey, Carole A., ed. *Give Them Roots, Then Let Them Fly: Understanding Attachment Therapy*. Evergreen, Colo.: The Attachment Center, 1995. P.O. Box 2764, Evergreen, CO 80437.

Melina, Lois Ruskai. *Raising Adopted Children*. New York: Harper and Row, 1986.

Verrier, Nancy. *The Primal Wound: Understanding the Adopted Child*. Baltimore: Gateway Press, 1993. (Order from the author, at 919 Village Center, Lafayette, CA 94549.)

Waldmann, Christopher, and Lynda Mansfield. *Don't Touch My Heart: Healing the Pain of an Unattached Child*. Colorado Springs, Colo.: Pinon Press, 1994.

Welch, Martha G. *Holding Time*. New York: Simon and Schuster, 1988.

Selected Resources

American Adoption Congress
1000 Connecticut Avenue NW, # 9
Washington, D.C. 20002
1-800-274-OPEN

Adoptive Families of America
333 Highway 100 North
Minneapolis, MN 55422
612-535-4829

The Attachment Center
  at Evergreen
P.O. Box 2764
Evergreen, CO 80437
303-674-1910
  This organization does attachment
  therapy and keeps lists of practitioners in other parts of the country who
  are knowledgeable about attachment
  problems.

Attachment Disorder Parent
  Network, Gail Trenberth
P.O. Box 18475
Boulder, CO 80308
303-443-1446

Concerned United Birthparents
200 Walker Street
Des Moines, IA 50317
1-800-822-2777

The North American Council on
  Adoptable Children
1821 University Avenue
Suite N 498
St. Paul, MN 55104
612-644-3036

RESOLVE, Inc.
1310 Broadway
Somerville, MA 02144
617-623-0744

Appendices

Appendix A

Tools for Family Growth

Even and Uneven Parenting
(to be used with pages 6–7)

Uneven versus Dysfunctional Parenting

People who were abused or abandoned may have been told that their families were dysfunctional. In *Growing Up Again,* families are not called dysfunctional because the authors believe that giving people such negative labels doesn't help them grow. If "dysfunctional" means "does not function," then anyone from a truly dysfunctional family would not be here. Think about using the term "uneven parenting" instead.

Probably most of us could describe an event from our growing up years that was helpful and another that was not. It is important to claim and celebrate the things we got that worked for us. It is also important to recognize and heal ourselves from the wounds of the things that did not support us.

Draw a Continuum

Think of your family of origin on a continuum. On one end are things that didn't help you. On the other end are things that did. Mark X on the spots where you got lots of parenting. At each end of the line write an example of an event or parental attitude or behavior that fits there.

Didn't help			Helped
✕ ✕	✕	✕ ✕	
Neglect of physical injuries		Consistent rules and attitudes about morals & ethical behaviors	

- You can draw a parenting line for your family of origin and identify some things at the middle and some toward the ends.
- You can draw a second line and record the ways you are parenting your children or yourself.
- You can draw a third line and indicate how you want to parent.

Stand and Explore

Family of Origin

To explore how focusing on each end of the continuum affects our ability to parent our children and care for ourselves, try the following standup exercise.

- Stand.
- Take one step to the right.
- Think about one specific positive thing you got from your *family of origin*. Notice your feelings.
- Now move one large step to the left.
- Think about one specific negative thing you got from your family of origin. Notice your feelings.
- Now move back to the right and recapture those strong positive feelings that help you make changes.

Parenting

- Now think about how you *parent your children*.
- Take one step to the right.
- Think about one specific positive way you related to your child. Notice your feelings.
- Now move one large step to the left.
- Think about one specific way you have parented that you wish you had done differently. Notice your feelings.
- Now move back to the right and recapture that strong feeling of having done well.

Caring for Self

- Now think about how you care for yourself.
- Take one step to the right.
- Think about one specific positive way you have taken care of yourself. Notice your feelings.
- Now move one large step to the left.

- Think about one specific way you have taken care of yourself that you wish you had done differently. Notice your feelings.
- Now move back to the right and recapture that strong feeling of having done well.

Describe how you felt at each end. Any time you feel stuck in your parenting or caring for yourself, move a step to the right, to that positive spot, and draw upon that good energy.

Using Contracts
(to be used with page 86)

Contracts can be a very helpful tool for starting new behavior in a family. Contracts can be initiated by a child or parent when they want to work together to solve a problem.

When you have developed a verbal contract with a child who is six or older, it is sometimes helpful to put the contract in visual form. Use symbols, pictures, drawings, or this written contract form.

Contract

Mutual Goal or Problem

John doesn't have clean clothes to wear to school.

	Child **John, age 10**	*Parent* **Mom and Dad**
BACKGROUND Describe current situation or behavior	Lends clothes and toys to others and doesn't get them back. Runs short of clothes between wash days.	Want John to wear clean clothes to school.
CHANGE Describe desirable situation or behavior	Will stop lending school clothes. May lend toys at his discretion.	Will not "bug" John about his clothes and toys not being at home.
BENEFIT Of proposed *behavior* *change*	Learns to say no to friends and be responsible for his clothes. Learns consequences of loaning toys.	Will not buy new clothes to replace loaned ones. Will not express anger to John.
EFFORT/ACTION When, where, what, how long	Will be sure he understands which clothes are school clothes. Will not loan school clothes. Will select several items of older clothes he can loan	Will not remind John or "bug" him. Will see that John has an adequate supply of school clothes and will wash them regularly.
SUPPORT **SOLICITED**	Mom and Dad will compliment John on his successes at weekly family meeting.	John will compliment Mom and Dad at the meeting for not bugging him.

| **REWARDS**
Positive
consequences,
celebrations | When John and parents have kept the contract for two weeks, they will play miniature golf to celebrate. | |

If someone breaks the contract,

| **PENALTIES**
Negative
consequences | John has to pay for lost school clothes from his allowance and make up the difference by doing yard work or errands. | Dad does one of John's chores for a week; mom buys him a new T-shirt. |

Sample Rules Charts
(to be used with page 73)

Families need to have rules that are clear and posted for all to see. Not posting rules invites confusion and manipulation. It is easier to challenge and change a posted rule to suit the needs of family members.

Two types of rules help families be successful. One set applies to interactions with others and respect for self. The other applies to jobs and responsibilities around the house. The items on these lists are suggestions and examples. Use the rules that fit your family and add the ones you need.

People Rules

1. Think and feel for yourself.
2. Tell the truth. Say yes when you mean yes and no when you mean no.
3. Figure out what you need.
4. Ask clearly for what you need and want.
5. Respect and be helpful to yourself and others.
6. Affirm yourself and others.
7. Be responsible for your behavior.
8. Cooperate.
9. _____
10. _____

House Rules

1. Make your bed before breakfast.
2. Put your dirty clothes in the hamper right after you take them off.
3. Clean your room by Saturday noon.
4. Finish your yard chores by Saturday at four o'clock.
5. Set the table for dinner by six o'clock or finish the dishes within one hour after dinner.
6. _____
7. _____

Getting Free of Double Binds
(to be used with page 136)

What Is a Double Bind?

A double bind is a set of two or more messages, each of which is or seems to be true when given separately, but when given in combination are contradictory, create a problem, and elicit confusion, anger, rage, fear, or helplessness. The messages may be:

- **Verbal, given simultaneously.** Heather says, "Tell me all about your vacation right now, but I have to leave in five minutes."
- **Verbal and nonverbal, given simultaneously.** Heather says, "Tell me all about your vacation right now," and then she walks out of the room.
- **Verbal or nonverbal, given at different times.** Heather says, "I want to hear all about your vacation soon. I'm interested!" During the next six months you offer to tell about the vacation four times. Each time Heather proclaims her interest but won't take time for the conversation.

Examples of Double Binds

"I love you." / "Don't inconvenience me."
"Be successful." / "Be dependent."
"Grow up." / "Don't grow up."
"Be unique." / "Do it my way."
"Be perfect." / "Don't be better than I am."
"Always please others." / "Stand up for yourself."

How to Counter Double Binds and Resolve the Problems They Create

Think of a double bind you have received, or choose one from the list above to practice on. Answer each of the following questions.

1. Is my relationship with the person who offered this bind an important one? Shall I ignore both messages and just walk away from this, or do I need to deal with it somehow?
2. If I need or want to deal with it, what is my goal? (For example, my goal is to keep my job.)
3. Can I reach my goal by confronting the double message?

Would it be wise to say to the person, "I can't go two ways at once. Will you pick one"?

4. If that would not be wise, is there something in one of the messages that I can use to help me reach my goal? If there is, can I ignore or circumvent the other message? Can I respond to the other message in a small, nondestructive way?

5. If this relationship or situation is important and none of the above questions help identify a way to resolve the double bind, it may be time to ask this question: Is this bind unimportant or do I need to be building a new relationship or looking for a new situation?

Children and Double Binds

Children, as well as adults, need skills for dealing with double binds. Because double binds are so immobilizing, they give rise to strong feelings. Children need help with their feelings and with thinking about what to do. Parents can

- Teach children what double binds are and how they are destructive.
- Teach children to identify options for resolving the dilemmas that double binds create.
- Let children hear and see adults deal with double binds.
- Encourage children to point out double binds so parents can re-place conflicting words and behaviors with loving nurture and clear structure.
- Teach children to honor their feelings and to use them to help recognize double binds.

Because double binds elicit more than one feeling, asking children to tell you how they feel may be less effective than helping them sort through their feelings with exercises like the Feelings faces board, page 284.

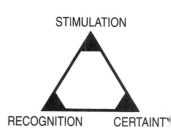

STIMULATION

RECOGNITION   CERTAINTY

The Feeling Faces Board: Let Your Finger Do the Talking[1]

Use the balloon faces on the Ups and Downs with Feelings faces board, page 284, to teach your child about double binds.

- Tell your child you are going to play a faces game to help learn how to deal with double binds.

- Say a double bind to your child ("I love you." / "I ignore you.") Ask him to point to the face or faces that show how he feels when you say those together. Mark or record which of the faces the child points to for later reference. Don't worry about naming the feelings at this time. Young children don't have many names for feelings.
- Say one of the messages, "I love you." Ask your child to point to the faces that show how he feels when he hears that message alone. Mark the face(s).
- Say the other message, "I ignore you." Ask your child to point to the faces that show how he feels when he hears that message alone. Mark the face(s).
- Tell your child that people have feelings to help them know what to do and that double binds are confusing, partly because we have more than one feeling about them.
- Teach your child that when he feels sad he is to get comfort. When he feels scared, he is to move to a safe place or get help from someone. When he is glad, he is to enjoy his gladness and maybe share it with someone else. When he is angry, he is to think how to get what he needs. When he is confused and needs more information, he is to get it. When he feels a mix of emotions, he may be dealing with a double bind.
- Go back over the faces your child pointed to and help him identify his needs and get comfort, safety, celebration, problem-solving ideas, information, or whatever is appropriate for each one. If you want to teach names for the emotions, this is a good time to do it.

When your child is facing a double-bind dilemma with friends or at school, you can use the Ups and Downs with Feelings faces board and the questions previously described to help your child feel, think, and decide what to do, and perhaps to help you decide how to give further support.

How Adults Can Reclaim the Ability to Recognize Feelings

Some adults who grew up with double binds learned to cope with them by ceasing to feel their confusion and by acting as if double binds are normal. As adults, these people will not have developed skills for protecting themselves from the destructive dilemmas of double binds and will probably give them without noticing it. One way adults can help themselves reclaim their feelings is by using their fingers to show them what their heads have had to forget. What the head had to forget, the body remembers. If you are such a person, you can use the Ups and Downs with Feelings faces board to help you reclaim your feelings. You can do this alone, with a partner, or in a support group. Don't use the word "feeling" or worry about naming the feeling. Just ask your finger to point to the face that shows *how it was when* he told you he loved you; when he was drunk; when she said he wasn't drunk, he was sick; or when she said it was your fault.

You can use the information your finger gives you to think about what you needed then and what you need to be aware of now.

Change Double Binds to Congruent Messages

As you think about double binds and reclaim your feelings about them, you will become more aware of giving them. If you think you may have set up a double bind, ask the person who received the messages if it felt like a double bind. You can think about whether the messages really do conflict, or you can pretend you are getting the messages and use the faces board to let your fingers do the talking. If, in fact, you have offered a double bind, take action to remove it and give clear, congruent messages about what you want.

UPS & DOWNS with Feelings

© 1985 Carole Gesme. Used with permission.

Top border: • needed • jealous • glad • hurt • lucky • tired • joyful • surprised •

Left border (top to bottom): disgusted • free • rejected • confident • depressed • guilty • smart • helpless • brave • stupid • special

Right border (top to bottom): carefree • embarrassed • scared • lovable • ashamed • capable • sad • excited • angry • alive • let down

Bottom border: • unwanted • trusted • alone • happy • dirty • worried • frightened •

Encouraging Responsibility through Language
(to be used with pages 186)

Encouraging responsibility in children is an important part of parenting. Becoming even more responsible for getting our needs met and for empowering others is an important part of growing up again for adults.

Parents can use these six guidelines for responsible language to help them act responsibly, to teach children to be responsible, and to grow into independence. Making a habit of speaking responsibly will help to move a family away from unhealthy enmeshment or codependence and into healthy caring, independence, and interdependence.

Guidelines That Support Responsible Language

1. Ask directly for what you want or need.
2. Think and feel for yourself, not for others.
3. Be responsible for your own feelings and responsive to the feelings of others.
4. Say yes and no straight.
5. Remember that people, not things, are responsible for behavior.
6. Respond to questions with straight answers.

Following are the six guidelines for responsible communication. Listed alongside them are irresponsible or codependent ways of communicating for each. These principles are especially important when going through or recycling the developmental stage indicated here and described in section VII.

Stage 1—Being

Responsible:
Ask directly for what you want or need. Say what is to be done and who is to do it.

Irresponsible:
Imply that someone should do something, manipulate.

Examples:
"Will you give me something to drink?" "Come and eat lunch now." "Do you have money to deposit in our checking account today?"

Examples:
"I'm thirsty." "The soup is getting cold." "The checkbook is overdrawn."

Stage 2—Doing

Responsible:
Think and feel for yourself, not for others.

Examples:
"I like this. Do you like it?"
"What do you think of this?"
"I am offended by that."

Irresponsible:
Think and feel for others.

Examples:
"You are going to love this."
"You will not approve of this."
"I know you mean to be kind, but . . ."

Stage 3—Thinking

Responsible:
Be responsible for your own feelings and responsive to the feelings of others.

Examples:
"I am furious." "I feel wonderful." "Here is what we are having for dinner. I hope you enjoy it."

Irresponsible:
Attempt to make others responsible for your feelings and ignore or redefine theirs.

Examples:
"You make me so mad!" "You make me happy." "I know you don't like the food I cook, but do eat it just to please me."

Stage 4—Power and Identity

Responsible:
Answer yes and no directly and don't ask "Will you . . ." unless you are willing to accept either yes or no for an answer.

Examples:
"Will you set the table?" / "No, not tonight."
"Have you finished your project?" / "No, it won't be ready until tomorrow."
"Do you want me to help you?" / "Yes, please."

Irresponsible:
Be indirect. Manipulate.

Examples:
"Will you set the table?" / "I might do it later."
"Have you finished your project?" / "I didn't know that you wanted it today."
"Do you want me to help you?" / "Oh, you are busy and I'm all right."

Stage 5—Structure

Responsible:

Remember that people, not things, are responsible for behavior.

Examples:
"What did you do today?" "I see that we are nearly finished." "You may be able to use the ideas in this book."

Irresponsible:

Act as if inanimate objects are responsible for people's behavior.

Examples:
"How did your day go?" "Things are falling into place." "This book will solve your problem."

Stage 6—Identify, Sexuality, and Separation

Responsible:

Respond to questions with straight answers without redefining or manipulating.

Examples:
"Where are your boots?" / "I left them at work."
"How much money do you need?" / "I need fifteen dollars."
"Do you have time to help me for half an hour?" / "Not today, but I can tomorrow if you still need me."

Irresponsible:

Don't reveal yourself. Manipulate.

Examples:
"Where are your boots?" / "I'm not going to wear them today."
"How much money do you need?" / "I don't need it until later."
"Do you have time to help me for half an hour?" / "Why?"

Self-Esteem: A Family Affair Leader Guide by Jean Illsley Clarke has six exercises that can be used in groups to help people practice recognizing irresponsible language and using responsible language.[2]

Supporting Spiritual Growth through the Early Developmental Stages
(to be used with pages 212)

Support for spiritual growth includes modeling, invitations, and direct teachings. Here youth minister Mary Kaye Ashley[3] describes how parents can support and enhance the spiritual growth of a child in each developmental stage within the loving atmosphere of a community of faith.

Stage 1—Being (Birth to Six Months)

The parent is laying the groundwork for the child to be able to trust anything beyond himself or herself. At this point, the parent is the "higher power." Trustworthiness on the parents' part in meeting the child's needs builds the child's ability to eventually trust others and God. It is not too early to begin praying with the infant, thus building patterns and habits of the heart.

Stage 2—Doing (Six Months to Eighteen Months)

Parents continue building strong attachments with the child and begin to expose the child to other strong attachments in the parents' lives. Nursery and parent/child classes within the faith community and with friends are invaluable. These safe, loving, nurturing environments build a sense that "this is a place where someone loves me." Parents who build supportive relationships with other parents of children this age within the faith community expand the circle of families the child can learn to depend on.

Stage 3—Thinking (Eighteen Months to Three Years)

Separation anxiety at the beginning of this stage underscores the importance of making separations in nurturing, supportive ways. This applies to separations at the place of worship as well. Take the child in for part of the worship if he or she is willing to go. If your child says no, remember that the ability to say NO means the child will also be able to say YES, not only to you, but also in other important relationships. Join in the awe of learning—watch butterflies, feel the soft fur of kittens, talk to trees, and stroke sleeping babies with love and prayers and gentle songs.

Stage 4—Power and Identity (Three Years to Six Years)

Loving rituals flourish with new meaning. Now children can think of people to pray for. Now children help us bring food for the foodshelf. Now we can teach new rituals for children to do all by themselves, such as praying, singing, talking about God's love for them at specific times like during baths. Expose them to the stories of your faith community in pictures, words, and songs, and they will carry them always. Table prayers and songs they can learn and say themselves give them great opportunities to lead, to be like big folks. If they learn many stories, they may act them out or retell them, pretending and changing them. Allow children those pretendings; they are making those stories their own.

Stage 5—Structure (Six Years to Twelve Years)

Now these precious ones are watching to see if you follow your own rules. Congruence in community life and faith is paramount. Let them ask questions; respond with "I believe . . . What do you believe?" They may enjoy visiting a friend's house of worship or celebrating someone's baptism, first communion, bar mitzvah, and so on. Explain as best you are able about how faiths differ. Encourage children to seek out all the answers they want to know in respectful ways. Model how to treat those we disagree with lovingly.

Stage 6—Identity, Sexuality, and Separation (Twelve Years to Nineteen Years)

If you have communicated your beliefs well, youth will now choose their own! Some may be like yours, and some may not. Continue to allow them to question, but you question, too, with respect and love as they "try on" new beliefs and behaviors. Love them through it all; love *them* even if they make choices that are hard for you to accept; point out your concern with love if you think they are being manipulated. Ask them all of your own whys; *listen* to their answers. Continue to live with your own faith choices, but be open to learning and sharing. Thank God for the children in your life.

Appendix B

Tools for Personal Growth

Developmental Affirmations:
How to Use Them with Your Family and Yourself
(to be used with pages 216–217)

When we offer developmental affirmations to children, we offer powerful support that strengthens their ability to accomplish their developmental tasks successfully.

Unfinished business from any prior developmental stage will demand to be addressed again until the child resolves it satisfactorily, so it is important to offer the affirmations from preceding stages as well as those corresponding to a child's current age. As adults, we are continually recycling previous stages from day to day so all sixty-one affirmations from the Becoming through the Adult stages (see pages 218–46) are appropriate for us.

Explore these affirmations. Photocopy the 54 ovals for stages 1 through 7. Cut them out. Color the ovals for each stage a different color: red, orange, yellow, green, light blue, dark blue, lilac or purple. Add the Integration affirmations in white if you are in that last stage or the prenatal ones in peach if you are focusing on prenatal work. Post them. Read them. Say them. Listen to them.

You can purchase colored laminated ovals if you wish. See page 312, Other Learning Materials Available.

Pay attention to how you give affirmations. Remember to offer the affirmations to other people as "*I* care about *you*" or "*You* can grow at your own pace" messages. Only when they have thought about and decided to trust the message should they change it to "*I* care about *myself*" or "*I* (do) grow at my own pace."

Read the affirmations to yourself, "*You* can grow at *your* own pace," speaking as your own nurturing parent to the child within. Your inner child may not believe you at first and may have to test and observe you before being able to say wholeheartedly, "It is okay for *me* to grow at *my* own pace" or "*I* do grow at my own pace." If we hurry the use of "I" in affirmations, we are only adding one more layer of adaptive behavior—one more layer of letting other people tell us how to think, feel, and do.

Here are several ways to use the Affirmation Ovals with children, yourself, and other adults. These exercises are from the book *Affirmation Ovals: 139 Ways to Give and Get Affirmations* by Jean Illsley Clarke and Carole Gesme.[4]

1. Finding Affirmations to Help You Identify What You Need

Read each Affirmation Oval and put the ones that sound especially good to you in a separate pile. Then read those and ask yourself what they have to do with what's going on in your life at the moment. Decide how you will get what you need based on this very personal assessment.

2. Introducing the Affirmations to Children Who Do Not Read

Put the Affirmations Ovals stages Birth through the age of the child in a basket. Ask a child to get the basket and hand you an affirmation. Read it to the child. Continue as long as the child shows interest in the activity or until all affirmations have been read.

3. Pairs[5]

This exercise can be led by a facilitator with any pair of people who have some commitment to each other (for example, couples, colleagues, siblings, or parent and child). Tell the partners that the affirmations can help them find out what they want and need from each other. Each person arranges a set of Stage 1 through 7 Affirmation Ovals by color rows; then looks at each row and picks which messages each *wish* the other person would give to him or her. Each goes through the chosen messages with the other person. Facilitator asks each person:

- "Did you know this person wants this affirmation from you?"
- "Do you give it now?"
- "How?"
- "If the other person isn't hearing, seeing, or getting it, how else can you give it?"
- "If you don't believe you can give it, what do you need that will enable you to give it? How can you get that?"
- "Will you give the affirmation right now?"
- (To the person who wishes to receive the affirmation) "Do you accept this? Anything else you need?"

4. Ask Your Family[6]

Ask family members to sit in a circle with a set of Affirmation Ovals spread in front of the group. Have each person pick one, two, or three affirmations and then ask the family member from whom he or she would like to hear each message to read it. If that person does not want to give the affirmation, the family can think about what each of them needs and if they need to improve their structure and rules so there is room for more love and self-esteem in the family.

5. Good Night (Especially for Kids)[7]

Keep a basket of Affirmation Ovals Stages 1 through the age of your child by each child's bed. Let the child pick three each night. Say those to the child as you tuck him into bed.

6. Helping Teenagers[8]

Picture your teenager as an infant and young child. Visualize what was going on at each developmental stage in her life and yours. If there were affirmations from any stage that you didn't know about or give, give them now. Use the Affirmation Ovals as your guide. Give the affirmations verbally, tell your child what was going on at that time, and then give the ovals. She may act as if she doesn't care or she may scoff. Give them anyway.

7. Problem Solving

Have each family member think of a problem that he or she needs or wants to solve. Then have each identify three possible solutions and choose Affirmation Ovals that will be helpful in resolving this problem.

8. You Can't Go Back But You Can Get What You Need Now

Work in pairs. Tell your partner a short story about a typical day in your life when you were a certain age or the age your child is now. Include your name and nicknames, family, house, school, friends, not-friends, activities, sports and what you liked to do, what you did well, and what your wishes were.

Lay out all of the Affirmation Ovals up to and including the age you are telling about. Pick up the affirmations that would have helped you on the kind of day you described. Take as many affirmations as you want. Of those, pick the most important three or four or the ones that feel best to you today. Have your partner read them to you, once with your eyes open and your partner handing them to you one at a time, and once again with your eyes closed.

Seeing Our Own Shields: A Visualization
(to be used with page 213)

This is a visualization. It is a way to get a picture of your ability to care for yourself and others using the metaphor of a shield. If you are a person who does not see pictures in your head easily, you can try doing the exercise anyway. You can imagine what your picture would look like. Remember that however it looks is okay because it is *your* shield *today*. Record the following directions onto a cassette tape, reading slowly. Then play the tape back and follow the directions. You could also ask someone to read the directions slowly to you.

> Seat yourself comfortably or lie down. Check out the various parts of your body to be sure you are comfortably situated. Keep your body straight, without crossed arms or legs. . . . Close your eyes to shut out the visual distractions. . . . Now be aware of your hearing. . . . Listen to the sounds of the room and make them louder. . . . Now let them go and hear only my voice. . . . Be aware of your body. . . . Feel the pressure of your body resting on the chair or the floor. . . . Feel the air going in and out of your lungs. . . . Now breathe deeply three or four times. . . . Become aware that you have something resting lightly at your side. . . . It does not bother you or distract you and it is always ready to be used. . . . This object represents your ability to take care of yourself and other people. . . . Look at it. . . . It may be a cloak or an umbrella of white light or something else. Whatever it is, it's yours so it is right for you. I will call it your shield. It may be the shape of the shields in picture books and museums . . . or it may look *very* different. . . . Pick it up. . . . Feel its weight. . . . Is it light or heavy? . . . Smell it. . . . Raise it over your head. . . . Is it large enough to protect you fully from the rain? . . . Can it extend over someone else to protect that person also? . . . Now hold it in front of you in a position that will deflect the arrows of life. . . . Notice how well it does that. . . . Look for holes or thin spots. . . . There may be a few or there may be many. . . . They may be large or they may be small. . . . However your shield is, accept it as it is for you today; it is your shield. . . . Thank your shield for being there for you and for all the good work it does for you. . . . After you have finished appreciating it, place it gently back at your side and become aware once again of your breathing and the sounds and smells around you. Open your eyes when you are ready. (This is the end of the visualization.)

Follow-up Activities

1. Write a description of your shield, or draw a picture of it, or describe it to someone.
2. Tell someone about a quality of your shield that you are happy you have developed.
3. Think of one way your shield could be improved.
4. Use the ideas in this book to help you find a way to do that.

The Great Variety of Shields

Remembering that your shield is the right one for you, you might like to hear how some other people have described their shields.

"White and loose and fluffy at the edges; can wrap all around me."

"A heavy iron cylinder from my feet to above my head with a small hole to look out."

"A bell of white light."

"A big mahogany bed with a wonderful canopy."

"A canoe shaped to take me through the calm water and the turbulent water."

"New and shiny with a price tag hanging on one side—the price of my recent therapy."

"Thicker over the genitals."

"A semipermeable membrane that lets love in and keeps the hate out."

"Looks great, but it is made of paper."

"Dark and conical and made of lead; it is not crowded inside, but there is no room for anyone else."

"A wall of flowers with thorns to use if I am in danger."

"Cylindrical, enter from one side, protects me all around."

"A wooden lattice or sieve that lets too much through."

"Honey-colored leather, smooth and round with a point in the center. It expands to cover other people."

Whatever your nurturing looks like, honor your ability to care for yourself and others and continue to strengthen it.

Where to Go for Additional Help

Here are some places to find help:

- Support groups and therapy groups
- Individual or family therapy practitioners (counselors, psychologists, psychiatrists, social workers, and other trained and accredited professionals)
- Community mental health centers
- Twelve Step groups
- Churches, hospitals, and crisis telephone lines

Twelve Step Groups

Look in your phone book for a number listed under Alcoholics Anonymous Intergroup or Information Services. Someone there will tell you about meetings in your area. If you live in a smaller town, that office may also have a listing for Adult Children of Alcoholics, Al-Anon, and other Twelve Step meetings available to you.

In a larger city, you may find a phone listing for the Twelve Step group you seek by looking for the group name directly: Overeaters Anonymous, Sex Addicts Anonymous, Parents Anonymous, Fundamentalists Anonymous, and so on.

Professional Help

One of the best ways to locate a therapist for individual, group, or family therapy is to ask friends and acquaintances for the names of professionals who have helped them. Although a therapist who is just right for another person may not be just right for you, this kind of research is a good way to begin.

If you seek help in recovering from a specific problem such as sexual abuse, you can ask for names of people who specialize in that work. Search out information from YWCAs, YMCAs, counseling centers, and other similar organizations. Ask about the services they provide and ask for referrals to other professionals in your community who may be suited to your needs.

It's okay for you to meet with the professionals and interview one or several before you decide on someone. Ask about their training, experience, and credentials. Ask how they would approach their work with you and what the cost will be. Ask what they expect of you. Pay attention to the information you receive and to your intuition.

When you agree to work with someone, keep several things in mind:

- You may benefit from working with several different helpers. Some people begin in family therapy and move to individual therapy. Some begin with individual therapy and move to group therapy. You and your therapist should discuss the most appropriate help for you at any point in your healing process. The decision is up to you. Trust yourself to know what you know and remember that it is important to get your needs met.
- Sexual contact between a therapist and a client is never okay. If this happens, leave immediately and report the person to his or her professional licensing board or association and get help for this abuse.

Therapy will probably generate some discomfort. This discomfort is a necessary part of growing. But if you should feel a particular discomfort about your therapist's behavior, it is important to find out why. Trust your intuition. Your needs are important and you deserve to feel safe.

Notes

CHAPTER 2, "THE HUNGER FOR STIMULATION, RECOGNITION, AND CERTAINTY"

1. Helen Neville and Diane Clark Johnson, *Temperament Tools: Working with Your Child's Inborn Traits* (Seattle: Parenting Press, 1997).

2. Michael D. Resnick, et al., "Protecting Adolescents from Harm: Findings from the National Longitudinal Study of Adolescent Health" (*JAMA*, Sept. 10, 1997, vol. 278, no. 10).

CHAPTER 5, "LIFE EXAMPLES OF THE NURTURE CHART"

1. Thanks to Jim Jump of Kalamazoo, Michigan, for suggesting and expanding upon the metaphor of the highway as a way to think about the nurture and structure continua.

2. See Carole Gesme and Larry Peterson, *Help for Kids! Understanding Your Feelings About Moving—For Kids Ages Six and Older* (4036 Kerry Court, Minnetonka, MN, 55345: Pine Press, 1991).

CHAPTER 6, "WHEN LOVE DOESN'T STICK"

1. Martha Welch, *Holding Time* (New York: Simon and Schuster, 1988).

2. Robert Karen, *Becoming Attached: Unfolding the Mystery of the Infant-Mother Bond and Its Impact on Later Life* (New York: Warner Books, 1994). See also John Bowlby, *A Secure Base: Parent-Child Attachment and Healthy Human Development* (New York: Basic Books, 1988).

CHAPTER 7, "NURTURING OTHER ADULTS AND OURSELVES"

1. Elaine Childs-Gowell, *Good Grief Rituals* (Barrytown, N.Y.: Station Hill Press, 1992).

CHAPTER 8, "STRUCTURE: WHAT IT IS AND WHY WE NEED IT"

1. See Jean Illsley Clarke, et al., *Help! for Parents of School-Age Children and Teenagers* (Seattle: Parenting Press, 1998).

2. Kathryn M. Hammerseng, *Telling Isn't Tattling* (Seattle: Parenting Press, 1995).

3. See Ruby K. Payne, *Poverty: A Framework for Understanding and Working with Students and Adults from Poverty* (Baytown, Tex.: RFT Publishing, 1995).

CHAPTER 10, "THE LESSONS OF DISCIPLINE"

1. "Mindworks," Minneapolis *Star Tribune*, March 6, 1997.

2. Diane Chelsom Gossen, *Restitution: Restructuring School Discipline* (Chapel Hill, N.C.: New View Publications, 1993).

3. Jean Illsley Clarke, *Time-In: When Time Out Doesn't Work* (Seattle: Parenting Press, 1998).

CHAPTER 12, "THE NURTURE/ STRUCTURE HIGHWAY"

1. Thanks to Gaye Hurtig for telling those of us who like to learn by doing to play with toy cars.

CHAPTER 13, "WHEN PARENTS DISAGREE ABOUT RULES"

1. John Bradshaw, *The Family: A Revolutionary Way of Self-Discovery* (Pompano Beach, Fla.: Health Communications, 1988), 53–54.

2. Thanks to Barbara Beystrom for contributing this section.

CHAPTER 16, "OVERINDULGENCE: MISGUIDED NURTURE, INADEQUATE STRUCTURE"

1. David J. Bredehoft, Ph.D., L.P., professor of psychology and family studies, Concordia University, St. Paul, Minn.

2. Jean Illsley Clarke, "What about Overindulgence?" *WE Newsletter,* March 1995 (Daisy Press, 16535 9th Ave. N., Minneapolis, MN 55447).

3. **Sample Characteristics:** 730 subjects were surveyed (84.5 percent female; 14.4 percent male). Subjects' ages ranged from 17 to 83 (mean age = 42.8); 78.2 percent of the subjects were parents with a mean of 2.39 children. The subjects were highly educated (4.2 percent doctorate; 34.2 percent masters; 34 percent bachelors; 23.2 percent less than or equal to twelfth grade diploma). The majority (86.4 percent) grew up in dual-parent families. Not all subjects responded to all survey questions.

Subsample Characteristics: of the 730 subjects, 124 (86.3 percent female; 12.1 percent male) identified themselves as an adult child of overindulgence (ACOs); 2.4 percent of ACOs had earned doctorates; 29 percent masters; 37.9 percent bachelors; 3.2 percent trade school degrees; 26.6 percent less than or equal to twelfth grade diplomas.

4. To procure a copy of the research survey questions to replicate the research with your population, send a request and $10.00 to David Bredehoft, Ph.D., 275 Syndicate Street North, Concordia University, St. Paul, MN 55104-5494.

CHAPTER 17, "THE HAZARDS OF OVERINDULGENCE"

1. Barbara Diamond Goldin, *Just Enough Is Plenty: A Hanukkah Tale* (New York: Viking Penguin Inc., 1988).

2. Betty Clark and Diane R. Houghton, *Too Many Toys: A Christmas Story.* (Boston: Little Friend Press, 1996).

3. Thanks to Heidi Caglayan and Sandra Agajanian for permission to include the affirmations for overindulgence and for all her helpful thinking on the topic.

CHAPTER 19, "WHAT TO DO INSTEAD OF OVERINDULGING"

1. See David Walsh, *Selling Out America's Children* (Minneapolis: Fairview Press, 1994). See also H. Stephen Glenn and Jane Nelsen, *Raising Self-Reliant Children in a Self-Indulgent World* (Rocklin, Calif.: Prima Publishing and Communications, 1988).

CHAPTER 20, "HOW WE DENY: THE FOUR LEVELS OF DISCOUNTING"

1. Rollo May, *Power and Innocence: A Search for the Sources of Violence* (New York: C. C. Norton, 1971).

2. Jacqui Lee Schiff et al., *Cathexis Reader: Transactional Analysis, Treatment of Psychosis* (New York: Harper and Row, 1975).

3. Thanks to Sandy Keiser for suggesting and helping with the design of this chart.

CHAPTER 21, "EXAMPLES OF THE FOUR LEVELS OF DISCOUNTING"

1. See William Sears and Martha Sears, *The Baby Book: Everything You Need to Know about Your Baby—From Birth to Age Two* (New York: Little Brown and Co., 1983). See also Laurie A. Kanyer, *The Journey of Becoming a Mother* (Golden, Colo.: Love and Logic Press, 1996).

CHAPTER 22, "STOP THE MANY WAYS OF DISCOUNTING"

1. Norman Cousins, *Anatomy of an Illness: Reflections on Healing and Regeneration* (New York: W. W. Norton, 1979).

2. Eric Berne, *What Do You Say After You Say Hello?* (New York: Grove Press, 1973), 324–37.

3. Janet Geringer Woititz, *Adult Children of Alcoholics* (Pompano Beach, Fla.: Health Communications, 1983), 72–73.

4. Thanks to Sandy Keiser for insisting that we address double binds and for conceptualizing and devloping this chart.

5. Robert Subby, *Lost in the Shuffle: The Co-Dependent Reality* (Pompano Beach, Fla.: Health Communications, 1987).

CHAPTER 23, "PROBLEM SOLVING: PUTTING IT ALL TOGETHER"

1. Thanks to Deane Gradous for the concept of combining Nurture, Structure, and Discounting in this way.

2. Thanks to Susan Legender Clarke for designing the Problem-Solving Worksheet.

CHAPTER 24, "BECOMING: THE PRENATAL AND BIRTH EXPERIENCE"

1. "Your Child from Birth to Three," *Newsweek Special Edition*, Spring/Summer 1997; J. Madeline Nastt, "Fertile Minds: From Birth a Baby's Brain Cells Proliferate Wildly, Making Connections That May Shape a Lifetime of Experience," *Time*, 3 Feb. 1997, 48–49.

2. Dr. Craig Ramey, professor of psychology and pediatrics and director of the Civilian International Research Center at the University of Alabama at Birmingham. Oral communication at a conference, 9 May 1997, in Minneapolis.

3. Lloyd de Mause, "Restaging Early Traumas in War and Social Violence," *The Journal of Psychohistory* 23 (Spring 1996) 344–92.

4. David B. Chamberlain, *Babies Remember Birth* (Los Angeles: Tarcher, 1988).

5. [deMause] Chairat Panthuraamphorn, "Prenatal Infant Stimulation Program" in *Prenatal Perception,* 187–220.

6. Thomas R. Verny with John Kelly, *The Secret Life of the Unborn Child* (New York: Dell Publishing, 1986).

7. Cheryl Kilvington and Robert F. Brunjes, *Affirmations for Your Healthy Pregnancy: Daily Affirmations with Fetal Developmental Stages* (St. Paul, Minn.: Affirmation Press, 1992).

8. Laurie Kanyer, *Journey of Becoming a Mother* (Golden, Colo.: Love and Logic Press, 1996).

9. [deMause] Adrian Raine, Patricia Brennan, and Sarnoff A. Mednick, "Birth Complications Combined with Early Maternal Rejection at Age 1 Year Predispose to Violent Crime at Age 18 Years," *Archives of General Psychiatry* 51 (1994): 984–88; Henry P. David, et al., *Born Unwanted: Development Effects of Denied Abortion* (New York: Sprinter Publications, 1988).

10. Lynda Share, *If Someone Speaks, It Gets Lighter: Dreams and the Reconstruction of Infant Trauma* (Hillsdale, N.J.: Analytic Press, 1994).

11. Verny with Kelly, *The Secret Life of the Unborn Child*.

CHAPTER 25, "AGES AND STAGES"

1. Claudia Black, *It Will Never Happen to Me* (Denver: M.A.C., 1981).

2. Pamela Levin, *Becoming the Way We Are* (Pompano Beach, Fla.: Health Communications, 1988).

3. Harriet Goldhur Lerner, *The Dance of Anger* (New York: Harper and Row, 1985).

4. Jean Illsley Clarke, *Self-Esteem: A Family Affair* (available from Hazelden 1998).

5. Thanks to Mary Boghdadi for wording the affirmation "Your life is your own," which gives the neonate permission to be born or to abort if necessary.

6. See Foster Cline and Jim Fay, *Parenting with Love and Logic* (Colorado Springs, Colo.: Pinon Press, 1990).

7. See Susan Beekman and Jeanne Holms, *Battles, Hassles, Tantrums & Tears* (New York: Hearst Books, 1993).

8. See Benjamin Bloom, *Developing Talent in Young People* (New York: Ballantine Books, 1985).

9. Thanks to Ruth Robinson.

10. After the title of a book of poems by Sharon Doubiago.

11. Brenda Ueland, unpublished manuscript.

CHAPTER 26, "GENERAL ACTIVITIES FOR DELIBERATELY GROWING UP AGAIN"

1. Muriel James, *Breaking Free: Self-Reparenting for a New Life* (Reading, Mass.: Addison-Wesley, 1981).

2. Laurie Weiss and Jonathan Weiss, *Recovery from Codependency: It Is Never Too Late to Have a Happy Childhood* (Pompano Beach, Fla.: Health Communications, 1988).

CHAPTER 27, "ADOPTION: PARENTING SOMEONE ELSE'S CHILDREN AS YOUR OWN"

1. David Kirk, *Shared Fate: A Theory and Method of Adoptive Relationships* (Port Angeles, Wash.: Ben-Simon Publications, 1984).

2. Marcy Wineman Axness, "Babies Separated from Mothers at Birth" (Interview with Dr. Wendy McCord in *New Parents,* September 1994).

3. Ted Bowman, *Loss of Dreams: A Special Kind of Grief* (2111 Knapp St., St. Paul, MN 55108, 1994); Elaine Childs-Gowell, *Good Grief Rituals* (Barrytown, N.Y.: Station Hill Press, 1992).

4. Foster Cline, and Jim Fay, *Parenting with Love & Logic* and *Parenting Teens with Love & Logic* (Colorado Springs, Colo.: Pinon Press, 1990, 1992).

APPENDIX

1. Thanks to Carole Gesme for permission to reproduce the faces board from her series of games *Ups and Downs with Feelings.*

2. Jean Illsley Clarke, *Self-Esteem: A Family Affair Leader Guide.* Available from author, see Other Learning Materials Available, page 312.

3. Thanks to Mary Kaye Ashley for contributing her thoughts on supporting spiritual development at each stage of growth.

4. Jean Illsley Clarke and Carole Gesme, *Affirmation Ovals: 139 Ways to Give and Get Affir-mation,* see Other Learning Materials Available, page 312.

5. Thanks to Gail and Harold Nordeman for designing this activity.

6. Thanks to Jean Koski for designing this activity.

7. Thanks to Julie Thomas for designing this activity.

8. Thanks to Linda Buranen for designing this activity.

Additional Readings

Brazelton, T. Berry. *Touchpoints: The Essential Reference. Your Child's Emotional and Behavioral Development.* Reading, Mass.: Addison-Wesley, 1992.

What to expect at each age and advice on handling the transitions from one stage to the next.

Brazelton, T. Berry, and Bertrand G. Kramer. *The Earliest Relationship: Parents, Infants, and the Drama of Early Attachment.* Reading, Mass.: Addison-Wesley, 1990.

Builds the bridge between prenatal development and development during infancy. It contains information for parents and professionals about the connection between early care and attachment formation.

Budd, Linda S. *Living with the Active Alert Child: Groundbreaking Strategies for Parents.* Seattle: Parenting Press, 1993.

Specific helpful strategies for daily life with a child who does not respond positively to the "good-parenting" methods that usually work.

Cline, Foster. *Conscienceless Acts, Societal Mayhem: Uncontrollable, Unreachable Youth in Today's Desensitized World.* Boulder, Colo.: Cline/Fay Institute, 1995.

An impassioned presentation of the connection between attachment failures and characterless behavior.

Elium, Don, and Jeanne Elium. *Raising a Daughter: Parents and the Awakening of a Healthy Woman.* Berkeley, Calif.: Celestial Arts, 1994.

Common-sense suggestions for the everyday problems of helping girls reach their potential.

————. *Raising a Son: Parents and the Making of a Healthy Man.* Berkeley, Calif.: Celestial Arts, 1994.

Encouragement and helpful ideas for raising a son in a social environment that is not always supportive.

Goleman, Daniel. *Emotional Intelligence.* New York: Bantam, 1995.

Self-awareness, self-discipline, empathy, impulse control, and other qualities have more to do with success in life than IQ.

Jones, Elizabeth, and Gretchen Reynolds. *The Play's the Thing: Teachers' Roles in Children's Play.* New York: Teachers College Press, 1992.

Parents as well as teachers can learn ways to arrange children's play to promote creativity, problem solving, and responsibility.

Karen, Robert. *Becoming Attached: Unfolding the Mystery of the Infant-Mother Bond and Its Impact on Later Life.* New York: Warner Books, 1994.

A readable and thorough discussion of the many facets and implications of attachment.

Kotulak, Ronald. *Inside the Brain: Revolutionary Discoveries of How the Mind Works.* Kansas, City: Andrews McNeel, 1997.

Based on interviews of more than 300 researchers and mounds of scientific articles by geneticists and molecular biologists, Kotulak reports the explosion of research on the brain. Easy to read.

Kurcinka, Mary Sheedy. *Raising Your Spirited Child: A Guide for Parents Whose Child Is More Intense, Sensitive, Perceptive, Persistent, and Energetic.* New York: HarperCollins, 1991.

To the parents of a spirited child, advice for helping the child and compassionate support for the perplexed or tired parent.

Levine, James A., and Todd L. Pittinsky. *Working Fathers: New Strategies for Balancing Work and Family.* Reading, Mass.: Addison-Wesley, 1997.

A hands-on guide for fathers, mothers, employees, and managers.

Lewis, Michael. *Shame: The Exposed Self.* New York: Free Press, 1995.

This book deals with the self-conscious emotion of shame and its place in human emotional development.

Miller, Alice. *The Drama of the Gifted Child: How Narcissistic Parents Form and Deform the Emotional Lives of Their Talented Children.* New York: Basic Books, 1981.

All children are gifted, especially in their ability to adapt to whatever circumstances adults create for them.

———. *Thou Shalt Not Be Aware: Society's Betrayal of the Child.* New York: New American Library, 1984.

Miller speaks eloquently of society's denial of the victimization of children by adults.

Oliner, Samuel P., and Pearl M. Oliner. *The Altruistic Personality: Rescuers of Jews in Nazi Europe.* New York: Free Press, 1988.

What personal qualities led some people, at great risk to themselves, to shelter the persecuted? Tales of moral heroism, the importance of justice, and caring.

Pipher, Mary. *Reviving Ophelia: Saving the Selves of Adolescent Girls.* New York: Putnam, 1994.

Insights into the pervasive, dangerous messages our culture sends to girls about being women. Stories help girls become aware of the subtle but persistent programming to be subservient.

Reitz, Miriam, and Kenneth Watson. *Adoption and the Family System.* New York: Guilford Press, 1992.

A thorough exposition of the assessment and treatment of families impacted by adoption.

Silverstein, Olga, and Beth Rashbaum. *The Courage to Raise Good Men.* New York: Penguin Books, 1994.

The authors assert that you don't have to sever the bond with your son to help him become a man, and the book offers many ways to keep that bond intact.

Index

About the Authors

Connie Dawson earned her Ph.D. in counselor education with a specialty in adoption counseling. She taught in the Counselor Education program at Portland State University where she helped integrate counseling ideas into teacher preservice education. She now lives in Evergreen, Colorado, where she has a private practice. She consults and conducts workshops with mental health professionals, child care providers, adoptive parents, and adult adoptees.

Jean Illsley Clarke holds an M.A. in Human Development and an Honorary Doctorate of Human Service. She is a parent educator, teacher trainer, the author of *Self-Esteem: A Family Affair,* and co-author of the *Help! for Parents* series. She is the 1995 recipient of the Eric Berne Memorial Award in Transactional Analysis in the area of Practice Applications for applied Transactional Analysis in parent education. She lives with her husband, Dick, in Minneapolis, Minnesota.

The authors based the content of this book not only on research, but also on their wide experience working with adult learners, their profound learnings from years of full-time parenting, and now from participating with their grandchildren. Connie and a colleague have created a group leader's guide to be used by mental health professionals and Jean has designed one for educators.

Other Learning Materials Available

Affirmation Ovals, laminated, colored ovals are available in pocket, table, or wall sizes or as bookmarks. Each set includes all Stages: Becoming through Integration. Adoption ovals are available in separate sets.

Affirmation Ovals: 139 Ways to Give and Get Affirmations, a book by Jean Illsley Clarke and Carole Gesme, is a collection of games and activities to help people of all ages use the affirmation ovals.

The **Sing Yes!** album by Darrell Faires contains six audio cassettes with sixty-three singable, easy-to-remember songs, based on the developmental affirmations. Sung in both male and female voices. Accompaniment tapes included. A sampler of eight songs is also available.

The Developmental Audio Cassette Tapes, **The Important Infants**, children birth to 6 months, **The Wonderful Busy Ones**, children 6 months to 18 months, **Exciting 3 to 6 Year Olds**, present important information about children and the nurturing they need. Told in both male and female voices, the tapes are 12 to 18 minutes long. Listening to each tape daily for three weeks helps the listener incorporate this information to help care for children or for the child within.

Growing Up Again: Helping Our Children, Helping Ourselves Leader's Guide, six meetings to be led by educators, by Jean Illsley Clarke.

Growing Up Again: A Course in Being an Affirming Parent to Your Children and Yourself, ten meetings to be led by mental health professionals, by Connie Dawson and Marj Ratliff.

Self-Esteem: A Family Affair Leader Guide, eight meetings to be led by educators, by Jean Illsley Clarke.

Carole Gesme's games that support building self-esteem and growing up again include *Ups & Downs with Feelings, The Love Game, The Family Puzzle: Putting the Pieces Together, Capture a Feeling,* and *Keyed Up for Being Drug-Free.* For more information about her games and books write to Carole Gesme, 4036 Kerry Ct., Minnetonka, MN 55345 612-938-9163.

For further information about these materials and Heidi Caglayan's games about overindulgence, write to Daisy Press, 16535 9th Avenue North, Minneapolis, MN 55447.

About Hazelden Publishing

As part of the Hazelden Betty Ford Foundation, Hazelden Publishing offers both cutting-edge educational resources and inspirational books. Our print and digital works help guide individuals in treatment and recovery, and their loved ones. Professionals who work to prevent and treat addiction also turn to Hazelden Publishing for evidence-based curricula, digital content solutions, and videos for use in schools, treatment programs, correction programs, and electronic health records systems. We also offer training for implementation of our curricula.

Through published and digital works, Hazelden Publishing extends the reach of healing and hope to individuals, families, and communities affected by addiction and related issues.

For more information about Hazelden publications,
please call **800-328-9000** or visit us online at **hazelden.org/bookstore**.